THE POLITICS OF HOUSEWORK

The Politics of Housework

edited by
ELLEN MALOS

Allison & Busby
London · New York

First published 1980 by
Allison & Busby Limited
6a Noel Street, London W1V 3RB, England
and
distributed in the USA by
Schocken Books Inc, 200 Madison Avenue, New York, NY 10016.
Revised edition 1982

The politics of housework.
  1. Housewives—Political aspects
  I. Malos, Ellen
  301.5'5   HQ759   79-41427

ISBN 0-85031-327-9
ISBN 0-85031-462-3 Pbk

Typesetting by Malvern Typesetting Services
and printed in Spain by Grijelmo S. A., Bilbao.

The extracts from *The Power of Women and the Subversion of the
Community*, by Mariarosa Dalla Costa and Selma James, which
appeared in the first edition of this volume, have been excluded
at the authors' request.

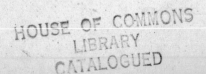

Contents

Epitaph for a Tired Housewife

Here lies a poor woman who always was tired
She lived in a house where help was not hired.
Her last words on earth were, ''Dear friend, I am going
Where washing ain't done, nor sweeping nor sewing;
But everything there is exact to my wishes,
For where they don't eat there's no washing of dishes.
I'll be where loud anthems will always be ringing:
But having no voice I'll be clear of the singing:
Don't mourn for me now, don't mourn for me never;
I'm going to do nothing for ever and ever.''

TRADITIONAL

Introduction

ELLEN MALOS

There will be no true liberation of women until we get rid of the assumption that it will always be women who do housework and look after children—and mostly in their own homes.

Marx and Engels believed that the problem would begin to be solved automatically when women became wage workers in industry on a large scale—but we have seen that this has not been so. In the capitalist West, women have been pushed and pulled from "housewifery" to waged work according to the laws of supply and demand and the needs of capitalism for a stable family base and a relatively healthy present and future workforce. Up to sixty years after revolutions that aspired to establish socialism and the emancipation of women, women in Eastern Europe have taken a full place in public industry without being relieved of the overall responsibility for housework and childcare. So, despite all advances toward legal "equality" in East and West—for the moment I am saying nothing of the colonial and ex-colonial countries—the sexual division of labour persists, not only in the apparently "natural" biological and domestic spheres but throughout society. No sooner do women make advances into a particular area of paid employment than it becomes "women's work" with lower pay than "men's work", leaving better-paid supervisory and managerial positions to men. And always the final responsibility for cooking, cleaning and childcare remains with women.

The new movements of the 1960s emphasised the dynamic unity of the personal and political, and the need to explore the ways in which oppression was internalised in the oppressed. In the new women's groups, the sexual and family roles of women were initially seen primarily as psychological or ideological, and the major focus was on relationships between individuals and the ways in which they embodied social norms, sometimes without conscious acceptance by the individuals themselves. Often these writings and actions highlighted neglected problems and described actual situations very vividly, emphasising common features of individual

experiences and laying the groundwork for new analyses, such as
Pat Mainardi's article "The Politics of Housework" in the United
States and similar publications in Britain in *New Left Review*
("The Housewife" by Susan Gail), and later in the London
Women's Liberation Workshop's *Shrew* ("Women and the
Family" by Jan Williams, Hazel Twort and Ann Bachelli).

These new attempts to analyse the historical roots and contemporary complexities of the situation of women led to a
rediscovery of the usefulness of marxism, despite its gaps and
failings. This was particularly true in Europe, where marxism had
not been driven so thoroughly underground by political repression.
Before the impact of the American movement was felt in Europe in
the late sixties, Simone de Beauvoir and Juliet Mitchell had already
begun to re-examine the the relationships between marxism and
feminism. But it was also true of a section of the movement in the
United States itself, as, for example, in Kate Millett's and Shulamith
Firestone's use of Engels's *The Origin of the Family, Private
Property and the State* in organising their ideas.

But none of these works gave more than passing attention to the
relationship between housework and the sexual division of labour.
Juliet Mitchell analysed the "biological differentiation of the sexes
and the division of labour" which she said had seemed an in-
terlocked necessity through history, in terms of the division between four "structures", Production, Reproduction (mainly
biological maternity), Sexuality and Socialisation. Domestic
labour, as such, was acknowledged in passing under Production as
"enormous if quantified in terms of productive labour" and in the
statement that women's liberation could be achieved only if "all
four structures in which they are integrated are transformed". She
concluded however that "the major structure which is at present in
rapid evolution is sexuality. Production, reproduction and
socialisation are all more or less stationary in the West today in the
sense that they have not changed in three or more decades".

The first target of the new women's movement, as we have seen,
was indeed in the area of sexuality, particularly sexism or the
ideology of male supremacy. The second has been in the area of
sexual reproduction, in the urgent concern for women to control
their own bodies and their own fertility.

In the area of economics, of production, we have had difficulty
formulating demands and strategies that go beyond those of the
earlier women's movement. We say "Equal Pay and Equal

Educational Opportunity", but most of us know we mean much more than that. As Juliet Mitchell put it:

> Economically, the most elementary demand is not the right to work or receive equal pay for work—the two traditional reformist demands—but *the right to equal work itself*. At present women perform unskilled, uncreative service jobs that can be regarded as "extensions" of their expressive familial role. They are overwhelmingly waitresses, office cleaners, hairdressers, clerks, typists. In the working class occupational mobility is thus sometimes easier for girls than boys—they can enter the white-collar sector at a lower level. But only two in a hundred women are in administrative or managerial jobs, and less than five in a thousand are in the professions. Women are poorly unionised (25 per cent) and receive less money than men for the manual work they do perform.[1]

Juliet Mitchell recognised the importance of the sexual division of labour in the paid workforce and saw that "the family as it exists at present is, in fact, incompatible with the equality of the sexes". Yet she thought that "the whole pyramid of discrimination" at work rested on

> a solid extra-economic foundation—education. The demand for equal work in Britain, should above all take the form of a demand for *an equal education system*, since this is at present the main single filter selecting women for inferior work roles.[2]

She apparently did not see that the "main filter selecting women for inferior work roles", and for their special oppression in many other areas, lay not in education so much as in the sexual division of labour within the family itself. Mitchell even spoke of the sphere of reproduction as if it were purely concerned with biological reproduction, and with the "need for intensive *maternal* care in the early years of a child's life",[3] thus accepting the very idea that lay behind the sexual division of labour.

Later writers from the women's movement, and many thousands of women in their everyday lives, have grappled with these problems. They have still not been solved either at a theoretical or a practical level. And this is not surprising, because housework, within which childcare is traditionally included, marks the point at which all four "structures" delineated by Juliet Mitchell interlock and fuse into each other. If we are unable to genuinely share housework and the caring for small children, then we shall never be able to share equally all other social tasks between the sexes, because as fast as we break down the inequalities associated with the sexual division of labour, unequal pay, for example, or unequal work, it will reassert itself: as in the Soviet Union, where recent studies have shown that women work longer hours than men because the housework, cleaning, cooking and shopping are still their responsibility. It can be seen that this question is not purely economic by the press discussion in the USSR that accompanied these revelations, in which at least one Soviet man wrote of a man's need for a "cool soft hand" to smooth his brow after a hard day's work.[4]

In the area of the division of labour the slogan "No Socialism without Women's Liberation" applies very much indeed. It has often been pointed out that the retention of small-scale private production in an otherwise "socialised economy" tends to create the conditions for capitalism to rebuild itself. It is not so very different with sexism and the sexual division of labour.

It has been historically clear, in Britain since the nineteenth century and in North America since the end of the Second World War, that the mere movement of married women into types of paid employment not previously open to them does not necessarily lead to any permanent gains for women. This is not only because women are seen as temporary interlopers in these areas, there "for the duration" until no longer needed. It is also partly because support services, such as childcare and good cheap public eating facilities, are rarely provided. But even more, it has seldom been questioned, even by women, that the ultimate responsibility for the children, the meals and the house cleaning is theirs.

That is why the gains of the first wave of the women's movement in the West and the attempt at the emancipation of women in the East left the few women who were able to take advantage of its impetus stranded singly on the shore while the rest of their sisters, especially lower-middle-class and working-class women, black and white, were washed back into the sea.

When Shulamith Firestone in *The Dialectic of Sex* attempted to get to the heart of this problem, the only solution she envisaged was to free women from the reproductive function itself through the application of science and technology. The majority of women in the women's movement rejected this solution, but Shulamith Firestone had highlighted the relationship between biological maternity, "mothering" and the whole complex of socially developed differences based on it.

Margaret Benston came at the question from another angle. She argued that "the roots of the secondary status of women are in fact economic" (rather than biological, or ideological), that "women as a group do indeed have a definite relation to the means of production and that this is different from that of men". In locating this difference in women's responsibility for domestic labour she laid the groundwork for a new analysis of "reproduction", which could now be seen to include not only biological maternity but also the work done by the housewife in the home and its relationship to production under capitalism or any other mode of production.

According to Margaret Benston, woman's production in the home was that of "use-values", that is, useful products and services consumed directly by the family, rather than commodity production for the market. Household labour therefore remained in a "pre-market" stage as in a peasant economy. (Her analysis was largely derived at this point from Ernest Mandel's discussion of peasant production.) This was one step forward from the idea of the housewife as a totally passive "consumer" which grew out of the analysis accepted by the women's movement up to this time that the nuclear family, and women located in these families as wives and mothers, were primarily, even solely, an ideological and psychological stabilising force in capitalist society. Margaret Benston, focusing on the economic function of the family, argued that in economic terms its primary function was not as a unit of consumption but that "the family should be seen primarily as a production unit for housework and child-rearing". She argued that women as a group are economically defined as responsible for household labour and therefore have a different relation to production from men as a group:

> We will tentatively define women, then, as that group of people which is responsible for the production of simple use-values in those activities associated with the home and family.
>
> Since men carry no responsibility for such production, the difference between the two groups lies here. Notice that women are not excluded from commodity production. Their participation in wage labour occurs but, as a group, they have no structural responsibility in this area, and participation is ordinarily regarded as transient. Men, on the other hand, are responsible for commodity production; they are not, in principle, given any role in household labour.

She specifically disagreed with Juliet Mitchell, who had argued that "in advanced industrial society, women's work is only marginal to the total economy".[5] For Margaret Benston "household labour, including child care, constitutes a huge amount of socially necessary production". She therefore argued that the problem of equality in work was not to be solved by integrating women into existing commodity production, because "so long as work in the home remains a matter of private production and is the responsibility of women they will carry a double work load". As the beginning of a solution she turned to Engels's and Lenin's traditional, though often forgotten, call for the socialisation of household labour,[6] though she recognised the many problems this involved, particularly, though not exclusively, in capitalism, and especially the possibility that the sexual division of labour would remain unchanged.

One problem with Margaret Benston's analysis was that her characterisation of housework as "pre-capitalist" production of "simple use values in those activities associated with home and family" still left household labour, even though "socially necessary", floating in a historical limbo somewhere quite outside the capitalist economy. But it is clear that her paper had completely changed the terms on which a discussion of women's work had to be carried on.

If Margaret Benston had attempted to explore the possibility that the specific oppression of women did itself have an economic base and women as a group a special relationship to the means of production, Mariarosa Dalla Costa and Selma James in "Women and the Subversion of the Community" (see note 28) began from the position that "the role of working-class housewife, which we believe has been indispensable to capitalist production, is *the* determinant for the position of all other women". They note that one thing reproduced in the home was what Marx called "that peculiar commodity, Labour power", both the labour power which the worker, male or female, presented each day for use at work and the future labour of the workers' eventual substitute in the labour force, the children. In this view women's labour only "*appears*" to be a personal service outside capitalism:

> The true nature of the role of housewife never emerges clearly in Marx. . . . We have to make clear that, within the wage, domestic work not only produces use values but is an essential function in the production of surplus value.

The outlines of a new approach to the question of housework

and the position of housewives in relation to the capitalist economic system had now emerged, though a number of new unresolved questions arose. Did women in the home produce purely "use values"? Or, because labour power was sold as a commodity, did they also produce exchange value? Was the housewife "productive" in capitalist terms because she produced a commodity for exchange, or "unproductive" even though her work was useful, even necessary in allowing a continuation of capitalist production at the present stage?

The problems were even greater in considering perspectives for action based on a definition of housework as economically necessary and central to an understanding of the relation of women to the mode of production. Margaret Benston had rejected the mere "integration of women into existing production" and looked to the absorption of housework into public industry with a long-term perspective of the socialisation of all industry. For James and Dalla Costa there was "no point in waiting for the automation of domestic work, because this will never happen". Their original perspective was for a mass refusal of housework as women's work so that women could become part of struggles in community and workplace alike. Later the demand for "wages for housework", which they had originally thought would risk the further entrenchment of "the condition of institutionalised slavery which is produced with the condition of housework", became the organising perspective for women in the women's movement who accepted their analysis, though it does not necessarily follow from the analysis.

The debates which have taken place on the theoretical and practical issues of housework since 1972 assume a knowledge of some aspects of marxist theory, particularly as they relate to a feminist critique of the inadequacies of the theory in overlooking the centrality of housework to any analysis of women's labour or the position of women in society. It would be useful, therefore, to take a moment to examine both the theory and practice of the marxist left on what it called the woman question and some historical reasons for the divergence of that theory and practice from the felt needs of a women's movement faced with the realities of mid-twentieth-century capitalism. From there we can go on to examine the development of the debate around these issues and its practical bearing on strategies for the women's movement.

For years, following a very selective reading of Engels's *The*

Origin of the Family, Private Property and the State, the marxist left had talked of women's emancipation following a socialist revolution and the full integration of women into social production. (The non-marxist socialists and liberal reformers usually thought that women were already "equal" by virtue of having the vote.) After the growth of the Women's Liberation Movement had forced a re-examination of the writings of Marx and Engels and some of their early followers, the notions of the "socialisation of housework", and for the more radical—and usually younger— "the abolition of the family", were added or revived.

The "normal" marxist approach to the woman question since the late twenties in the West had been to avoid the problems of the relationship between sex and class, by defining the task as that of reaching and mobilising only women of the industrial working class. Partly as a reaction to the catastrophic decline of working-class living standards during the depression, the communist parties, despite their confirmation of the importance of the entry of women into industry and their struggle for equality in the workplace, placed their chief emphasis on programmes "to defend the working-class family" in which, inevitably, the stress lay on the man's role as breadwinner and the woman's as housewife.*

Even after the growth of the women's movement, and despite a

---

*As late as the 1970s this emphasis can be seen. In a draft document for the 32nd national conference of the British Communist Party, though not in the pamphlet on women published subsequently ("Women, the Road to Socialism and Equality", by Rosemary Small), we read the following:

Most married women in Britain go to work primarily because they need to supplement their husbands' income. As most of them have had little or no training or further education they are forced to accept uninteresting and wearying jobs at low rates of pay, with no opportunity to widen their horizons. In order that these mothers should have real freedom to choose whether to remain at home with their young children or return to work or training, their husbands must be earning an adequate wage, and there must be a massive expansion of social provisions by government and local authorities.

For millions of working-class families, good modern housing at a low cost is the first consideration. . . . A modern, well equipped house would relieve millions of working-class women of a vast amount of drudgery.

A swing back and forth occurred between "socialisation of housework" and the need to "build labour-saving houses for women" as the answer to the question of housework, because no leading marxist theoretician had yet questioned the domestic division of labour; so until domestic drudgery was abolished, it was necessary to provide the best possible conditions for housewives to work under.

long-term, somewhat utopian commitment to the socialisation of housework or the abolition of the family, several left organisations still saw the main or even the only task of the women's movement as reaching women already in the paid labour force, and organising them in and around the trade unions on economic issues; a strategy often summarised as "getting women into unions". In this view such issues as sexism or abortion or contraception were often regarded as "only of interest to bourgeois women", while childcare was sometimes regarded as important almost purely to make things easier for working-class women needing to take paid jobs.*

This approach saw the only possibilities for action by women outside the paid labour force to be organisation around issues like prices, rents and perhaps childcare. It differed very little from the approach followed by the left after the political and economic shocks of the thirties. It also corresponded to a simplification of the belief of Marx and Engels that, besides legal reforms, it was the large-scale entry of women into industry that was the necessary precondition for the equality which would only be realised when a socialist revolution had brought about the socialisation of housework and childcare.

Marx had said that production and reproduction were interlinked parts of a whole. In *Capital* Marx was concerned with the production and reproduction of capital itself because he was interested in understanding the mechanisms by which the economic system worked in order to overthrow it, but he did attempt to summarise the relationship between the "productive consumption" or reproduction of the working class and the reproduction of capital:

> The individual consumption of the labourer, whether it proceeds within the workshop or outside it, whether it be part of the process of production or not, forms therefore a factor of the production and reproduction of capital; just as cleaning machinery does, whether it is done while the machinery is working or while it is standing. The fact that the labourer consumes his means of subsistence for his own purposes, and not to please the capitalist, has no bearing on the matter. The consumption of food by a beast of burden is none the less a

---

*Of course there were very important differences between the groups here so crudely lumped together; but what they seemed to have in common was an uneasiness or hostility towards any actions against displays of sexism other than those of an economic or judicial character, and a fear of taking up demands that could not be seen to have a clear class content.

necessary factor in the process of production, because the beast enjoys what it eats. The maintenance and reproduction of the working class is, and must ever be, a necessary condition to the reproduction of capital. But the capitalist may safely leave its fulfilment to the labourer's instincts of self-preservation and propagation. All the capitalist cares for is to reduce the labourer's individual consumption as far as possible to what is necessary. [7]

This statement and what it leaves unanalysed mark the point at which the question was left for about a hundred years, only now to be picked up and elaborated by feminists and socialists. [8] What it leaves out is the fact that the responsibility for the major part of the "maintenance and reproduction of the working class" in the home is that of women, and of course that "the labourer" might be "she" as well as "he", facts of which Marx showed himself aware in other contexts.

Another part of the problem with conventional marxism was that it was based on a faulty historical perspective on women. In *Capital*, when he spoke of women's pre-industrial work as "free labour at home within moderate limits", Marx appeared unaware of the considerable participation by women both in production for the market in pre-industrial capitalism and in petty artisan production, as described by Alice Clark [9] and Catherine Hall. But more important was the fact that at the point of British capitalist development at which Marx and Engels were writing it seemed that individual workers would become more and more responsible for the reproduction of their own labour power as individuals because women, especially married women and mothers, were being drawn into the labour market in large numbers.

Although contemporary reformers almost certainly exaggerated the proportions of married women factory workers, Ivy Pinchbeck [10] and Margaret Hewitt [11] have both shown that there were many married women working for wages in England in the nineteenth century, especially at the growing points of capitalism, on the large farms of East Anglia worked by the gang system, in the textile industry, the metal shops of the Midlands and the potteries, as well as in the older domestic industries. Figures for the cotton manufacture and pottery industries given by Margaret Hewitt, though of varying reliability, suggest that at some times between a quarter and a third of the women workers were married and/or widowed. [12] One assumption underlying *Capital*, *The Condition of the Working Class in England in 1844* and *The Origin of the Family*,

Private Property and the State, therefore, was that the traditional sexual division of labour was being broken down in working-class families because of the entry of married women into paid work in "public industry". It also seemed to Marx and Engels that the whole of the working-class population above a very low age would become wage labourers and, since the work of the women in the family to reproduce the labour power of the male labourer would be broken down, all would be exploited *individually* as wage labourers reproducing their own individual means of consumption/reproduction almost in terms of the model outlined by Marx above. By the 1960s it should have been clear that this, like the socialist revolution Marx and Engels expected in the more developed capitalist countries, had not happened. Yet the marxist left's attitude to "working women" in the 1960s was hardly different from what it might have been if those expectations had come true.

The reorganisation of women's work

What did happen to the family in nineteenth-century England was that both liberal reformers *and* working-class organisations recognised that if things continued the way they were going, the working class would be unable to reproduce itself adequately; and so there was a whole series of reforms in the nineteenth and early twentieth centuries, the overall effect of which was to restore the family as the centre in which the maintenance of the working class and the reproduction and socialisation of their children took place in conditions as near as possible to what had become a middle-class ideal (as redefined by capitalism since industrialisation) of a wife whose sole function lay inside the home and the family.

First came the series of measures to regulate the hours of work of women and children and then to stop the employment of very young children. On the evidence, especially of mortality among the children of employed women, much of this was of vital importance, but it went along with attempts to restrict the field of employment of *all* women and especially of all married women and mothers.[13] There was a great deal of accompanying propaganda against women working outside the home at all, except as domestic servants, particularly after they were married, particularly alongside men in so-called "male jobs", particularly the better paid ones. This coincided with an attempt by the trade unions to institute a "social wage" which would enable the working-class family to live adequately on the man's wage.[14]

After the reduction of women's hours of work, which were often specifically described as allowing time for the housework, came a prohibition against women working within a given period before and after childbirth; much later still came the institution of state insurance schemes to enable women to live while prohibited from earning. Later again came "positive" incentives to housewifery, health centres for babies, domestic education and so on. One thing that was hardly even thought of, as Margaret Hewitt has shown, was the provision of nurseries so that the babies of wage-earning women could escape the consequences of inadequate feeding and hygiene that attended the full-time work of mothers in industry or agriculture at that time.[15] Such a course, which would have involved adequate artificial feeding beyond the means of working-class parents, besides being expensive, would have contradicted the prevailing ideology in Britain, though it did happen in France to some extent.

The survival of working-class infants as well as the comfort and moral welfare of husbands[16] was therefore promoted through the cheaper and more acceptable means of a redefinition of the sexual division of labour along "traditional" lines, but with girls and unmarried women now carrying out "women's work" in industry and commerce as they already did in paid domestic service. Over the period between the seventeenth century and the early twentieth century married women of the working class, having little chance of competing with capitalist industry by the production of goods and services under the old "domestic system",[17] were gradually more and more confined to childcare, cooking and cleaning, as their contribution to the family and to capitalism. What domestic industry remained became largely integrated, as "outwork", into capitalist industry, but it was worse paid than wage-work proper. The "family wage" now came to mean the man's wage rather than the pooled contributions of the different family members. The term "breadwinner", which had once meant that in the smallholder's family the man's wage usually bought wheat for bread that the family could not grow for itself, now meant that the entire family would often depend entirely on the husband for their subsistence. According to society's rulers this was how it ought to be, and it fitted in with traditional ideas about the subordination of women to their husbands.[18]

Even so, capitalism could never wholly do without women in the labour force, married and unmarried, though its needs fluctuated, and would never pay a full "social wage" to all men with families to support, let alone female workers in the same position. And so women remained in an ambivalent position, half in and half out of the paid labour force, and whether in or out they were expected to play the major part in the "nurturing" of the working class and of men and children in general, and to remain subordinate to their husbands, the major breadwinners.

Though this may have allowed more children of the working class to survive their first year, it failed to produce a healthy workforce, as the examination of working-class recruits to the Boer War and the First World War demonstrated, to the alarm of many.[19] Its effect on the health of working-class mothers was even less beneficial, as the investigation of the Women's Health Commission in the 1930s revealed (see the excerpt from Margery Spring Rice's *Working-Class Wives*).

The pioneer historical research in this area by Alice Clark (*The Working Life of Women in the Seventeenth Century*), Ivy Pinchbeck (*Women Workers and the Industrial Revolution*) and Margaret Hewitt (*Wives and Mothers in Victorian England*) and others in both Europe and North America, whose work has been out of print for long periods, is just now being continued and extended by contemporary women's historians, so that our detailed historical knowledge still remains sketchy and incomplete, just as does our theory.[20]

In North America these developments began later and were rather different. It was probably not until late in the nineteenth century, with mass immigration from Europe and an end to the "frontier" era, that conditions began to approximate to those of Britain.[21] They therefore occurred at a time when the effects of industrialisation and the wage-earning mother on the family had already been much discussed and had been subject to legislation. Contemporary reformers and such studies as *Mothers in Industry* by Gwendolyn Salisbury Hughes show themselves very aware of British ideas and developments.

It is also true that industrialisation in the United States was much more rapid and made very far-reaching inroads into traditional domestic functions. Charlotte Perkins Gilman in America, Margaret Bondfield in England and to a lesser extent the members of the English Women's Health Commission looked towards taking housework out of the home, leaving it as a place of relaxation for both sexes, but the prevailing viewpoint was very different.

Barbara Ehrenreich and Deirdre English show in "The Manufacture of Housework"[22] some of the effects of the industrialisation of such domestic tasks as soap-making and canning, and also how at a later time the growth of the "Scientific Home Management Movement" turned housework into a "a vocation", so that the time that might have been saved by the industrialisation of domestic functions was absorbed in other new domestic tasks. So, retained as women's prime task but redefined in a way which was to lead to "consumerism", housework became first a crusade against dirt and disease and later a quest for family health and happiness. In both, the purchase of the right products of capitalist industry became a major element in the definition of what housework involved, and the essential work of women in maintaining the workforce was hidden. As "consumers" they appeared inessential and parasitic, in the labour market they were seen as temporary and not quite legitimate, at best a necessary evil, even though many women, like those studied in the Bermondsey district of London by Pearl Jephcott, Nancy Seear and John Smith, continued to combine paid labour with housework.[23]

Capitalism has not been able totally to submerge the reality of housework under the joys of "pure" commodity consumption. For a while it seemed possible, but, as Jean Gardiner has pointed out,[24] in a period of economic stagnation such as that we have now entered there is a strong attempt to hold down the wages and consumption of the majority of the working population. This means, for example, that the unpaid labour of women in converting unprocessed foodstuffs into palatable meals will tend to become more important, so that in this and other ways the work of women at home will increase, to soften the effect of austerity on their families. She points to the fact that in England in 1971, a year of growing unemployment and acceleration in the rise of food prices, "convenience food sales fell by 5 per cent while seasonal food sales rose by 4 per cent, a dual reversal of long-term trends". Since then the cutback in public spending on social services, childcare, education, health, etc. has accentuated this trend.

If it seemed to Juliet Mitchell in the mid-sixties that the relationships between production, reproduction and socialisation were more or less stationary in the West today, it is certainly no longer true, and the debate about the relationships between production and reproduction, especially between women's unpaid work in the home and paid work outside, and a whole host of other related questions, have grown in importance within the women's movement and outside, though they ought not in their turn to lead to a denial of the non-economic, non-workplace issues but be united with them in an integrated whole.

Wages for housework

It was not until 1969–70 that a Women's Liberation Movement came into being in the United Kingdom, the impetus coming almost equally from struggles of women of the traditional working class around workplace issues such as equal pay and from the "middle class" and student left. Significant numbers of the women who became involved from the beginning were socialists with a marxist orientation, of whom many were unaligned and seeking a redefinition of marxism in relation to women. But some were members of left groups or parties which believed that only industrial (or "productive") workers, organised in their workplaces around primarily economic demands, were capable of playing a significant role in transferring capitalist society to socialism, after which the "emancipation" of women would automatically follow. This gave a particularly sharp edge to all of the discussions at the series of national meetings and conferences organised after February 1970.

In this context and in opposition to the traditional left approach the demand for Wages for Housework was first raised as part of a series of demands in a paper written by Selma James for the National Women's Liberation Conference in Manchester in March 1972. "Women, the Unions and Work: Or What is Not to be Done" was specifically directed against left organisations and their perspective of unionising women because, in Selma James's view, unions "structurally make generalised struggle impossible":

This is not *because they are bureaucratised, this is why*: their functions are to mediate the struggle in industry and keep it separate from struggles elsewhere. Because the most concentrated potential power of the class is at the point of production of commodities which are things, the unions have convinced the wageless that only at that point can a struggle be waged at all. This is not so, and the most striking example has been the organisation of the black community. Blacks, like women, cannot limit themselves to struggle in factories. And blacks, like women, see the function of the union within the class writ large in relation to them. For racism and sexism are not aberrations of an otherwise powerful working-class weapon. They are its nature.[25]

The paper drew on the ideas of "Women and the Subversion of the Community", which had only had a limited circulation in Britain, but went beyond it, both in putting forward the Wages for Housework demand and in other ways.

Where "Women and the Subversion of the Community" had described "the role of the working-class housewife" as "*the* determinant for the position of all other women", and "the struggle of women of the working class against the family" and against "the role of housewife" as crucial, "Women, the Unions and Work" regarded as equally decisive "the struggle of the woman of the working class against the union" because "like the family, *it protects 'the class' at her expense* (and not only hers) and at the expense of offensive action. Like the family, we have nothing to put in its place but the class acting for itself and women as integral, in fact pivotal to that class." The six demands were put forward as a programme for the movement to replace four demands which had been used since the International Women's Day March in 1971. In shortened form, the new demands were:

1. We demand the right to work less.
2. We demand a guaranteed income for women and for men, working or not working, married or not . . . we demand wages for housework. All housekeepers are entitled to wages (men too).
3. It is in this context that we demand control of our bodies . . . we demand the right to have or not have children.
4. We demand equal pay for all.
5. We demand an end to price rises.
6. We demand free community-controlled nurseries and childcare.[26]

At two successive national conferences the debate on the paper stuck on two issues—the attitude the paper spelled out towards trade unions and left organisations, and the "wages for housework" demand (rather than "a guaranteed income for all" under which it had originally been included). The six demands themselves were never debated or voted on as such and the present seven demands of the movement remain the original four, hastily assembled for International Women's Day 1971—equal pay, equal education and opportunity, twenty-four-hour childcare, and free contraception and abortion on demand—with the addition of three more since 1974, financial and legal independence for women, the right to determine our own sexual orientation, and freedom for all women from the use or threat of sexual violence.

The debate on the perspective of "Women, the Unions and Work" generated more heat than light. There was an almost instant polarisation from the first between "orthodox marxists" on the one hand, some of whom refused to recognise the importance of housework, as work, to capitalism, and the partisans of "Wages for Housework" who, under pressure to defend the paper, made that single demand the focal point of their argument. The debate about the nature of the trade unions, though not irrelevant, became secondary, as did all the other issues raised in the paper, although a debate on the subject was held in *Red Rag* (two of these contributions by Sheila Rowbotham and Ros Delmar, are reprinted in this volume).

From the beginning the debate tended to make a separation between the practical issues and agitational tactics discussed at several national Women's Liberation conferences, and the theoretical and strategic issues discussed at a series of conferences about Women's Liberation and Socialism, which related more to "Women and the Subversion of the Community" than to "Women, the Unions and Work".

The theoretical debate, although complicated and often confusing and heated, was less bitter and more fruitful than the practical one. It was centred around the question of the relationship between housework and the capitalist mode of production. On the whole it was accepted that housework, as part of the total reproductive process of capitalism, was economically important as well as ideologically functional (and that was a big, largely underrated, addition to the thinking of most marxists); but problems remained in working out the nature of the housewife's link with capitalism.

Some argued, as Margaret Benston had done, that the housewife produced "simple use values" for consumption in the family which benefited and indirectly profited capital and allowed the woman herself to be manipulated in and out of the paid labour force to meet the changing needs of capitalism. According to this argument the housewife's link with capitalism through housework came not so much through her reproduction of labour power as through her work in processing the articles of consumption and in reproducing "the relations of production", less an economic than an ideological function.

Those campaigning for wages for housework argued that the housewife was producing a commodity for capital via her man and her children (and herself if she was in waged work), that her work therefore produced surplus value and was "productive in the marxist sense" and that therefore she should be paid a wage for the production of that commodity. There was a third position[26] which accepted a link with capitalism economically through the economic function of the housewife's role in the reproduction of labour power, without arguing that the housewife thereby became a productive labourer.

By now there is a considerable body of detailed argument on the theoretical implications of these questions, much of which is relatively difficult to obtain, and there is no comprehensive work which covers all the issues. It would be impossible to discuss the issues fully here, but two seem essential: the question of what Marx meant by the terms "productive and unproductive labour", and the question of what a wage is and what it is paid for. Other issues which came within the theoretical debate and are useful to look at here are the relationship between housework and class, and the way in which the demand for wages for housework became enlarged from part of one single demand to a total strategy.

The argument about whether housework is productive or unproductive is based on questions about what Marx actually said, or meant. Silvia Federici, in her article "View from a Kitchen", states: "Marx . . . said that this reproduction of labour power, housework, was productive labour, and that our consumption as workers was productive."[27]

"Women and the Subversion of the Community" itself is not consistent here, partly because the article, the introduction and the notes to the Falling Wall Press editions were not all composed at the same time and therefore represent different stages in the development of the argument. The text says that "domestic work . . . is essential in the production of surplus value", but the note says that "housework . . . is productive in the Marxian sense, that is, is producing surplus value".[28]

It is therefore useful to look at what Marx did in fact say. In volume one of *Capital* he did say that the reproduction of labour power was *productive consumption*, but he did not say it was productive *labour*. In *Theories of Surplus Value* he specifically excluded this kind of work, whoever it was done by, from his definition of "productive labour". Having said that the work of a seamstress, carpenter or cook or any servant working for wages for a private master is unproductive because "the same labour can be productive when I buy it as a capitalist, as a producer, in order to produce more value, and unproductive when I buy it as a consumer, a spender of revenue, in order to consume its use-value", Marx goes on to say that the working class must perform this kind of labour for itself:

> But it is only able to perform it when it has laboured "productively". It can only cook meat for itself when it has produced a wage with which to pay for the meat and it can only keep its furniture and dwellings clean, it can only polish its boots, when it has produced the value of furniture, rent and boots. To this class of productive labourers itself, therefore, the labour which they perform for themselves appears as "unproductive labour". This unproductive labour never enables them to repeat the same unproductive labour a second time unless they have previously laboured productively.[29]

Marx also explicitly stated that the labour of such people as "the doctor and the schoolmaster", although "services which yield in return 'a vendible commodity etc' namely labour power itself", is not productive because it "does not directly create the fund out of which they are paid, although their labours enter directly into the production costs of the fund which creates all value whatever—namely the production costs of labour power".[30] Yet he says that these services can be "industrially necessary".

It seems clear then that to Marx the reproduction of labour power, whoever it was carried out by and whether it was paid or not, was *not* productive labour even if it was socially and industrially necessary. But although Marx was always careful to make clear that the distinction he was making was a technical one which did not describe the usefulness or importance of the work that fell into either category, those who followed him have not always been so clear and have spoken as if "productive" was the same as useful or "important to capitalism". This may have arisen partly because in Marx's time the majority of unproductive workers were domestic servants. In our time, because of the massive expansion of the service sector, both private and public, unproductive workers are an increasingly important group, including the majority of office workers, teachers and public servants of all kinds as well as nurses, canteen workers, cleaners and others whose work is "industrialised housework". It is important for both the women's movement and socialists to be aware of the importance of these groups and of their particular relationship to capitalism. And it is probably for this reason that there was felt a need to assert the "productiveness" of housework. However, the productive/unproductive argument is a red herring in the debate about whether women should receive wages for housework, since both forms of labour can be paid.

Because there was also a great deal of confusion around the question of what a wage is and what it is paid for, it is important to look briefly at this question, which is discussed very clearly by Caroline Freeman in "When is a Wage not a Wage". She points out that the term "wages for housework" is not the same as "money for women who are housewives". "Women and the Subversion of the Community" itself made a distinction between a wage and a "pension" or allowance, which may not be so closely tied to the performance of a task. This is important when we come to consider whether a wage for housework would tend to strengthen the sexual division of labour. It is clear that for marxists the *wage* is paid for a given measured amount of time during which the capitalist buys the labour power of the worker, or for a given measured number of commodities which the worker produces in a piecework system. While it is clear that domestic labour can be so measured and paid, it is not clear from attempts to measure the work of housewives whether privatised housework, in which the worker has an undefined work-day and almost limitless number of tasks and responsibilities, could be measured in this way. What is fairly clear, though, is that if a wage were to be paid, by capitalists or the state, they would demand some kind of measurement of the labour time involved, so that women would not easily be able to take the money and refuse to do the work any more than any group of wage workers can for any significant period. Arguments about the degree of absenteeism in industry do not alter this. Wage workers can negotiate to shorten their hours and they can lengthen their holidays and sometimes take unauthorised days off, but they cannot altogether refuse to do the work for which they are receiving a wage and continue to receive it. Having looked at some of the issues involved in the relationship between housework and capitalist production, we must also consider the relationship between housewives and the working class before going on to examine the strategic and practical issues.

Margaret Benston's approach had suggested that women constituted a separate economic category because of their relationship to the means of production, but the approach initiated by Dalla Costa and James swept such questions to one side by declaring that women's struggle around their oppression and exploitation as wageless housewives subsumes all else. The process of the argument is complex but it is summed up in the slogan "Power to the sisters and *therefore to the class*". Many women wish to reject a "caste" definition of feminism whereby the success of the feminist movement is measured in terms of women managing directors and women presidents or prime ministers, without seeing women's struggles as being simply that of a section of waged workers "and their wives" which has too often been offered as a class analysis. But the problem of the relationship between sex oppression and class cannot be solved by declaring women or housewives to *be* The Class or to include The Class. Nor can it be solved by way of an analogy with blacks in the United States or by putting women and people in the Third World in the one category of "wageless of the world". Though such analogies have been important in pointing to similarities between different groups of oppressed people, they are only analogies, not an analysis.[31]

Nor is it clear how the *wagelessness* of the housewife is really the central issue in international feminist and class politics. It is true that housewives earn no wage for performing absolutely vital work in reproducing labour power and the labour force; but some women who are housewives reproduce the other side of the capitalist relation, the capitalist class itself. It is also true that the wagelessness of housewives means that they are more powerless than if they had money of their own and that they are directly dependent economically and therefore much more subordinated to their husbands. And it is clear that the discovery of the consequences of their economic dependency and powerlessness was one of the reasons for the dissatisfaction of many housewives and a driving force behind the formation of the women's liberation movement in the 1960s (rather than only the heavily overpublicised revolt of young college women against male domination in the civil rights movement and the New Left). But it is also true, as articles written by members of Wages for Housework groups themselves make clear, that a wage for women does not necessarily bring the power to end the rule of capital or subordination of women to men, any more than a wage for men ends their subordination to capital.

Wage labour is only the form by which the owners of the means of
production put to use the labour power of those who do not own
the means of production. It is true that capitalists do not wish to
purchase directly all aspects of the reproduction of labour power
itself and incorporate them in the wage system. That is why, as
Jean Gardiner and others have argued, housewives still represent,
even in a purely economic sense, a convenient form of flexible
labour who are performing useful work for capital even when
"unemployed". But they are not performing that useful work only
in serving and reproducing the working class. However powerless
they may be themselves, the wives and mistresses of the capitalist
class serve and maintain that class also. The problem of the
relationship between sex and class, therefore, is not solved by
basing our politics on the wagelessness of housewives, particularly
if we are looking for an anti-capitalist and anti-imperialist perspective for the women's movement.

Yet more and more "wages for housework" is seen by the
women who put it forward as more than a demand. To them it
seems to have become the embodiment of a total strategy for the
women's movement as a whole under which all other demands can
be included and by means of which all other perspectives can be
judged:

> What emerged from the debate was that this demand was more than a
> demand, and represented a new organising perspective. In the process
> of building an international network of Wages for Housework
> organisations and launching our campaign for our wage, we have
> redefined who is the working class, and clarified what organisational
> practices flow from this perspective, what are the state's plans for our
> productivity in the home and out of it and what kind of struggle women
> are waging against these plans. We have seen more and more clearly
> that we women everywhere are daily struggling against work and for
> wages, and that the unions are *for* work and against us. We can see,
> too, that although women have previously been defined by the class of
> their fathers or husbands, and many of us had seen ourselves as
> "middle class", our exploitation as unwaged housewives and our
> common struggle against that exploitation is a working-class experience
> and a working-class struggle.[32]

Yet it has never become clear how this demand, which was
specifically rejected in "Women and the Subversion of the
Community" because of the risk of "entrenchment of the conditions of institutionalised slavery in which housework is carried

out'' became the ''mobilising goal'' for a movement. The case for the demand was first put as a footnote to the case against it in the Falling Wall Press edition of 1972:

> Today the demand for wages for housework is put forward increasingly and with less opposition in the women's movement in Italy and elsewhere. Since this document was first drafted (June 1971) the debate has become more profound and many uncertainties that were due to the relative newness of the discussion have been dispelled. But above all, the weight of the needs of proletarian women has not only radicalised the demands of the movement. It has also given us greater strength and confidence to advance them. A year ago, at the beginning of the movement in Italy, there were those who still thought that the State could easily suffocate the female rebellion against housework by "paying" it with a monthly allowance of £7–£8 as they had already done especially with those "wretched of the earth" who were dependent on pensions.
>
> Now these uncertainties are largely dissipated. And it is clear in any case that the demand for a wage for housework is only a basis, a perspective, from which to start, whose merit is essentially to link immediately female oppression, subordination and isolation to their material foundation: female exploitation. At this moment this is perhaps the major foundation of the demand for wages for housework. . . .
>
> The practical, continuous translation of this perspective is the task the movement is facing in Italy and elsewhere.

But pointing to the militancy of a movement based on the demand was not an answer to the case against it, which argued that it would intensify the sexual division of labour.

This case has never been answered, although the arguments have been repeated many times. It is still not clear whether campaigners for wages for housework really want what they are asking for. To ask for money for women is not the same as to ask for a wage for housework, especially when the "wage" is seen as a means of refusing the work. In the beginning there were those in the wages for housework movement who pointed out some of the dangers; but increasingly the "wage" is seen as *the* answer to all problems of women, including rape and domestic violence, because "money is power", or even "money is capital".* The wages for housework

---

*Silvia Federici, *Wages Against Housework*, but compare Marx, *Capital*, vol. 1, chap. 6: "For *the conversion of money into capital*, therefore, the owner of money must meet in the marketplace with the free labourer, free in this double sense, that as a free man he can dispose of his labour power as his own commodity, and that on the other hand he has no other commodity for sale, is short

analysis holds that the oppression and exploitation of women is based on their lack of a wage, and seems to assert that the wage and the factory rather than capitalist relations of production are the foundations of capitalism. However, the precondition for the development of capitalism and the capitalist version of the sexual division of labour is not the wage but the private ownership of the means of production by a relatively small class of capitalists. The tendency for women to be excluded from wage labour after capitalism passed from its early domestic form—though it never became universal—is based on the tendency for the reproduction of labour power to be perceived as a "natural" function outside of capitalism or any other economic system. The fact that it is un-waged is based on its privatisation and on the fact that it is not measured in terms of the expenditure of labour power over a given time. In other words "wagelessness" is secondary, just as the wage is, to a system in which the mass of women and men who do not own the means of production face the power of those who do. It is difficult to see how a wage for housework could alter that fundamental situation.

This is not to say that money is not important or that those who have a wage do not have more power than those without, but it is to point again to the very obvious fact that real power lies with those who can transform their money into capital rather than with those who only have the means to purchase the necessities of life.

Focusing on the wages for housework demand has tended to blur the original main intentions of "Women and the Subversion of the Community" which seem to have been to analyse women's oppression and exploitation in relation to economic functions of the sexual division of labour under capitalism, to assert the critical importance of the working-class housewife in examining women as a "caste" or sex, and to try to establish a theoretical basis from which to argue against the idea that women are "peripheral" to the working class and to revolutionary struggle except as waged workers. It seems clear that although the theoretical analysis is still incomplete, it is increasingly accepted among socialist and radical feminists in Britain at least that the position of the housewife is

---

of everything necessary for the realisation of his labour power." Marx was concerned to *distinguish between* money and capital, whereas for Silvia Federici to gain wages for housework is "to reappropriate the money which is the fruit of our labour", an idea Marx would have found puzzling in the extreme. In this view surplus value seems to have disappeared.

crucial to an understanding of women as workers, that women in the home are doing work which is of economic value for capital and not merely serving an economic function inside the individual family, and that although this work cannot be described as "productive of surplus value" in the sense that Marx defined it, it nevertheless contributes to the production of surplus value. But it is less clear what perspectives for action should be based on that position. The women's movement as a whole, and socialist feminists too, especially since the onset of the present economic crisis, have taken up issues that seem important as they have arisen without much more than a vague sense of priorities and a feeling that it is important for the movement to fight on all fronts at once.

The women's liberation movement as a whole has not adopted the perspective of wages for housework, nor has the practical debate really asked whether it would be to the advantage of women that their housework be waged or, in the long term, what effect it would have on the sexual division of labour. The answer to the first question, in particular, is dependent on particular conditions of time and place. Margaret Benston was writing from Canada where, as in the United States and Britain, the percentage of women, and of married women in particular, in the paid labour force was rising. The problem for the women's movement in those countries, was, and still is, to develop an analysis and a strategy which would integrate women's struggles in and outside the workplace adequately. Peggy Morton, in "Women's Work is Never Done", starting from a critical analysis of Margaret Benston's article, argued for "the need to integrate the demand for the socialisation of household labour with the demand for the socialisation of labour outside the home" keeping in mind the aim of building "a revolutionary cadre among women" and seeing the need to "figure out which sectors of women will move fastest".

In Italy, however, according to one set of figures only about 20 per cent of women between the ages of fifteen and sixty-four work outside the home, and, for married women in particular, one of the important means of paid work is still domestic service. It may have been partly for this reason that a programme for action based on a perspective of the industrialisation or socialisation of housework seemed to make no sense at all. France, on the other hand, with a tradition of significant numbers of married women working outside the home, also has a family allowance system which seems to approach "wages for housework", in that a sum of money is paid to mothers at home in order to encourage them to stay there. It apparently operates in a way that allows the wives of better paid workers to avoid the "double shift" and helps women wage workers with childcare, but imposes a sort of bureaucratic "quality control" by forcing women to produce health dossiers on their children to qualify.[33]

At the present moment no one has a formula of demands which will give us the right terms in which to organise a fully effective struggle of women against their own oppression and against the social system which perpetuates it, let alone telling us exactly what to do *after* we have got rid of that system. But I think we have at least some outlines on which to work, which allow us to link the housework struggle with the workplace struggle, which is extremely important because women are situated in both. While wages for housework does not seem viable as a single mobilising demand or long-term perspective for the women's movement, the demand for the "socialisation of housework" is itself also inadequate, only looking at part of the problem, as "wages for housework" does.

The most fundamental objection to wages for housework as a perspective was stated by Shulamith Firestone in 1970, before it was raised as a demand:

> In official capitalist terms, the bill for her economic services might run as high as one fifth of the gross national product. But payment is not the answer. To pay her, as is often discussed seriously in Sweden, is a reform that does not challenge the basic division of labour and thus could never eradicate the disastrous psychological and cultural consequences of that division of labour.[34]

"Women and the Subversion of the Community" itself seemed to support this position in its original version:

> The proposal for pensions for housewives (and this makes us wonder why not a wage) serves only to show the complete willingness of those parties [of the left] further to institutionalise women as housewives and men as wage slaves.[35]

Also:

> Hence we must refuse housework as women's work, as work imposed upon us, which we never invented, which has never been paid for, in which they have forced us to cope with absurd hours, 12 and 13 a day, in order to force us to stay at home.
> We must get out of the house; we must reject the home, because we want to unite with other women, to struggle against all the situations

which presume that women will stay at home, to link ourselves to the struggles of all those who are in ghettos, whether that ghetto is a nursery, a school, a hospital, an old-age home, or a slum. . . . This alteration in the terms of the struggle will be all the more violent the more the refusal of domestic labour on the part of women will be violent, determined and on a mass scale.[36]

"Women and the Subversion of the Community" clearly recognised that, if women were in a position analogous to slaves who had the product of their labour power appropriated without payment, the remedy was not payment but the destruction of the system "which institutionalised women as housewives and men as wage slaves". But what happened after "Women, the Unions and Work" was that this perspective was blurred and a possible *tactical* issue, "payment for housework" or "a guaranteed income for all", became confused with the strategic issues, just as in the labour movement the necessity to defend and improve the conditions of workers under the wage system often seems to imply a necessity to preserve the wage system and even the capitalist system itself.

As I see it there are three crucial objections to the idea of individual women being paid wages to care for their individual families (or, for that matter, for individual *people* to be paid wages for caring for their individual families or themselves). First, as Shulamith Firestone pointed out, it does not challenge the sexual division of labour, especially since it is now put forward within the women's movement as a demand for women primarily, the bisexual implications of "a guaranteed income for all" having been dropped from the campaign as it developed, and it therefore does little to challenge the low-paid status of women's work or the conditions which give rise to the special oppression of women—the assumption that her primary role is that of wife and mother. Secondly wages, however generous, would not end the isolation, the twenty-four-hour responsibility of the housewife with children (which is what most of us mean when we say housewife) or of a woman caring for sick or aged relatives, nor would they create a situation in the long run whereby those burdens would be lightened.

Thirdly no society, whether capitalist, socialist or anarchist/utopian, could afford to pay a proper wage for the work, because in terms of the hours spent and functions carried out the burden would be enormous. The Chase Manhattan Bank gave an estimate of $257.573 per woman per week in June 1970 which, according to *The Houseworkers' Handbook* would have amounted to twice the total US government budget. And as the writers of the *Handbook* said,

> It is clear that this potential cost of housework is due to the incredibly inefficient organisation of housework in 50 million isolated, identical (in terms of production) domestic factories. The same results could be produced at far less monetary cost, (were it paid for) to the government and health and sanitary costs to women by the socialisation and community control of this labour and the facilities for its performance.[37]

Why then does the idea of "wages for housework" have such initial appeal for so many women? The context of "Women, the Unions and Work" suggests that the idea crystallised out of a search for demands which would mobilise women for this wave of the women's movement as the demand for a vote did the last, but without suffering the limitations of being a single-issue demand— just as, for example, "Peace, Bread and Land" did for the Russian revolution. If there has been such a slogan so far for this phase of the movement, it has been the demand for control over our own bodies and our own lives. "Wages for Housework" has been an attempt to give that demand for control over our own lives the kind of bite that the campaigns for freely available contraception and abortion had and at the same time to be more revolutionary. But, for all the reasons given above, it is a demand that represents more a short-term means of self-defence and survival by housewives who at present have *no other alternative but to be housewives*, whether or not they are also in paid work outside the home, while it also appeals to younger, usually radical women from the professional or white-collar sectors, who see no viable way of reconciling the apparently contradictory desires to be women and to claim the right to have a decent, interesting, varied life, including the right to have children. Therefore, while wages for housework is not the perspective for the women's movement that its supporters think it to be, neither is it the totally reactionary and backward-looking demand that many radicals and socialists in the movement and outside think it is. If the demand for a *wage* is illusory, the impetus behind it, shorn of its mysticism, could be a valuable part of a total strategy if it could avoid the utopianism involved in the pure "wages for housework" and the pure "socialisation of housework" formulations.

A perspective based on wages for housework is not necessarily the same thing as campaigns for money payment or money benefits in recognition of the important function of housework, childcare, and care for the aged and ill by women in the home, in the economy at present, such as adequate welfare payments, family allowances payable to women caring for children regardless of whether they have a paid job or not, and recognition of years spent as housewives in assessing rights to state retirement pensions.

At its most basic the wages for housework demand has at least taken to women the proposition that housework is indeed work, and not merely a natural function like eating and sleeping. It lays, if imperfectly, the basis for separating "womanhood" from the work that societies have given to women as a result. Perhaps it is the crystallisation of a particular stage of consciousness, in which a woman might think as she is washing or sweeping the floor, "If someone else was doing this she would be paid for it" or "If I was doing this somewhere else I would be paid for it"; that is, the division of labour no longer appears "natural" like eating and sleeping, though it still might appear inescapable.

But this useful core is distorted and obscured by some of the arguments used by the Wages for Housework campaign to counter suggestions that the demand is only partial and limited, for example the argument already mentioned that wages for housework will not tie women more to the home because once women have the money they can refuse to do the work, or that all the work done by women in their homes, like putting on lipstick or making love, should be waged. Another is that wages for housework will not tend to confirm the sexual division of labour because most women's work outside the home is *really* only housework anyway. While it is true that a great deal of women's waged work, in the textile and clothing industries, in nursing, catering and cleaning for example, *is* "industrialised housework" and does not challenge the division of labour by sex, it is also true that other kinds of work, such as clerical work, which have *become* women's work are "feminised" to include personal services like making coffee because it is assumed that this kind of work is "naturally" women's work. And it is difficult to see how a campaign which identifies "money for women" with "wages for women for housework" can fail to strengthen that assumption. Although moving service work and the reproduction of labour-power into the labour market does not in itself challenge the sexual division of labour, it does make it possible to challenge it by way of action for equal pay or equal opportunity, or actions such as the recent one by New York secretaries against personal services being part of their job. Many of us know from experience how much more difficult, if not impossible, that kind of action is when we are more emotionally involved with those we serve than workers with their bosses.

But if we are to recognise that most women, whether they work outside the home or not, are housewives, especially if they have children, and believe that the housework issue is of critical importance to women's liberation, if we also accept that the Wages for Housework groups have helped focus attention on the problem while not accepting their solution, what can we put in place of that demand?

—Refusal to accept the division of labour, inside or outside the home, as "natural". We must make a clear statement of the importance of the work done by housewives and of the fact that it has a crucial economic function.

—A study of what housework is and has been, including a study of the parts of it that have already been socialised through industrialisation. The recognition that jobs done in the home are not necessarily menial and uninteresting in themselves, but that it is the context in which they are carried out that makes them oppressive. Housework is inefficient and time-consuming not because housewives are inefficient but because of the system in which and for which they work. Such a study should include an analysis of the different components of housework and, in particular, the separation of childcare from personal maintenance and care of the home.

—Financial recognition for women who have spent years of their lives as housewives. Campaigns for full pension rights, grants for job training and jobs if they want them.

—For women in the paid workforce, a fight for *real* equal pay, which must mean *at least* getting "the price of women's labour power calculated on the same basis as that of men: in terms of the means of subsistence necessary to reproduce as well as to live".[38]

—Workplace demands for maternity/paternity leave; time off for parents of sick children, etc. Shorter hours (rather than part-time work), no compulsory overtime, etc. The "right to work less" is also part of a revolutionary perspective for both men and women, especially in advanced capitalist societies.

—Campaigns for the recognition of childcare as a *social* function and need. This is one of the most difficult areas, because we are here questioning some of the strongest traditional assumptions about parental, and above all maternal, responsibilities and rights. Such a campaign must be coupled with genuine concern for the needs of children as well as women. Possibly campaigns for free community-controlled childcare facilities with short-term either/or campaigns (for example, either provide community-controlled childcare or give us the money to provide our own).

—Campaigns for adequate social service and welfare benefits, especially for women bringing up children on their own. The pittances paid to "welfare mothers" is some kind of indication of what a "wage" for housework paid by the state might be.

—We must also be ready to resist attempts by way of cuts in social services, public health care, or education and childcare to intensify the unpaid labour of housewives.

—A struggle for *both* socialised housework *and* shared tasks of personal maintenance across sex lines in the home. The marxist left's perspective of socialisation is important, otherwise the isolation and oppression of housewives would continue whether recognised financially or not, along with pointless duplication of effort and of expensive, underused equipment. But sharing of necessary housework with men (and children) is important too, since not all housework can be taken outside the home.

—A constant fight to end the sexual divison of labour and sexual discrimination in jobs outside the home. The insistence that "equal opportunity" must mean an attack on the idea of a sex-divided labour market, not just a few women in "men's jobs" or new areas being opened up to become "women's jobs"; otherwise low pay and women's work remain synonymous and women will end up doing the "socialised" housework outside the home for low pay.

—Beyond these essentially economic issues the continued fight against sexism in all its forms, including combating the sex dominance that expresses itself in rape and domestic violence against women, and fighting for women's rights to control their own bodies and their own lives.

Such an approach is clearly relevant mainly to industrial capitalist countries, and would need to be geared in to the particular situation in each society. For the colonised countries, or for what might be called the "transitional" societies like China or the USSR, a different strategy would have to be formulated which still tried to hold a dual perspective of improving the immediate situation of women while challenging as far as possible assumptions about the ''naturalness'' of a sexual division of labour and sexist institutions in general.

We must absolutely agree with the *goal* of the wages for housework campaign—to free women from a choice between unpaid work at home and badly paid work outside but their demand is a case in which a short cut might turn out to be a short circuit. Nor can we take a pure ''socialisation of housework'' line, because the wages for housework groups are right when they say that on its own socialisation would only chain women more firmly to working in laundries, cafeterias, clothing and food factories, typing pools, kindergartens and schools for lower wages than even men get for their work, without removing the irreducible minimum of housework and childcare at home that still gives them an extra job in *any* society we look at.

What we have to say instead is: ''Socialise housework and end the sexual division of labour and sexual discrimination in *all* jobs and sexism in society as a whole.'' It also has to have the spoken or unspoken accompaniment that at the same time we have to be finding ways of undermining capitalism and building a real non-sexist socialist society. And we all know by now that this is not going to be easy.

Finally it is important to fight against the reduction of women's liberation to a narrowly economic issue. One of the strengths of the women's movement has been its insistence that social relations are not a mere reflex of economic relations and has therefore been one of the forces helping to rescue revolutionary theory and practice from economic determinism. Women are not only housewives; the position of women in the family cannot be reduced to the housework issue, any more than the position of women in society as a whole. The family in our society, based as it is on heterosexual monogamy, is more than merely a device for servicing the male workforce, though it is that too. We would hopelessly oversimplify the relationships between sexism and capitalism, and hinder our struggle, if we were to reduce it simply to a fight for money.

The selection that follows, after looking at the history of the housework issue, concentrates on attempts to clarify its economic significance and the political consequences for women's liberation—that is liberation for all women, not just an illusion of self-fulfilment for a few. It separates housework and the housewife from the living institution in which it takes place—the family. But we must never forget that it is not a separate issue, that the housewife and her work in the home cannot really be separated from the emotions that surround family relationships, however hard we might try. In its ideal representation, perhaps seen in its purest form in television advertising, the work of the housewife is an act of pure love. In real life it may be made up of more complex emotions. And those represented in the "recipe" from Shirley Moreno's "Story" are of a very sombre cast:

> Take one heart
> soak it
> salt it
> shake it
> braise it
> add finely chopped nut
> graized word
> $\frac{1}{2}$ baked book
> 2 pinches of love and lump it
> 1 bay leaf
>
> Bash the heart well, stuff it and rape it, roll it well around, mix it with essence of hate and sprinkle it liberally with loneliness and isolation.[39]

In the same way, as Jan Williams, Hazel Twort and Anne Bachelli recognised, the work of the housewife is inseparable from the condition of being "in the family". The housewife quoted in Lee Comer's *Wedlocked Women* expresses the same idea:

> There was one time when I was getting close to breaking down. I really needed a break and I told S. He didn't understand. He said he'd give me a rest and take over for a day or two but when I said I wanted to get right away, out of the house and away from the children, he got very mad. I mean what would have been the use of me sitting here in the house listening to him struggling with the children? I couldn't get any peace out of that could I?

But even such a temporary escape from the condition of housewife implied a rejection of what is understood as the loving relationship of a woman with her man and her children. Lee Comer comments:

> The husband got mad because his wife's demand was unintelligible. He interprets her need for solitude as a rejection of him and the children, as a denial of her role. This woman's husband also misunderstood her need for a break as a need for a rest from housework. It wasn't the burden of the work that was bothering her. It was the burden of *being a housewife*.[40]

Yet "being a housewife" is seen as "caring for the family", so it is not surprising that an attempt to escape is interpreted "as a rejection". Such a feeling of rejection by the man implies more than an expectation of service to the material needs of reproduction of labour power, and women themselves find it difficult to separate the loving and caring—however onesided—from the work it involves.

However distorted heterosexual relationships might be they do embody one kind of love, and one which is the only kind many women want, or can envisage, between adults at least. In *For Her Own Good*, Barbara Ehrenreich and Deirdre English sum up the problem—and the challenge—before the feminist movement:

> Claustrophobia or agoraphobia. Suffocation or free fall. Neither projects a vision of moral redemption or social transformation. Neither upholds any higher value than material self-interest in a world of scarcity. . . . The reason we hang back is because there are no answers left but the most radical ones. We cannot assimilate into a masculinist society without doing violence to our nature which is, of course, *human* nature. But neither can we retreat into domestic isolation . . . A synthesis which transcends both the rationalist and romanticist poles must necessarily challenge the masculinist social order itself. . . . This is the most radical vision but there are no human alternatives. The Market, with its financial abstractions, deformed science, and obsession with dead things—must be pushed back to the margins. And the "womanly" values of community and caring must rise to the centre as the only *human* principles. [41]

An examination of the economic history and political economy of housework can be a way of opening up the contradictions in the heart of the family, that group in which all, including women, are supposed to find solace from the rigours of the outside world—but which too often only reproduces in a horrifying parody all the unequal power relationships and injustices of the wider society in the goldfish bowl of the home. But a concentration on this problem alone would solve nothing. Whatever might be gained in terms of a kind of brutal honesty by transforming into market transactions all the work and the caring and loving that take place in the family, even the sexual relationship itself, the result would not even begin to realise the hope for the future embodied in the Women's Liberation movement. If sexual relations within marriage are often intrinsically no more than a disguised commercial transaction, removing the disguise cannot lead to freely chosen relationships.

And if "caring" for children or other members of the family is often one-sided, unpaid drudgery, little will be gained by turning it purely into *paid* drudgery, either in or outside the home.

> No more the drudge and idler—ten that toil where
>   one reposes,
> But a sharing of life's glories: Bread and roses!
>   Bread and roses.[42]

NOTES

1. Juliet Mitchell, "Women: The Longest Revolution", in *New Left Review*, no. 40, London, November–December 1966. Reprinted in Edith Hoshino Altbach (ed.), *From Feminism to Liberation*, Cambridge, Mass., 1971, p. 121.
2. Ibid., p. 123.
3. Ibid., p. 122.
4. George St George, *Our Soviet Sister*, London, 1973, p. 121. See also Natalia Baranovskaya, "A Week Like Any Other", in *Spare Rib*, nos. 53–59, London, December 1976 to June 1977.
5. Altbach, op. cit., p. 93.
6. See F. Engels, *The Origin of the Family, Private Property and the State*, and V. I. Lenin, "On the Emancipation of Women", in *Collected Works*, vol. 37.
7. Marx, *Capital*, vol. 1, chap. 23.
8. See for example Collected Papers from British Socialist Feminist Conferences; *Red Rag*, London; *Power of Women Journal*, London; *New Left Review*, nos. 83 and 89; *The Bulletin of Socialist Economists*, London, June 1975; "The Political Economy of Women", Conference of Socialist Economists pamphlet, London, 1976; *Latin American Perspectives*, nos. 12–13, Riverside, California, 1977.
9. Alice Clark, *The Working Life of Women in the Seventeenth Century*, London 1919. See also Marx, *Capital*, vol. 1, chap. 15, pp. 391–2.
10. Ivy Pinchbeck, *Women Workers and the Industrial Revolution*, London, 1930.
11. Margaret Hewitt, *Wives and Mothers in Victorian Industry*, London, 1958.
12. Ibid., chap. 2.
13. Ibid., chaps. 3, 9–10, 14.
14. For an account of opposing views at the Leicester Trades Union Congress of 1877 see Marion Ramelson, *Petticoat Rebellion*, pp. 102–3, London, 1972.
15. Hewitt, op. cit., chap. 11.

16. Ibid., p. 70ff.

17. See Alice Clark, op. cit., and Ivy Pinchbeck, op. cit.

18. See for example Doris Mary Stenton, *The English Woman in History*, London, 1957, on homilies and sermons.

19. See the work of Anna Davin, especially "Imperialism and Motherhood", History Workshop Publications, Oxford.

20. Besides those mentioned, see Sheila Rowbotham, *Hidden from History*, London, 1973; Juliet Mitchell and Ann Oakley (eds.), *The Rights and Wrongs of Women*, London, 1976; Catherine Hall, "The History of the Housewife" in *Spare Rib*, no. 26.

21. See Brownlee and Brownlee, *Women in the American Economy*, Yale, 1976; Gwendolyn Salisbury Hughes, *Mothers in Industry*, New York, 1925; Charlotte Perkins Gilman, *The Home: Its Work and Influence*, Chicago, 1972; Women's Study Group, "Womb, Broom and Loom", in *Radical America*, vol. 10, no. 2, Madison, March–April 1976.

22. Barbara Ehrenreich and Deirdre English, "The Manufacture of Housework", in *Socialist Revolution*, No. 26, San Francisco, October–December 1975, reprinted in an expanded version as "Microbes and the Manufacture of Housework" in *For Her Own Good*, New York, 1978, and London, 1979.

23. Pearl Jephcott, Nancy Seear and John Smith, *Married Women Working*, London, 1962.

24. Jean Gardiner, "Women's Domestic Labour", in *New Left Review*, no. 89, January–February 1975.

25. Selma James, *Women, the Unions and Work*, London, 1972 (reprinted Bristol, 1976).

26. See for example Papers from the Women and Socialism Conference, 1972; see also *Red Rag*, nos. 2 and 5.

27. In *Falling Wall Book Review*, no. 5, 1976, p. 25.

28. Mariarosa Dalla Costa, "Women and the Subversion of the Community", in *Radical America*, vol. 6, no. 1, Boston, January-February 1972 (originally published in Italian as "Donne e sovversione sociale", in *Potere femminile e sovversione sociale*, Padova, 1972). Revised and expanded version in M. Dalla Costa and Selma James, *The Power of Women and the Subversion of the Community*, Bristol, October 1972, see p. 31 and p. 52 note 12; in third revised edition (September 1975, with new Foreword noting that original article was co-authored by Dalla Costa and and James), p. 33 and p. 53 note 12.

29. Marx, *Theories of Surplus Value*, Moscow, 1964, p. 161.

30. Ibid., p. 162.

31. See Selma James, "Wageless of the World", in Wendy Edmonds and Suzie Fleming (eds.), *All Work and No Pay*, Bristol, 1975.

32. Selma James, "Women, the Unions and Work", introduction to Second Edition, Bristol, 1976, p. 1.

33. Nicole Questiaux and Jacques Fournier, "Family Policy in France", in *International Working Party on Family Policy*, New York, 1977, p. 112 ff.

34. Shulamith Firestone, op. cit., pp. 207–8.

35. Mariarosa Dalla Costa, op. cit., p. 32 and 34.
36. Ibid., p. 39; see also p. 36.
37. Betsy Warrior and Lisa Leghorn, *The Houseworker's Handbook*, Cambridge, Mass., 1974, pp. 17–18.
38. See Caroline Freeman, "When Is a Wage Not a Wage?", in this volume, p. 202.
39. In *Women's Liberation Review*, no. 1, October, 1972, p. 77.
40. Lee Comer, *Wedlocked Women*, Leeds, 1974, p. 110.
41. Barbara Ehrenreich and Deirdre English, *For Her Own Good*, New York, 1978, pp. 290–2.
42. From the song by James Oppenheim, inspired by banners carried by young mill girls in the 1912 Lawrence USA textile strike. Reprinted in Altbach, op. cit.

1

The History of the Housewife

CATHERINE HALL

Housewives have rarely thought of themselves as having a history—and historians have not thought of the housewife as worthy of academic study. The history of women in the home—of the changing nature of marriage, childcare and domestic labour, for example—is an area which badly needs exploration.

Every society has rules about which activities are suitable for which sex but these rules are not constant—the sexual division of labour is not a rigid division. The activities of men and women are always patterned and the patterning always reveals relations of domination and subordination in relation to the major productive spheres. But the actual patterns of male and female activities within any one society at any one stage in the development in its mode of production differs. Women may do no heavy work in one society and only heavy work in another. The way in which the sexual division of labour is defined and decided will depend on both the real relations of sexuality, reproduction and work and the attitudes and beliefs about them. The sexual division of labour is not given in nature but constant in history.

Being a housewife, then, is a condition which is socially defined and its definition changes at different historical moments. When we talk about a housewife now we mean a woman whose work is to maintain and organise a household and look after her husband and children—we think of washing, cooking, cleaning and the full-time care of pre-school children. That work is unpaid: the woman is paid through her husband who is supposed to receive enough to support himself and his family. If, as Marx suggested, wages represent only the reward for necessary labour time—that is, what is necessary for the worker to reproduce the conditions of his own labour—then in modern capitalism the housewife has become one of those hidden conditions, and thus the invisible support for the generation of surplus value. Around this real, objective, but heavily disguised role the ideological definitions and supporting definitions have clustered. Since the "real" labour of the world consists of public work, being a housewife now is seen as a job with little if any status; women often say when asked what they do, "Oh, I'm only a housewife," or, "I'm just a housewife." It has not always had such a limited or despised status.

To be a housewife in fourteenth-century England meant something very different to what it does today, when it has been decisively separated from the productive and industrial sphere. It still involved domestic work and the care of children, and it was still unpaid: but for a large proportion of women it would also involve many other kinds of work besides—brewing, baking, looking after a dairy, keeping the poultry and so on. Part of the reason for that was the fact that the family itself, both among the peasants, and in the towns, was a productive unit.

The family means in this context father, mother, often unmarried brothers and sisters, possibly grandparents, children, servants and—in an urban situation—apprentices. In this family the labour power of each individual member is only a definite portion of the labour power of the family. Women were, therefore, themselves centrally related to production, and not only through their husbands. The pre-industrial family was a self-sufficient economic unit and consequently domestic work had a much wider definition than it does now. It might well involve brewing, dairy work, the care of poultry and pigs, the production of vegetables and fruit, the spinning of flax and wool and also medical care—nursing and doctoring. These areas were rougly defined as "women's work": but there is much more flexibility in the drawing of lines around women's work and men's work—work was done on the basis of task-orientation rather than by way of a rigid and formalised division of labour.

There were some jobs which were always specifically connected with one sex. The higher manorial officers were always men and the dairymaid, for example, was always a woman. A thirteenth-century manual on "The Duties of Manorial Officers" gives us an account of the dairymaid's work: "The dairymaid ought to be faithful and of good repute, and keep herself clean, and ought to know her business and all that belongs to it. She ought not to allow any under-dairymaid or another to take or carry away milk, or butter, or cream, by which the cheese shall be less and the dairy impoverished. And she ought to know well how to make cheese and salt cheese, and she ought to save and keep the vessels of the dairy that it need not be necessary to buy new ones every year." [1]

The two most powerful medieval theories about women were the creations of the Church and the aristocracy. The Church's view of women was heavily influenced by St Paul and saw women as the creation of the devil and as both inferior and evil. Marriage was an institution set up to contain the unavoidable sin of sexuality; as Our Lord put it in a vision to Margery Kempe the fifteenth-century mystic, "for though the state of maidenhood be more perfect and more holy than the state of widowhood, and the state of widowhood more perfect than the state of wedlock, yet, daughter, I love thee as well as any maiden in the world." [2] The aristocracy on the other hand developed the counter doctrine of the superiority of women. This was connected with the cult of the Virgin Mary, the adoration of the Virgin in Heaven and the lady on earth. Though the two theories were at different poles, in one sense both combined to give women an other-worldly role—they were seen as in no way central to political or economic life. This split between the wicked and the divine, the prostitute and the saint, represents an ideological split and projection by men which has recurred in many forms. Women provided either an explanation for evil or a haven of good. Neither view had much to do with reality. In Chrétien de Troyes's romance *Lancelot* the hero gets into Queen Guinevere's bedroom but Lancelot "holds her more dear than the relic of any saint" and "when he leaves the room he bows and acts precisely as if he were before a shrine". [3] Neither of these theories was taken at face value outside the Church and the aristocracy; but what was clearly already accepted was that women were secondary and inferior.

Because of the need for their labour, women in the village were in a better position than aristocratic women, in the sense that they were involved in productive relations. What this means in fact is that they were free to be exploited in an equal way with men. The feudal economy was based on the ownership of land, which was the major source of power, by a relatively small number: the land was worked by both free and unfree peasants. Few received money wages—the unfree worked on the lord's land in return for renting some of the lord's land. Every peasant was subject to a lord and in a hierarchical society every lord was subject to another who was ultimately subject to the king. Supposedly there was a system of rights and obligations at each level but at the bottom of the ladder the obligations which the lord owed to the peasant were absolutely minimal whereas his rights were extensive.

Peasant women were able to hold land though the normal assumption was that heads of households would be male—the position of widows in particular has long been recognised as of importance, both because of their longevity and their established rights. Manorial records, as Rodney Hilton has shown, do record a substantial number of women holding land—even as minors.[4] It seems that unmarried women with holdings would usually quickly marry—the labour of the man was as important to the woman as vice versa. However, their right to hold land was only because the holdings were small and would not affect the distribution of power on the feudal estate. Aristocratic women, with few exceptions, could not hold land since land was the key to the feudal economy and once the property rights of a family or aristocratic line came into question women were simply a marriageable commodity. It is clear that peasant women did do heavy work on the land as can be seen from the illustrations of clod breaking and there is evidence that at some points they got equal pay. The question as to whether women labourers were paid the same as their male counterparts seems to have something to do with job definition and bargaining power. Female domestic servants were low paid, for example, because they were subject to non-economic compulsion since they tended to live in the lord's household and could have all kinds of personal pressure put on them. But it would be wrong to associate the respect given to women's labour with a society free from discrimination. Distinctions were of course made in the law, education, the Church and in political and property rights between men and women. Peasant women could not assume the limited rights to property which men had—their rights were much less clear and would probably depend on the customs of a particular locality.

Women were, furthermore, subject to particular kinds of exploitation by the feudal lord. At Pattingham in Staffordshire in April 1369, Juliana, the daughter of Roger Baroun, was "deflowered" by a Welshman and had to pay a five-shilling fine to the lord of the manor. A woman who was not a virgin had less monetary value to her feudal lord since a well-to-do peasant might refuse to marry her and consequently the cut of the marriage settlement which the lord got would be less. In 1388 Agnes, the daughter of Juliana Prynce, had to pay ten shillings to the lord of the manor to be able to marry and go as a free woman with her goods.[5]

But abstract theories about the proper role of women were not allowed to stand in the way of meeting familial and social needs. Peasant women were able to play a relatively independent role in day-to-day economic life—they were open to the same kind of exploitation by the feudal lord as were men whereas at other times the appropriation of women's labour has been effected in a more indirect way. This means that women were likely to organise themselves politically in the same way as men. In Halesowen in Worcestershire in 1386, "A certain John atte Lythe and Thomas Puttewey, serfs, by the advice, procurement and maintenance of a certain Agnes, wife of John Saddler, assembled an illegal conventicle of unknown rebels against the abbot . . . saying openly that they did not wish any more to be considered as serfs of the abbot and would not do any of the previously owed services."[6]

The social, political and ideological dominance of the male was clear, however, at the local level. Women were not the heads of tithings, they didn't sit on local juries, they didn't fill the office of constable or reeve. Women with a legal title to a holding could often be obliged to marry and they had to suffer a regular barrage from the Church about their evil influence. Women played a variety of economic roles within the village—they were not all housewives and housewife had a much wider definition than it does now. They were not all housewives because there was a much smaller number of households to the population and there might be several women living in a household whose jobs were as domestic servants or labourers. Peasant women might, according to their age and marital status, be doing a variety of different jobs. They might be doing specifically women's work, such as spinning and carding or in the dairy; they might be doing work which was not rigidly defined as men's or women's—in the fields—ploughing or harvesting; they might be working centred around their own household—cooking, brewery and caring for children or as domestic servants either in the lord's house or in the house of a richer peasant.

Housewife in fourteenth-century England tended to mean the co-ordinator and organiser of an establishment and of a centre of production. The condition of being wedded to a house was a more substantive one than it is now because the fourteenth-century house had a different function and meaning from the twentieth-century equivalent. It did imply a status which was, however, considerably limited by the current ideology on the position of women. This reminds us that the ideological forms do not merely reflect the economic but have a life and relative autonomy of their own which can even serve in certain instances to limit and restrict the economic sphere. The economic and ideological demands on women in the village were to a considerable degree in contradiction to each other.

The situation was very similar in the towns—being a housewife was recognised as a particular job but it involved a wide range of domestic activity. Generally there were no frontiers between professional or business life and private life. These activities all tended to go on in the same living/working area. The household was the centre both of domestic activity and mercantile activity. This integration of work and home contributed to the fact that it was not necessary to regard the socialisation of children as one of the most important functions of the family. Children were not seen as a special group—once they were past infancy they were absorbed into the adult household and were educated by the process of life and work going on around them. Domestic service and apprenticeship were two of the major ways of educating and these applied to boys and girls alike (though the evidence as to girls being formally apprenticed is unclear, they certainly were apprenticed and trained informally).

In a feudal society the notion of service was central both to the relations between lord and master, parents and children, lover and mistress. Transmission of a way of life from one generation to another was ensured by the everyday participation of children in adult life. In the towns, as in the villages, women were engaged in a wide range of economic activities connected with the family as a unit of production. Women figure in guild records as barbers, furriers, carpenters, saddlers, joiners, and in many other trades. There are relatively few trades which explicitly exclude women. All the female members of a merchant's household would be engaged in some form of economic activity—the housewife herself might spend a good deal of her energies organising other men and women to fulfil the necessary domestic tasks so that she would be free to engage in mercantile activities. Women in smaller scale households might take up one of the entrepreneurial activities which were often associated with women because they were extensions of domestic activity—Margery Kempe who was the daughter of one of Lynn's leading citizens describes how ''she now bethought herself a new housewifery'' and went in for milling—this was after the failure of her brewing enterprise which she ascribes to God's disapproval of her involvement in such activities: ''Then for pure covetousness, and to maintain her pride, she began to brew, and was one of the greatest brewers in the town of N. for 3 years or 4, till she lost much money. . . . For, though she had ever such good servants, cunning in brewing, yet it would never succeed with them.''[7]

But the degree to which it was considered the duty of the good wife to look after her husband should not be underestimated. ''The Goodman of Paris'', a late fourteenth-century text, instructs the wife. ''Wherefore love your husband's person carefully, and I pray you keep him in clean linen, for that is your business, and because the trouble and care of outside affairs lieth with men, so must husbands take heed, and go and come, and journey hither and thither, in rain and wind, in snow and hail, now drenched, now dry, now sweating, now shivering, ill-fed, ill-lodged, ill-warmed and ill-bedded. And naught harmeth him, because he is upheld by the hope that he hath of the care which his wife will take of him on his return, and of the ease, the joys and the pleasures which she will do him, or cause to be done to him, in her presence, to be unshod before a good fire, to have his feet washed and fresh shoes and hose, to be given good food and drink, to be well served and well looked after, well bedded in white sheets and nightcaps, well covered with good furs, and assuaged with other joys and desports, privities, loves and secrets whereof I am silent. And the next day fresh shirts and garments. . . . Wherefore, dear sister, I beseech you thus to bewitch and bewitch again your husband that shall be, and beware of roofless house and smoky fire, and scold him not, but be unto him gentle and amiable and peaceable. Have a care that in winter he have a good fire and smokeless and let him rest well and be well covered between your breasts, and thus be with him. . . . And thus shall you preserve and keep your husband from all discomforts and give him all the comforts whereof you can bethink you, and serve him and have him served in your house, and you shall look to him for outside things, for if he be good he will take even more pains and labour therein than you wish, and by doing what I have said, you will cause him ever to miss you and have his heart with you and your loving service and he will shun all other houses, all other women, all other services and households.''[8]

The position of aristocratic women in the fourteenth century was much more rigidly circumscribed and narrowly defined than that of their lower class sisters and this was paradoxically because they could not be housewives. Their position was much more determined by ideological considerations than by economic ones because their husbands and fathers were wealthy enough to free them from the economic necessity of engaging in domestic activity with all its ramifications. There are cases of widows who were heavily involved with estate management or of queens who were actively involved politically but in general most upper-class women were almost entirely without political or juridical rights and they spent their lives under the perpetual wardship of a father, a husband or a guardian. They had minimal rights over their own property—it simply made them into suitable marriage alliances.

The lack of freedom of aristocratic women was fundamentally connected to the centrality of private property. It was essential for a lord to defend the property rights of his family against any intrusion. He wanted to be sure that his land would be passed on to his heirs and them alone. A major interest of every feudal land-owning family was to extend their property—to make good marriages which would result in this, to buy up whatever they could to consolidate their estates and to increase them by force if the occasion arose. Because property was naturally inherited through the male line and property meant land, men and power, women were inevitably seen as decorative pawns. In a period when conspicuous consumption was becoming an increasingly important symbol of power within the ruling class, to have a leisured lady as a wife followed round by a company of young men who were dying of love for her was one aspect of that consumption. It increased the status of the husband in the eyes of the world.

We can see from the medieval definition of housewife how close a relationship there is between the position of women at work and at home—in pre-capitalist society, because there is no split between the two, being a housewife means being engaged in a whole range of productive activities centred both in domestic activity for private consumption and in domestic activity which would be marketable. There are two sets of considerations at work in defining women's proper work—firstly what it is on the whole thought right and proper for women to do and, secondly, what is—given the circumstances of production at the time—practicable for women to do. These two continuously interact on and constrain one another. It is the interaction of the ideological with the economic—both levels within the same social formation but having a relative autonomy of their own—which are the major factors in the definition of housewife.

The extended activities of the fourteenth-century household were

beginning to disappear by the seventeenth century. The emergence
of capitalism led to extensive changes in the organisation and
function of the family. The family started to be less important in
production but at the same time far more important in the creation
of the relations of capitalist production—in the production we
might say of bourgeois men. Women became considerably less
important in the direct creation of surplus value but more important in the reproduction of conditions for labour power—the
family had to become the training ground of rational men. With
the development of capitalism comes the separation of capital from
labour, the separation of the home from the place of work and the
separation of domestic labour and commodity production. With
the development of a capitalist mode of production the household
is no longer the central unit of production. We are already
beginning to discern the family as a centre of consumption.

This was, of course, a very long-term change, but the separation
of work from home has a vital effect on women since it brings with
it a much changed conception of the sexual division of labour and
what constitutes women's work.

Two of the major functions of the family within capitalism are to
act as a centre of consumption and to act as the unit which is
responsible for the maintenance and reproduction of labour
power.[9] The change in the family from being the major unit of
production in the society does have quite specific effects on the
position of the housewife. As more consumer goods and services
become available on the market so there is less need for the
household to be a self-sufficient economic unit—a narrowing down
of the conception of domestic activities takes place. Alice Clark in
her excellent study of *The Working Life of Women in the
Seventeenth Century* documents, for example, the way in which
services which were performed within the family in a pre-capitalist
economy became professionalised in the seventeenth century and
were taken over by men.[10] This professionalisation—which was
particularly marked in the medical and educational spheres—was
partly a result of the scientific and intellectual developments of the
seventeenth century but it was also due to the new division of
labour which was taking place in the capitalist organisation of trade
and industry. Nursing and doctoring which had been a part of
domestic activity began to be organised and require training and as
women were excluded from this specialised training so domestic
handling of it came to seem inadequate. A similar kind of

limitation on domestic activity took place because of the developing capitalist organisation of those trades which had previously been part of an extended household. Brewing is a classic example: it was, as we have seen, an entrepreneurial area which had been particularly popular with women but by the end of the seventeenth century brewing had become an organised trade and was no longer open to women. The skills which could be acquired domestically were not enough to establish women's position in trade—women could still, of course, brew for their own families if they wanted to, but that became a privatised activity which could not easily be extended into the social sphere. Gradually a change was taking place in the relative efficiency of domestic and capitalist production—a slow decline had set in for the self-sufficient household or country estate as a unit of production. It became more important for men to organise their trades protectively once the separation of capital and labour and of the home from the place of work took place: the separation of commodity production from domestic labour was an inevitable result. Male workers were gathered together and employees began to form associations in addition to the employers' guilds which existed. For journeymen in their new position as wage labourers to be able to bargain well they had to maintain their exclusive position by long apprenticeships and many restrictions on entry: the easiest group to exclude were women. Both guilds and workers' associations had power and influence stemming from their collective organisation which women did not have at their command. A large number of poor women had managed to make a living by selling domestic produce from door to door—the established shopkeepers disliked this competition and managed to restrict unlicensed selling because of their political influence in the localities.

We defined a second function of the capitalist family as the maintenance and reproduction of labour power. This can be divided into two areas—firstly the material reproduction of the labour force and secondly the ideological reproduction of the relations of production. The seventeenth-century housewife is directly responsible for the first and has a limited responsibility for the second. The material reproduction of the labour force is ensured by giving labour power the material means with which to reproduce itself—that is to say, wages. The notion of the individual "social" wage—enough to support a man and his family—is only beginning in the seventeenth century and it does not receive full recognition until the era of industrial capitalism. But with the separation of work and home within the capitalist organised trades there comes the much clearer division of labour between the man who goes out to work and the woman who stays at home and organises the household—which has in any event, as we have seen, come to mean far less than it did and is being progressively reduced to the physical care of husband and children. The maintenance and reproduction of labour power is and must always be a necessary condition to the reproduction of capital. But the capitalist, as Marx points out, can safely leave this to the labourers' instincts of self-preservation and propagation.[11] Workers, even when not directly engaged in the labour process, are still, therefore, an appendage of capital while an appearance of independence is kept up by the fiction of a free contract between the employer and the labourer. The reproduction of labour power requires not only material care but also ideological care. Labour power must both reproduce its skills and its submission to the rules of the established order—in other words, as Althusser puts it, the reproduction of submission to the ruling ideology for the workers and the reproduction of the ability to manipulate the ruling ideology correctly for the agents of exploitation and repression.[12] The family, the Church, the army and the schools are all crucial in the reproduction of the relations of production—they socialise people in ways which ensure subjection to the ruling ideology or mastery of its practice. In the medieval period the Church was the most important institution of this type, in that it provided the ideology of feudalism—it deified hierarchical relations. It was for this reason of course that religious struggle and dissent was so crucial to the decline of feudalism and the transition to capitalism. With the crisis in the Catholic Church, the Reformation and the development of Puritanism, the Anglican Church in the seventeenth century no longer combined within itself religious, educational, and cultural functions. Consequently the family had become much more formative in the education and socialisation of children. As a prayer in the Primer of 1553 put it: "To have children and servants is thy blessing, O Lord, but not to order them according to thy word deserveth thy dreadful curse."[13]

The changes which capitalism began to effect in the organisation of the household were not experienced in the same way by all women. Up to the Restoration it had been seen as quite natural that the wives of merchants and large farmers should play an active part in business affairs but from 1660 onwards this seems to become increasingly unusual.[14] The idea develops of the upper-class woman as a lady of leisure—a shift takes place from the image of women as active and energetic to the old aristocratic ideal of women as passive and dependent. As Sheila Rowbotham points out, not to work becomes a mark of superiority for upper-middle-class women just as men establish work as a crucial criterion of dignity and worth.[15] The spread of capitalism brought with it a great increase in wealth which made possible the idleness of a much larger group of women. The bourgeois revolution brought with it not only an extension of the ruling class but also a new set of values for the wives of the successful bourgeoisie. This process had in fact been going on for a long time. There is a considerable amount of popular literature in the preceding hundred years which documents the emergence of a new leisured middle class and the resulting ambivalent attitudes to women. Most of the literature revolves around the position and behaviour of middle-class wives. The main attacks were on their love of luxury and their vanity. Rich, in a typical pamphlet on ''The Excellency of Good Women'', says: ''and what is it that doth make so many citizens and trades men, so commonly to play bankrupt, but the excessive pride that is used by their wives. By this pride of women Hospitality is eaten up and good Housekeeping is banished out of the Country. . . .''[16] Or Gainsford, an early seventeenth-century spokesman for the commercial classes: ''A citizen is more troubled with his wife than his wares: for they are sorted, locked up, and never brought out, but by constraint for the profit of their master; but his wife is decked, adorned, neatly apparelled, sits for the gaze, goes at her pleasure, and will not be restrained from any sights or delights, or merry-meetings; where they may shew their beauties, or riches, or recreate themselves.''[17] The objections were to middle-class women behaving in ways which were not suitable to their position—overreaching themselves. There are many references to the increasing difficulty in distinguishing between countesses, courtesans and merchants' wives. In the more prosperous commercial families the role of the wife was increasingly that of a leisured lady—the most that she would do would be to supervise the domestic activities of her servants. This also resulted to some extent in a bourgeoisification of the aristocracy. There is a tendency in the seventeenth century towards a reduction in the size of households which was probably connected with the development of bourgeois patterns. Aristocratic ladies might, as in the fourteenth century, be concerned with the supervision of the household but essentially their lives were leisured. We do have records of some exceptional figures who were deeply involved with the organisation of their estates but what is striking about the diary of Lady Anne Clifford as seen through her biographer, for example, is the extent to which she regards private or domestic events as scarcely worth recording.[18] Time and again the seventeenth-century private records demonstrate the degree to which the inferiority of women and the unimportance of household activities were a part of the cultural apparatus. Public events were the things which were worth recording.

Lady Anne Clifford filled several volumes with the records of her long and active life, but the major issues dealt with are public ones. She had a long struggle over a disputed inheritance which took up a great deal of time and energy. She was obviously an unusual woman in that she would not give in despite very strong pressure from both her husband, who wanted a settlement, and the king—until finally an agreement was made over her head. An arrangement which was only possible, of course, because she was a woman. Once she eventually got hold of her inheritance because of the death of the surviving male heir, her major concern was with the administration of her estates. The only private issue that she deals with is her religious sentiments, and this seems to be a common pattern in seventeenth-century diaries.

In the less wealthy families and in the gentry and clerical families of middling status the housewife continued to play an active part in the organisation of the domestic economy. The general impression from Ralph Josselin's diary is that the bond between husband and wife was very strong.[19] There is evidence that they worked together on the farm and it seems as if all important decisions were taken jointly. At the end of one account of some advice to his son he says "their mother gave them the same advice".[20]

Ralph Josselin was a clergyman, but his wife clearly worked. The idea of the leisured lady was only possible when there were no financial problems. Ralph records in his diary felling a tree with his wife—she was used to hard physical labour.

Housewifery seems to have been a valued skill. Thomas Isham of Lamport when he was looking for a wife had one possible candidate described to him as "very vertuously educated by a careful and vigilant mother, and is of an excellent temper and disposition, naturally brisk and cheerful, a notable Housewife and may prove a very endearing consort if well managed''.[21] It seems to have been a common pattern in these sorts of families for the children—both boys and girls—to leave home when they were adolescent. The boys would be apprenticed out to learn a trade, the girls would be sent as servants into other families—presumably to learn housewifery.

The beginning of the separation of the place of work from the home made it more difficult for lower-class women and children to be engaged in productive activity. The wives of journeymen found themselves no longer on the work premises and seriously disadvantaged because of this. If their husbands made enough money they could become dependent—and in the seventeenth century we find the idea developing of husbands keeping their wives rather than a couple being engaged together in economic activity: or they could attempt to find work themselves. But women were in a weak position in the labour market. Once a woman lost the ability to support herself and her family through domestic activity centred on the household, she found herself very disadvantaged compared with men—her family ties now operated as a severe handicap. Capitalism undermined the position of considerable economic independence enjoyed by married women and widows in the tradesmen and middling farmer groupings.[22] The value of a woman's productive capacity to her family was greatly reduced when through poverty she was obliged to work for wages—spinsters, for example, suffered from extremely low wages because of the combination of disorganisation and a lack of bargaining power, both of which resulted mainly from the fact that they worked at home.[23] Consequently a large proportion of the produce of a woman's labour was diverted from her family to the capitalist or consumer, whereas when a woman was fully employed in the household the whole value of what she produced was retained by the family. Capitalist organisation tended to deprive women of the opportunities to share in the more profitable forms of production—it confined them as wage-earners to the unprotected trades. Any family which had sufficient resources would employ the woman within the household in some form of domestic industry—women were only driven on to the labour market from necessity.

The development of Puritanism marked a change in the importance given to the family. In using the example of the Puritans I am not claiming that they were a representative group in the society but rather that they reflected the emergence of new attitudes to the family which were centrally related to the development of a capitalist ethic. As the Puritans did not have control of the ruling institutions and indeed for much of the seventeenth century were subject to active persecution and repression, it was essential for them to develop counter-institutions, of which the family was one. In the spiritual withdrawal of "the saints" for the years to come, the family became a focus of organisation and discipline. The Puritans were extremely well aware of the centrality of proper socialisation and they saw the family or household unit as vital to this. For the Puritans the lowest unit in the hierarchy of discipline was the household—for "Who is anywhere," says a preacher in 1608, "but is of some man's family, and within some man's gates?"[24] They believed in the spiritualisation of the whole life and the household was a starting point for this process. The influence of God must be felt at all levels and in all spheres. One of the key elements in socialisation was the taboo on idleness and the imposition of a labour discipline, as Christopher Hill has demonstrated.[25] The father and master of the household was given the main responsibility for this but the mother was seen as his lieutenant. Elizabeth Joceline in *The Mother's Legacie To Her Unborne Childe* of 1632 says, "Be ashamed of idleness as thou art a man, but tremble at it as thou art a Christian. . . . What more wretched estate can there be in the world? First to be hated of God an idle drone, not fit for this service; then through extreme poverty to be contemned of all the world."[26] A Puritan homily against idleness stresses that children must be trained to work so as to be able "not only to sustain themselves competently, but also to relieve and supply the necessity and want of others".[27] From the seventeenth century onwards there is much more emphasis on work in the parish provisions for orphaned children. The fact that the father was charged with the responsibility for the moral welfare of his household enhanced his dignity and made everyone else more dependent on him—as the Hallers put it: "In the society which the preachers were helping to shape, the family household, with its extensions in farmstead and shop, and in its relation to religious life, was assuming an importance it had not had in feudal, monastic or courtly society. The preachers described it again and again as a little church, a little state—for which the head of the household was responsible."[28] Calamy in *England's Looking-Glasse* of 1642 says, "First reform your own families and then you will be the fitter to reform the family of God. Let the master reform his servant, the father his child, the husband his wife."[29] Yet there were contradictory influences within Puritanism; one of these was the emphasis on regarding morality as an affair of the inner spirit rather than depending on the opinion of the world. Paradoxically, this emphasis on the inner spiritual life was, it has been argued, one of the major reasons for the Puritan success in the business world, in that subjecting the spiritual life to godly discipline and setting the whole of a man's life under the eye of God led to the extension of rational calculation and organisation in the world of trade as well. Thus in assisting the husband to discipline the family women no doubt played a crucial role in the character formation and training of the children who were to grow up to be "proper bourgeois men". Within the Puritan family, however, strict hierarchy was maintained—the man remained the head of the household. As Benjamin Wadsworth put it in *The Well Ordered Family*, "Though the husband is to rule his Family and his Wife, yet his government of his wife should not be with rigour, hautiness, harshness, severity; but with the greatest love, gentleness, kindness, tenderness that may be. Though he governs her he must not treat her as a servant, but as his *own flesh*: he must love her as himself, Eph. 5 33. He should make his government of her, as easie and gentle as possible; and strive more to be loved than feared; though neither is to be excluded."[30] The Puritan God was undoubtedly masculine and Puritanism in abolishing the cult of the Virgin Mary had undoubtedly abolished whatever moderating feminine influence the Virgin had had on rampant Catholic male chauvinism! Some of the radical Puritan sects recognised the spiritual equality of the woman with the man and this produced at the ideological level at least some early and quite radical statements on the position of women. Even they, however, as Keith Thomas has suggested, did not carry this beyond the spiritual arena.[31] The dominant tendency in Puritanism remained that of seeing women as subordinate helpmeets—the image of the sun and moon is very often used for the husband and wife. As Adam says in *Paradise Lost*:

> For nothing lovelier can be found
> in woman, than to study household good
> and good works in her husband to promote.[32]

Milton makes it clear that Adam should have exercised his proper authority over Eve—he attributes Adam's failure to his dependence on his wife and insufficient control over his instincts. Lucy Hutchinson, the wife of a Puritan commander in the Civil

War shares Milton's attitudes—she firmly believed in the subjection of women. When describing her husband she says, "For conjugal affection to his wife it was such in him as whosoever would draw out a rule of honour, kindness and religion to be practised in that estate, need no more but to draw out exactly his example. Never man had a greater passion for a woman, nor a more honourable esteem of a wife; yet he was not uxorious, nor remitted not that just rule which it was her honour to obey, but managed the reins of government with such prudence and affection that she who would not delight in such an honourable and advantageable subjection must have wanted a reasonable soul. He governed by persuasion. . . . all that she was, was him, while he was here, and all that she is now at best is but his pale shade."[33] She describes her own mother's role as "The care of the worship and service of God, both in her soul and her house, and the education of her children."[34] But what authority the mother did have over her children was received from the father. Daniel Rogers in his *Matrimonial Honour* of 1642 illustrates how unimportant it was if a mother objected to a marriage alliance—it was the father that mattered.[35]   Women were expected to give some religious instruction—special "mothers' catechisms" were produced—but again it was as the father's lieutenant. The Puritans assumed that babies were born evil and ignorant but that this could be overcome by education. The task of instruction and discipline must be started very early—they realised how much easier it was to train young children than adolescents. The mother's role as educator and socialiser of her children was certainly recognised in the seventeenth century but it was a limited and narrowly defined and ultimately dependent responsibility which she had. Lucy Hutchinson remarks in her few autobiographical notes that her mother did not approve of the amount of intellectually oriented education which her father arranged for her.[36]

We can see from the seventeenth-century definition of housewife the way in which the role is subject to change. The establishment of a more clearly defined sexual division of labour within the developing capitalist mode of production has a crucial effect on the position of women both inside and outside the home. It would be wrong to over-emphasise the separation of work from home—even the big London merchants did not begin to live systematically away from their counting-houses until the eighteenth century and for the shopkeeper separation comes very much later. However, the economic status of women was declining—often no doubt with their active connivance since there were clearly many advantages in being "leisured". Women are now defined both economically and ideologically as secondary—as people who care for and support others rather than themselves being active in the world. There is less tension between the economic and the ideological spheres than there was in pre-capitalist society because the woman's two main economic functions have become, firstly, the organisation of a household which is no longer the central unit of production; and secondly, the provision of a cheap supply of labour. There are increasing numbers of ladies at one end of the social scale and exploited women at the other end: somewhere in the middle, the traditional housewife is trying to defend her position.

The third definition of housework that I want to look at is the one which was current in early Victorian society. The dominant ideal definition was one which was established by the Victorian middle class and which was highly unsuited to working-class experience. One of the major functions of the Victorian family was to provide a privatised haven for the man who was subject day in and day out to the pressures of competition in the new industrial world. This feminine role was, one might say, a new aspect of the material reproduction of labour power—to provide men at home with the emotional support to face the world of work outside. As Engels says, the family is not only the sum of its economic functions; it is not just a serving-house for capitalism, standing in a one to one relationship with the mode of production—it is also itself a system of relations and emotional needs which shape responses in the world and are created and defined with peculiar strength within the intimate sphere of the family.[37] So just as we have seen how in the seventeenth century women became much less directly concerned with the creation of surplus value and much more concerned with the production of the proper conditions for capitalist production— so, with the coming of industrial capitalism, the more total separation of work from home and the public from the private, the proper role of women was increasingly seen to be *at home*. The family was at the centre of Victorian middle-class social life and the fulcrum for the complex set of social values which comprised middle-class respectability. We now know something of the degree of double standards and the mechanism of psychological projection which sustained this ethic. As Marx was the first to point out the respectable middle-class lady and the prostitute were two sides of the same coin—one might almost say bedfellows! The rich harvest of Victorian pornography would not exist without the Victorian gentleman's ability to travel constantly between virginal ladies upstairs and easy prey below stairs. So it became essential for the preservation of family life that women should be at one and the same time exalted and despised. Thomas Arnold talked of that peculiar sense of solemnity with which the very idea of domestic life was invested: the conception of the home was a source of virtues and emotions which could not be found elsewhere. As Ruskin puts it in *Sesame and Lilies*, ''This is the true nature of home—it is the place of peace—the shelter not only from all injury, but from all terror, doubt and division. In so far as it is not this, it is not home; so far as the anxieties of the outer life penetrate into it, and the inconsistently minded, unknown, unloved, or hostile society of the outer world is allowed by either husband or wife to cross the threshold, it ceases to be   home.''[38] William Thompson in his *Appeal on Behalf of One Half of the Human Race* was somewhat sceptical of the male-oriented view of the home. ''Home'', he writes, ''was the eternal prison house of the wife; her husband painted it as the abode of calm bliss, but took care to find outside its doors a species of bliss not quite so calm, but of a much more varied and stimulating description.''[39] The Victorians needed to sentimentalise the home in order to give themselves some relief from the anxieties of the public world. Tennyson ironically epitomises the new tradition in *The Princess*:

> Man for the field and woman for the hearth;
> Man for the sword, and for the needle she;
> Man with the head and woman with the heart;
> Man to command, and woman to obey;
> All else confusion.[40]

As endless manuals reminded the Victorian wife and mother, their job was to be ''a companion who will raise the tone of a man's mind from low anxieties and vulgar cares'' and preserve an exalted love free from the taint of sexuality or passion. Love should be an uplifting experience and belonged at home—sex was a different matter. Middle-class women who saw themselves as tending the household and maintaining its moral tone provided sex on demand for their husbands along with preserves, clean linen and roast meat. The notion of autonomous sexual pleasure for themselves was unthought of: sex was a necessary obligation owed to men and not one which women were permitted to talk or think about as owed to themselves. Mrs Ellis in her manual *Daughters of England* gives us a rich Victorian middle-class definition of love: "What, then, I would ask again, is love in its highest, holiest character?" It is woman's all—her health, her power, her very being. Man, let him love as he may, has ever an existence distinct from that of his affections. He has his worldly interests, his public character, his ambition, his competition with other men—but woman centres all in that one feeling, and "in that *she* lives, or else *she* has no life". In woman's love is mingled the trusting dependence of a child, for she ever looks up to man as her protector, and her guide; the frankness, the social feeling, and the tenderness of a sister—for is not man her friend? The solicitude, the anxiety, the careful watching of the mother—for would she not suffer to preserve him from harm? Such is love in a noble mind. . . .'[41]

As the rapidly expanding bourgeoisie extended its range of power and influence—as it established itself not only economically but also politically, so it took on—as the seventeenth-century bourgeoisie had done—the ideas of the ruling class about the proper activities of women: namely, economic idleness. As a result of the increase in wealth and consumer developments which came with the industrial revolution women's activities were restricted in various directions. The employment of servants and the mass production of articles formerly made in the home gradually made such idleness physically possible for the privileged. The industrialisation in textiles made redundant one of women's most traditional skills—that is spinning—and the invention of the sewing-machine, for example, altered conditions even further in the direction of the leisured lady. Increasing wealth brought new standards of luxury and new ideas of refinement which prevented women in the trading and business classes from taking any further share in their husband's concerns. In the eighteen century many of women's entrepreneurial activities had been based on experience rather than training—but as the division of labour developed and education and skill became more important there was no provision for the training and education of women. The process which had begun in the seventeenth century with the emergence of capitalism was carried several stages further and affected much greater numbers of women in the nineteenth century. Margaretta Grey in her diary in 1853 wrote: "A lady, to be such, must be a mere lady and nothing else. She must not work for profit, or engage in any profit that money can command. . . . The conventional barrier that pronounces it ungenteel to be behind a counter, or serving the public in any mercantile capacity, is greatly extended. The same in household economy. Servants must be up to their offices which is very well; but ladies, dismissed from the dairy, the confectionery, the store room, the still room, the poultry yard, the kitchen garden and the orchard, have hardly yet found themselves a sphere equally useful in the pursuits of trade and art to which to apply their too abundant leisure."[42] The mid-nineteenth-century feminists were extremely concerned with the lack of useful employment available to women. By the 1870s there were complaints that women were no longer involved even in supervising servants. George Eliot says of Mrs Amos Barton, "You would never have asked, at any period in Mrs A. B's life, if she sketched or played the piano; you would even, perhaps, have been rather scandalised if she had descended from the serene dignity of being to the assiduous unrest of doing."[43] For women not to work reflected the success of their men—whether father or husband. The education and training of girls was to prepare them for courtship and marriage. Much more attention was paid to the education of boys for they had to make their own way in the world—a woman could if she was lucky rely on somebody else doing it for her. If she did not marry—her life was likely to be a hard one. Fathers tended to be responsible for the education of their sons—for after all their mothers could scarcely carry this out given their own limited experience. The importance of the mother as a primary agent in the socialisation of children only emerges in the nuclear family when the mother is more or less solely responsible for the pre-school child. The twentieth-century "myth of motherhood" associated with Bowlby, Spock and others is one of the end products of this historical process of narrowing the definition of the family. Victorian middle-class mothers usually had limited contact with their children so they were not seen as the key person in the reproduction of the ideological relations of production. The utilitarian educators of the nineteenth century located the crucial years as those at school and laid great emphasis on the importance of establishing through education either a proper ruling ideology or a proper work discipline. They saw working-class parental attitudes as both inadequate and decadent and sought to substitute the teacher and the school as the dominant inculcators of values.[44] The Schools Enquiry Commission of 1867 complained that the major problem in the education of girls was heir parents' attitude.[45] As Mr Gibson put it in *Wives and Daughters*, "Don't teach Molly too much: she must sew and read, and write and do her sums. . . . After all, I'm not sure that reading or writing is necessary."[46] Music, drawing, painting, French, fancy work, gossip and fashion were the stuff of a Victorian girl's life—all designed to prepare her to catch a man. Mrs Ellis in her chapter on the training of girls says: "It is sometimes spoken of as a defect in women, that they have less power of abstraction than men; and certainly if they were required to take part in all the occupations of the other sex, it would be so; but for my own part, I must confess, I never could see it an advantage to any woman, to be capable of abstraction beyond a certain extent . . . a woman, I would humbly suggest, has no business to be so far absorbed in any purely intellectual pursuit, as not to know when water is boiling over on the fire."[47] There was no training in the practical duties of a housewife even in many lower-middle-class households for it was seen as an unladylike activity. Once married, housekeeping presented many problems as Rosamund Vincy in *Middlemarch* experienced so bitterly. Even Lydgate—a thinking man in many ways—wanted for a wife "an accomplished creature who venerated his high musings and momentous labours, and would never interfere with them".[48] The Victorian middle-class obsession with cleanliness hardened the division between the housewife as organiser and those who actually did the work. A lady must have white shapely hands free from dirt and must never be seen outside the house without gloves. A. J. Munby gives us considerable insight into the symbolic power of hands as distinguishing between those who worked and those who didn't.[49]

The leisure of the Victorian lady was necessarily bound up with the exploitation of her less fortunate sisters. She relied on lower middle- and working-class women to nurse and train her children and to do the domestic work associated with her household. Her own involvement would be confined to supervision. Servants were of course found right down the social scale—even in some working-class households. But whereas in upper-class households the mistress would be engaged in a system of labour relations, in small units with only one or two servants the "housewife" would be more actively engaged herself—in thinking out menus for example. The image of the housewife as lady, therefore, was the one propagandised by the dominant class in the nineteenth century. Middle-class women who were driven by economic necessity out to work, mainly as governesses, were able despite the poverty and loneliness of their situations to maintain an aura of gentility. Middle-class women did have to work to earn money in considerable numbers—but they were a depressed minority. Feminists argued that it was vital to recognise the existence of this group and allow them to work. As Mary Carpenter put it, "It is work we ask, room to work, encouragement to work, an open field with a fair day's wages for a fair day's work; it is an injustice, we feel, the injustice of men, who arrogate to themselves all profitable employments . . . and . . . drive women to the lowest depths of penury and suffering. . . . Could Providence have created several thousand superfluous women for the purpose of rendering them burdens on society, as inmates of our prisons, workhouses and charitable institutions? Or is it that there is something wrong in our social arrangements, whereby they are unfairly deprived of occupations?"[50] Being themselves Victorians the feminists could not help arguing within those terms. Their new model woman would "become, in a better sense than they have ever been before, companions and helpmeets to men".[51] But the idea of women working was very much disapproved of by the Victorian middle class—it did not go well with the deification of the home and the idea of women and children as helpless dependants who had to be protected.

However, this ideology of domesticity was far in advance of the practice. Not only did considerable numbers of middle-class women have to go out to work but the vast majority of working-class women were engaged in work either inside or outside the home. A working-class woman at home might very well be engaged in something else as well as running the house—taking in laundry, for example, or outwork, or running a trading sideline or a shop. Practice was wildly at variance with the social ideal canvassed by bourgeois and clerical moralists. What changes, as Margaret Hewitt points out, is that the middle class try and impose their new standards on the working class[52] and the power of their dominant ideology is such that it would seem to have been to some extent adopted and internalised by working-class men and women as early as the mid-nineteenth century. There were of course many contradictory influences at work and attitudes and expectations would vary very much from region to region according to the work available and other factors. The situation was clearly different in areas like Lancashire where there was factory work available for women, from areas where the only kind of available employment was as servants. In addition patterns of housewifery would be different in towns from those in rural areas. It was typical of Victorian hypocrisy that they should combine the exploitation of women as factory workers, domestic servants, needlewomen and agricultural workers with lectures and homilies on the disgraceful way in which these women were neglecting the care of their families. A factory deputation from Yorkshire on the ten-hour day pressed for the gradual withdrawal of women from factories on the grounds that "the home, its cares and employments are the woman's true spheres".[53] No doubt fears on the men's part about losing their own jobs combined with a degree of acceptance of the prevailing view that woman's place was in the home. Engels reminds us that the early heavy employment of women in the textile industries particularly brought about something of a reversal of the economic position of men and women.[54] This exacerbates the internal divisions in the working class created by the sexual division of labour. Of course, this was hardly a new view—one of the major changes which industrialisation brought was that women who had been employed as outworkers in the home were now employed in factories in some areas, and their hours and conditions were on view in a way that they had never been before. "The idea of women's work outside the home in industry", as Winifred Holtby puts it, "became associated with squalor, fatigue, bad cooking and neglected children, just as women's work in the professions became associated with celibacy aggressiveness or impropriety and with everything contradictory to the ideal of ladyhood."[55] The articulate and interfering sections of the Victorian middle class were united in their disapproval of the disastrous effects of factory labour in particular on the family. By keeping women at work, thought Ashley, "You are poisoning the very sources of order and happiness and virtue; you are tearing up root and branch all relations of families to one another; you are annulling, as it were, the institution of domestic life decreed by Providence Himself, . . . the mainstay of peace and virtue and therein of national security."[56] Dr Andrew Ure, usually the most hard-headed of political economists, remarked what a good thing it was that women were paid low wages since it would make the idea of staying at home and doing their natural job more attractive to them.[57] However, economic necessity did send many women out to work and households had to be organised on that basis. Domestic obligation

was outridden on the labour market. In the early days of industrialisation in Lancashire when father, mother and children
would all be working the home was little but a shelter. When both
parents were working it was generally understood that the woman
organised the household as well. In Birmingham in the 1840s
Monday was still often regarded as a holiday but only for the
men—the women then had to do the washing, shopping and other
domestic work.[58] Hawkins, a factory inspector in the north,
reported in 1861: "I scarcely need argue that there can be comparatively no comfort in the dwelling of a working man whose wife
is away from home from 5.30 in the morning till 6.30 in the
evening, except at mealtimes, for she is compelled to leave her
children and her household to other hands; and, having so little
experience of her own, is quite unable to teach her daughter those
attractive qualifications with which women keep their husbands
from disreputable associations."[59] Large numbers of women were
employed in service capacities to the mill women—to fulfil the
domestic activities which they had not time to do themselves—as
tea-makers, washerwomen, needlewomen, cleaners and to nurse
children. The critics of the new factory age attacked this whole
system of domestic economy—they were shocked by the handing
out of laundry and that women did not know how to sew and
mend. The middle-class commentators were particularly shocked
by the standards of housewifery of the factory operatives but it
seems that they were very little different from those of other
working-class women—and how could it be otherwise. It was a
piece of double-think, as Ivy Pinchbeck points out, to go on about
the dirt and squalor and lack of domestic pride among the working
class—given the material circumstances in which they lived.[60] But
the combination of the doctrine of *laissez-faire* with the ideal of the
sanctity of the home made it impossible for a long time for the
Victorian moral entrepreneurs to do more than bemoan the
inadequacies of working-class family life. Again the hypocrisy was
quite astounding—the conditions of that life were the creation of
that same bourgeoisie which imposed quite other standards in
ideological terms. By the mid-century the importance of educating
working women was beginning to attract considerable attention.
Household Words in 1832 describes a new school for wives in
Birmingham—the first evening school which taught sewing including mending, reading, writing, arithmetic—so that they could
check whether they were being swindled by shopkeepers—and the

Bible.[61] From about 1870 domestic economy did begin to be introduced in some schools.

So we can see how in the nineteenth century the pattern established in the seventeenth century with the development of the capitalist mode of production has been strengthened and extended with the formation of industrial capitalism. The sexual division of labour rigidifies as the capitalist division of labour becomes more refined and job specialisation increases. The bourgeoisie make their wives into ladies in a position of dependence economically and subordination ideologically and then use lower middle-class and working-class women to service their households and produce their textiles. It is only when the capitalist economy needs women in large numbers that the image of the idealised wife and mother changes somewhat and a new note is introduced. The society can organise crèches and canteens and substantially reduce the need for privatised domestic labour as can clearly be seen from the experience of the two world wars. To understand the position of women in the home it is necessary to see the way in which women provide an industrial reserve army of labour which can be drawn upon in different ways at different times. The ideology of domesticity which ties women into the home and stresses their role as wife and mother has, since the early nineteenth century, been a key to the sexual division of labour as we know it. The fact that a woman's place is in the home justifies the definition of her work outside the home as secondary—and, therefore, typically low-paid and unskilled. But this is not a natural phenomenon, it is a cultural creation. A crucial missing element in our knowledge of the past is a history of the housewife.

NOTES

1. From *Senechaucie*, quoted in *The Portable Medieval Reader*, Viking (1949), p.135.
2. *The Book of Margery Kempe.* A modern version of W. Butler-Bowden, Cape (1936), p.82.
3. Chrétien de Troyes, *Arthurian Romances*. Everyman (1965). The *Lancelot* romance is particularly interesting.
4. R. H. Hilton, *The English Peasantry In The Later Middle Ages*, The 1973 Ford Lectures. Cf. the chapter on "Women In The Village". I have greatly benefited, in preparing the medieval section of the paper

and especially in this paragraph, from discussions with Professor Hilton and access to his unpublished material.

5. Pattingham, Staffs. Court Rolls, 1369, 1388.
6. Halesowen, Worcs. Court Rolls, 1386.
7. Margery Kempe, op.cit., p.28.
8. *The Goodman of Paris*, trans. E. Power, in *The Portable Medieval Reader*, op.cit., p. 155.
9. For the developing marxist-feminist analysis of the family under capitalism, cf. *inter alia*, Juliet Mitchell, *Women's Estate*, Penguin (1972); Sheila Rowbotham, *Woman's Consciousness, Man's World*, Pelican (1973); M. Dalla Costa and S. James, *The Power of Women and the Subversion of the Community*, Falling Wall Press
10. Alice Clark, *Working Life Of Women In The Seventeenth Century*, Frank Cass (1968), ch. 6, "Professions".
11. Karl Marx, *Capital* Vol. I, Foreign Languages Publishing House, Moscow (1961).
12. L. Althusser, "Ideology And Ideological State Apparatuses", in *Lenin And Philosophy, & Other Essays*, New Left Books (1971).
13. Ed. J. Ketley, *The Two Liturgies in the Reign of King Edward VI*, Parker Society, 1844, p. 465. Quoted in C. Hill, *Society And Puritanism In Pre-Revolutionary England*, Secker & Warburg (1964).
14. Alice Clark, op.cit., especially Ch. 2, "Capitalists".
15. Sheila Rowbotham, *Women, Resistance and Revolution*, Allen Lane (1972), especially Ch. 1.
16. Rich, *The Excellency Of Good Women*, quoted in L. B. Wright, *Middle-Class Culture In Elizabethan England*, p. 483.
17. Gainsford, quoted in L. B. Wright, op. cit., p. 491.
18. Williamson, *Lady Ann Clifford, Countess of Dorset, Pembroke, Montgomery* 1596–1676.
19. Alan MacFarlane, *The Family Life of Ralph Josselin, Seventeenth-Century Clergyman*.
20. Ibid., p. 109.
21. *The Diary of Thomas Isham of Lamport*, ed. Sir Gyles Isham, p. 43.
22. For more detail on this, see Alice Clark, op. cit., chs. 3, 5.
23. Ibid., especially ch. 4.
24. Quoted in Keith Thomas, "Women And The Civil War Sects", *Past and Present*, no. 13 (1958).
25. Christopher Hill, op. cit.
26. Elizabeth Joceline, *The Mother's Legacie to Her Unborne Child* (1632), p. 28–9. Quoted in C. Hill, op. cit.
27. *Homily Against Idleness*, quoted in C. Hill, op. cit.
28. W. and M. Haller, "The Puritan Art Of Love", *Huntingdon Library Quarterly* V, p. 247.
29. E. Calamy, *England's Looking-Glasse* (1642), p. 31, quoted in C. Hill, op. cit., p. 445.
30. Benjamin Wadsworth, *The Well Ordered Family*, quoted in *The Puritan Family*, Boston, Mass. (1956), p. 11.
31. Keith Thomas, op. cit.

32. John Milton, *Paradise Lost*, Book 9, ed. Alistair Fowler, Longmans (1968), p. 552.

33. Lucy Hutchinson, *Memoirs of the Life of Colonel Hutchinson*, ed. James Sutherland, Oxford U.P. (1973), p. 9.

34. Daniel Rogers, *Matrimonial Honour*, 1642, quoted in L. L. Schuking, *The Puritan Family*, Routledge & Kegan Paul (1969), especially the chapter on "Marriage".

35. Lucy Hutchinson, op. cit., "Autobiographical Notes", p. 288.

36. F. Engels, *The Origin of the Family, Private Property and the State*, Laurence & Wishart (1940).

37. Thomas Arnold, quoted in Houghton, *The Victorian Frame of Mind*, Yale U.P. (1957), p. 343.

38. Ruskin, in Houghton, op. cit., p. 343, *Sesame and Lilies*.

39. William Thompson, *Appeal of One Half of the Human Race, Women, Against the Pretensions of the Other Half, Men, to Retain them in Civil and Domestic Slavery* (1825), Lennox Hill (1970), p. 79.

40. Tennyson, *The Princess*.

41. Mrs Ellis, *The Wives of England. Their Relative Duties, Domestic Influence and Social Obligation*, London (1843), p. 99–100.

42. Quoted in Ivy Pinchbeck, *Women Workers and the Industrial Revolution 1750–1850*, Routledge (1930), p. 315–16.

43. George Eliot, *Scenes of Clerical Life*, "Amos Barton".

44. Richard Johnson, "Educational Policy And Social Control in Early Victorian England", *Past and Present,* no. 49, November 1970.

45. See Wanda Neff, *Victorian Working Women 1838–50*, Allen & Unwin (1929), especially chapter on "The Idle Woman".

46. Mrs Gaskell, *Wives and Daughters*, pp. 104–5.

47. Mrs Ellis, *Mothers of England* (1843), p. 321.

48. George Eliot, *Middlemarch*.

49. Derek Hudson, *Munby: Man of Two Worlds*.

50. Quoted in Lee Holcombe, *Victorian Ladies at Work 1850–1940*, New York (1973), especially ch. 1.

51. Ibid.

52. Margaret Hewitt, *Wives and Mothers in Victorian Industry*, London (1958).

53. Quoted in Hewitt, op. cit. p. 23.

54. F. Engels, *The Condition Of The Working Class In England, 1844*, Blackwell (1958).

55. Winifred Holtby, p. 37.

56. Ashley, quoted in Hewitt, op. cit., p. 49.

57. Dr Andrew Ure, quoted in Neff, op. cit., p. 29.

58. There are complaints in the diaries and accounts of small masters in particular of the problems posed by "Saint Monday".

59. Quoted in Hewitt, op. cit., p. 63.

60. Ivy Pinchbeck, op. cit.

61. *Household Words*, quoted in Neff, op. cit., p. 78.

from

The Home: Its Work and Influence

CHARLOTTE PERKINS GILMAN

The housewife

The housewife . . . still predominates by so large a majority as to make us wonder at the noisy prominence of "the servant question". (It is not so wonderful, after all, for that class of the population which keeps servants is the class which makes the most noise.) Even in rich America, even in richest New York, in *nine-tenths* of the families the housewife "does her own work". . . .

The iron limits of her efficiency are these: First, that of average capacity. Just consider what any human business would be in which there was no faintest possibility of choice, of exceptional ability, of division of labour. What would shoes be like if every man made his own, if the shoemaker had never come to his development? What would houses be like if every man made his own? Or hats, or books, or wagons? To confine any industry to the level of a universal average is to strangle it in its cradle. And there, for ever, lie the industries of the housewife. What every man does alone for himself, no man can ever do well—or woman either. That is the first limit of the "housewife".

The next is the maternal character of this poor primeval labourer. Because of her wealth of power and patience it does not occur to her to make things easier for herself. The fatal inertia of home industries lies in their maternal basis. The work is only done for the family—the family is satisfied—what remains? There is no other ambition, no other incentive, no other reward. Where the horizon of duty and aspiration closes down with one's immediate blood relations, there is no room for growth.

Next comes her isolation. Even the bottom level of a universal average—even the blind patience of a working mother—could be helped up a little under the beneficent influence of association. In the days when the ingenious squaw led the world, she had it. The women toiled together at their primitive tasks and talked together as they toiled. The women who founded the beginnings of agriculture were founders also of the village; and their feminine constructive tendencies held it together while the destructive tendencies of the belligerent male continually tore it apart. All through that babyhood of civilisation, the hunting and fighting instinct made men prey upon the accumulated wealth resultant from the labouring instinct of women—but industry conquered, being the best. As industry developed, as riches increased, as property rights were defined, as religions grew, women were confined more and more closely at home. Later civilisations have let them out to play—but not to work. The parasitic female of the upper classes is allowed the empty freedom of association with her useless kind; but the housewife is still confined to the house.

We are now giving great attention to this matter of home industry. We are founding chairs of Household Science, we are writing books on Domestic Economics; we are striving mightily to elevate the standard of home industry—and we omit to notice that it is just because it is home industry that all this trouble is necessary.

So far as home industry had been affected by world industry, it has improved. The implements of cooking and cleaning, for instance—where should we be if our modern squaw had to make her own utensils, as did her ancient prototype? The man, in world industry, makes not only the house, with all its elaborate labour-saving and health-protecting devices; not only the furniture of the house, the ornaments, hangings, and decorations, but the implements of the home industries as well. Go to the household furnishing store of our day—remember the one pot of the savage family to boil the meat and wash the baby—and see the difference between "home-made" and "world-made" things.

So far as home industry has progressed, it is through contact with the moving world outside; so far as it remains undeveloped, it is through the inexorable limitations of the home in itself.

There is one more limitation to be considered—the number of occupations practised. Though man has taken out and developed all the great trades, and, indeed, all trades beyond a certain grade, he has left the roots of quite a number at home. The housewife practises the conflicting elements of many kinds of work. First, she is cook. Whatever else is done or undone, we must eat; and since eating is ordained to be done at home, that is her predominant trade. The preparation and service of food is a most useful function; and as a world-industry, in the hands of professionals, students, and experts, it has reached a comparatively high stage of development.

In the nine-tenths of our homes where the housewife is cook, it comes under all these limitations: First, average capacity; second, sex-tendency; third, isolation; fourth, conflicting duties.

The cook, having also the cleaning to do, the sewing, mending, nursing, and care of children, the amount of time given to cooking is perforce limited. But even the plainest of home cooking must take up a good proportion of the day. The cooking, service, and "cleaning up" of ordinary meals, in a farmhouse, with the contributary processes of picking, sorting, peeling, washing, etc., and the extra time given to special baking, pickling, and preserving, take fully six hours a day. To the man, who is out of the house during work-hours, and who seldom estimates woman's work at its real value, this may seem extreme, but the working housewife knows it is a fair allowance, even a modest one.

There are degrees of speed, skill, intelligence, and purchasing power, of course; but this is a modest average; two hours for breakfast, three for dinner, one for supper. The preparation of food as a household industry takes up half the working time of half the population of the world. This utterly undeveloped industry, inadequate and exhausting, takes nearly a quarter of a twelve-hour day of the world's working force.

Cooking and sewing are inimical; the sewing of the housewife is quite generally pushed over into the evening as well as afternoon, thus lengthening her day considerably. Nursing, as applied to the sick, must come in when it happens, other things giving way at that time. Cleaning is continuous. Cooking, of course, makes cleaning; the two main elements of dirt in the household being grease and ashes; another, and omnipresent one, dust. Then, there are the children to clean, and the clothes to clean—this latter so considerable an item as to take two days of extra labour—during which, of course, other departments must be less attended.

We have the regular daily labour of serving meals and "clearing up", we have the regular daily labour of keeping the home in order; then we have the washing day, ironing day, baking day, and sweeping day. Some make a special mending day also. This division, best observed by the most competent, is a heroic monument to the undying efforts of the human worker to specialise. But we have left out one, and the most important one, of our home industries—the care of children.

Where is Children's Day?

The children are there every day, of course. Yes, but which hour of the day? With six for food, with—spreading out the washing and ironing over the week—two for laundry, with—spreading the sweeping day and adding the daily dusting and setting to rights—two for cleaning; and another two for sewing—after these twelve hours of necessary labour are accounted for, what time remains for the children?

The initial purpose of the home is the care of children. The initial purpose of motherhood is the care of children. How are the duties of the mother compatible with the duties of the housewife? How can child-culture, as a branch of human progress, rise to any degree of proficiency in this swarming heap of rudimentary trades?

Nothing is asked—here—as to how the housewife, doing all these things together her life long, can herself find time for culture and development; or how can she catch any glimmer of civic duty or public service beyond this towering pile of domestic duty and household service. The particular point herein advanced is that the conditions of home industry *as such* forever limit the growth of the industry so practised; forever limit the growth of the persons so practising them; and also tend to limit the growth of the society which is content to leave any of its essential functions in this distorted state.

Our efforts to "lift the standard of household industry" ignore the laws of industry. We seek by talking and writing, by poetising and sermonising, and playing on every tender sentiment and devout aspiration, to convince the housewife that there is something particularly exalted and beautiful, as well as useful, in her occupation. This shows our deep-rooted error of sex-distinction in industry. We consider the work of the woman in the house as essentially feminine, and fail to see that, as work, it is exactly like any other kind of human activity, having the same limitations and the same possibilities. . . .

A house does not need a wife any more than it does a husband. Are we never to have a man-wife? A really suitable and profitable companion for a man instead of the bond-slave of a house? There is nothing in the work of a house which requires marital or maternal affection. It does require highly developed skill and business sense—but these it fails to get.

Would any amount of love on the part of that inconceivable house-husband justify him in depriving his family of all the fruits of progress? What a colossal charge of malfeasance in office could be brought against such a husband—such a father; who, under the name of love, should so fail in his great first duty—Progress.

How does the woman escape this charge? Why is not she responsible for progress, too? By that strange assumption does she justify this refusal to keep step with the world? She will tell you, perhaps, that she cannot do more than she does—she has neither time nor strength nor ambition for any more work. So might the house-husband have defended himself—as honestly and as reasonably. It is true. While every man had to spend all his time providing for his own family, no man ever had, or ever could have, time, strength, or ambition to do more.

It is not *more* work that is asked of women, but less. It is *a different method* of work. Human progress rests upon the interchange of labour; upon work done humanly for each other, not, like the efforts of the savage or the brute, done only for one's own. The housewife, blinded by her ancient duty, fails in her modern duty.

It is true that, while she does this work in this way, she can do no more. Therefore she must stop doing it, and learn to do differently. The house will not be "neglected" by her so doing; but is even now most shamefully neglected by her antique methods of labour. The family will not be less loved because it has a skilled worker to love it. Love has to pass muster in results, as well as intentions. . . .

The housemaid

The performance of domestic industries involves, first, an enormous waste of labour. The fact that in nine cases out of ten this labour is unpaid does not alter its wastefulness. If half the men in the world stayed at home to wait on the other half, the loss in productive labour would be that between half and the fraction required to do the work under advanced conditions, say one-twentieth. Any group of men requiring to be cooked for, as a ship's crew, a lumber camp, a company of soldiers, have a proportionate number of cooks. To give each man a private cook would reduce the working strength materially. Our private cooks being women makes no difference in the economic law. We are so accustomed to rate women's labour on a sex-basis, as being her "duty" and not justly commanding any return, that we have quite overlooked this tremendous loss of productive labour.

Then there is the waste of endless repetition of "plant". We pay rent for twenty kitchens where one kitchen would do. All that part of our houses which is devoted to these industries, kitchen, pantry, laundry, servants' rooms, etc., could be eliminated from the expense account by the transference of the labour involved to a suitable workshop. Not only our rent bills, but our furnishing bills, feel the weight of this expense. We have to pay severally for all these stoves and dishes, tools and utensils, which, if properly supplied in one proper place instead of twenty, would cost far less to begin with; and, in the hands of skilled professionals, would not be under the tremendous charge for breakage and ruinous misuse which now weighs heavily on the householder. Then there is the waste in fuel for these nineteen unnecessary kitchens, and lastly and largest of any item except labour, the waste in food.

First the waste in purchasing in the smallest retail quantities; then the waste involved in separate catering, the "left overs" which the ingenious housewife spends her life in trying to "use up"; and also the waste caused by carelessness and ignorance in a great majority of cases. Perhaps this last element, careless ignorance, ought to cover both waste and breakage, and be counted by itself, or as a large item in the labour account. . . .

So far our sufferings under the present rapid elimination of the housemaid have taught us little. Our principal idea of bettering the condition is by training servants. We seriously propose to establish schools to train these reluctant young women to our service; even in some cases to pay them for going there. This is indeed necessary; for why should they pay for tuition, or even waste time in gratuitously studying, when they can get wages without?

We do not, and cannot, offer such graded and progressive salaries as shall tempt really high-class labour into this field. Skilled labour and domestic service are incompatible. The degree of intelligence, talent, learning, and trained skill which should be devoted to feeding and cleaning the human race will never consent to domestic service. It is the grade of work which forever limits its development, the place, the form of service. So long as the home is the workshop the housewife cannot, and the housemaid will not, even if she could, properly do this work for the neglected world.

Is it not time that the home be freed from these industries so palpably out of place? That the expense of living be decreased by two-thirds and the productive labour increased by nine-twentieths? That our women cease to be an almost universal class of house-servants; plus a small class of parasitic idlers and greedy consumers of wealth? That the preparation of food be raised from its present condition of inadequacy, injury, and waste to such a professional and scientific position that we may learn to spare from our street corners both the drug-store and the saloon? That the care of children become at last what it should be—the noblest and most valuable profession, to the endless profit of our little ones and progress of the race? And that our homes, no longer greasy, dusty workshops, but centres of rest and peace; no longer gorgeous places of entertainment that does not entertain, but quiet places of happiness; no longer costing the laborious lives of overworked women or supporting the useless lives of idle ones, but properly maintained by organised industries; become enjoyed by men and women alike, both glad and honourable workers in an easy world?

Lines of advance

... The mother cannot herself alone do all that is necessary for her children, to say nothing of continuing to be a companion to her husband, a member of society, and a still growing individual.

She can sacrifice herself in the attempt,—often does,—but the child has a righteous indifference to such futile waste of life. He does not require a nervous, exhausted, ever-present care, and it is by no means good for him. He wants a strong, serene, lovely mother for a comfort, a resource, an ideal; but he also wants the care of a trained highly qualified teacher, and the amateur mama cannot give it to him. Motherhood is a common possession of every female creature; a joy, a pride, a nobly useful function. Teacherhood is a profession, a specialised social function, no more common to mothers than to fathers, maids, or bachelors. The ceaseless, anxious strain to do what only an experienced nurse and teacher can do is an injury to the real uses of motherhood. . . .

Our houses are threaded like beads on a string, tied, knotted, woven together, and in the cities even built together; one solid house from block-end to block-end; their boasted individuality maintained by a thin partition wall. The tenement, flat, and apartment house still further group and connect us; and our claim of domestic isolation becomes merely another domestic myth. Water is a household necessity and was once supplied by household labour, the women going to the wells to fetch it. Water is now supplied by the municipality, and flows among our many homes as one. Light is equally in common; we do not have to make it for ourselves.

Where water and light are thus fully socialised, why are we so shy of any similar progress in the supply of food? Food is no more a necessity than water. If we are willing to receive our water from an extra-domestic pipe—why not our food? The one being a simple element and the other a very complex combination makes a difference, of course; but even so we may mark great progress. Some foods, more or less specific, and of universal use, were early segregated, and the making of them became a trade, as in bread-stuffs, cheese, and confectionery. Where this has been done we find great progress, and an even standard of excellence. In America, where the average standard of bread-making is very low, we regard "baker's bread" as a synonym for inferiority; but even here, if we consider the saleratus bread of the great middle west, and all the sour, heavy, uncertain productions of a million homes, the baker bears comparison with the domestic cook. It is the maintenance of the latter that keeps the former down; where the baker is the general dependence he makes better bread.

Our American baker's bread has risen greatly in excellence as we make less and less at home. All the initial processes of the food supply have been professionalised. Our housewife does not go out crying, "Dilly-dilly! Dilly-dilly! You must come and be killed"— and then wring the poor duck's neck, pick and pluck it with her own hands; nor does the modern father himself slay the fatted calf—all this is done as a business. In recent years every article of food which will keep, every article which is in common demand, is prepared as a business.

The home-blinded toiler has never climbed out of her hogshead to watch this rising tide, but it is nearly up to the rim, ready to pour in and float her out. Every delicate confection, every pickle, sauce, preserve, every species of biscuit and wafer, and all sublimated and differentiated to a degree we could never have dreamed of; all these are manufactured in scientific and business methods and delivered at our doors, or our dumb-waiters. Breakfast foods are the latest step in this direction; and the encroaching delicatessen shop with its list of allurements. Even the last and dearest stronghold, the very core and centre of domestic bliss—hot cooked food—is being served us by this irreverent professional man. . . .

Turning to the other great domestic industry, the care of children, we may see hopeful signs of growth. The nursemaid is improving. Those who can afford it are beginning to see that the association of a child's first years with low-class ignorance cannot be beneficial. There is a demand for "trained nurses" for children; even in rare cases the employment of some Kindergarten ability. Among the very poor the day-nursery and Kindergarten are doing slow, but beautiful work. The President of Harvard demands that more care and money be spent on the primary grades in education; and all through our school systems there is a healthy movement. Child-study is being undertaken at last. Pedagogy is being taught as a science. In our public parks there is regular provision made for children; and in the worst parts of the cities an incipient provision of playgrounds.

There is no more brilliant hope on earth today than this new thought about the child. In what does it consist? In recognising "the child", children as a class, children as citizens with rights to be guaranteed only by the state; instead of our previous attitude toward them of absolute personal ownership—the unchecked tyranny, or as unchecked indulgence, of the private home. Children are at last emerging from the very lowest grade of private ownership into the safe, broad level of common citizenship. That which no million separate families could give their millions of separate children, the state can give, and does. Our progress, so long merely mechanical, is at last becoming personal, touching the people and lifting them as one.

Now what is all this leading to? What have we to hope—or to dread—in the undeniable lines of development here shown? What most of us dread is this: that we shall lose our domestic privacy; that we shall lose our family dinner table; that woman will lose "her charm"; that we shall lose our children; and the child lose its mother. We are mortally afraid of separation. . . .

Now the father goes out every day; does the home cease to exist because of his hours away from it? It is still his home, he still loves it, he maintains it, he lives in it, only he has a "place of business" elsewhere. At a certain stage of growth the children are out of it, between say 8.30 and 3.30. Does it cease to be home because of their hours away from it? Do they not love it and live in it—*while they are there?* Now if, while the father was out, and the children were out, the mother should also be out, would the home disappear into thin air?

It is home *while the family are in it*. When the family are out of it it is only a house; and a house will stand up quite solidly for some eight hours of the family's absence. Incessant occupation is not essential to a home. If the father has wife and children with him in the home when he returns to it, need it matter to him that the children are wisely cared for in schools during his absence; or that his wife is duly occupied elsewhere while they are so cared for?

Two "practical obstacles" intervene: first, the "housework"; second, the care of children below school age. The housework is fast disappearing into professional hands. When that is utterly gone, the idle woman has but one excuse—the babies. This is a very vital excuse. The baby is the founder of the home. If the good of the baby requires the persistent, unremitting care of the mother in the home, then indeed she must remain there. No other call, no other claim, no other duty, can be weighed for a moment against this all-important service—the care of the little child.

But we have already seen that if there is one thing more than another the home fails in, it is just this. If there is one duty more than another the woman fails in, it is just this. Our homes are not planned nor managed in the interests of little children; and the isolated homebound mother is in no way adequate to their proper rearing. This is not disputable on any side. The death rate of little children during the years they are wholly in the home and mother's care proves it beyond question. The wailing of little children who live—or before they die—wailing from bodily discomfort, nervous irritation, mental distress, punishment—a miserable sound, so common, so expected, that it affects the price of real estate, tenants not wishing to live near little children on account of their cries— this sound of world-wide anguish does not seem to prove much for the happiness of these helpless inmates of the home.

Such few data as we have of babies and young children in properly managed day nurseries, give a far higher record of health and happiness. Not the sick baby in the pauper hospital, not the lonely baby in the orphan asylum; but the baby who has *not* lost his mother, but who adds to mother's love, calm, wise, experienced professional care. . . .

The home that is coming will not try to be a workshop, a nursery, or a school. The child that is coming will find a more comfortable home than he ever had before, and something else besides—a place for babies to be happy in, and grow up in, without shrieks of pain. The mother that is coming, a much more intelligent person than she has ever been before, will recognise that this ceaseless procession of little ones requires some practical provision for its best development, other than what is possible in the passing invasion of the home. "How a baby does tyrannise over the household!" we complain, vaguely recognising that the good of the baby requires something different from the natural home habits of adults. We shall finally learn to make a home for the babies too.

This involves great changes in both our idea of home, and our material provision for it. Why not? Growth is change, and there is need of growth here. Slowly, gradually, by successive experiments, we shall find out how to meet new demands; and these experiments are now being made, in all the living centres of population.

3

Women as Domestic Workers

MARGARET G. BONDFIELD

Labour women have studied the question of domestic work from two points of view—(1) that of the paid worker and (2) that of the vast body of unpaid workers: the housewives and home-makers. The basis of discontent which affects and unconsciously irritates both paid and unpaid workers, is the utter lack of any attempt so to adjust the household work as to enable the worker to attain the best results, with the least waste of time and least expenditure of energy. In the fact that women engaged in housework are becoming conscious of this lack, lies the greatest hope of revolutionary change.

At a recent interview between some unemployed munition workers and a few members of Parliament, the subject of alternative employment was discussed.

"My wife says she cannot get servants," urged an elderly MP. "Wouldn't you like to go back to domestic service?"

"No!" was the prompt reply: "*Would you*?"—and then followed an animated description of pre-war servitude—long hours—many spent in the dark ill-equipped kitchens, unhealthy sleeping rooms, poor pay, the petty tyranny of little minds, and above all the consciousness of inferior status, which had been endured while they knew no other life, but which had become intolerable after the experience of the greater freedom of factory life.

The ex-domestic, who, during the war, has worked at harder, dirtier work in the factory than any cook or housemaid has had to undertake, who has worked alternate night and day shifts of twelve hours, who has taken uncomfortable journeys in all winds and weathers, who has lived dangerously in filling factories and in air-raid areas—revolts from the thought of a return to "the shelter of quiet domestic life", as she knew it before the war. For the majority, paid domestic service is an unregulated, sweated industry, conducted by ill-trained, unorganised employers and work-people. It has remained unorganised largely because the employing class could draw upon an almost unlimited supply of cheap, and for the most part docile young labour: because in fact there still existed a servile class, and a class which desired servile labour.

To avoid misunderstanding it may be well to state that we are quite aware there still exists a class of "gentleman's servants", who look down from the Olympian heights upon mere labour folk, and to whom nothing in this chapter would apply. There is also a large class of really happily placed domestic workers, between whom and their mistresses there exists a feeling of mutual dependence and good-will, loyal service lovingly rendered to those who appreciate and suitably reward such service.

The former group we have no time nor inclination to consider, and the latter group we have no desire to disturb; we are concerned with those whose lives are made miserable and ineffective by conditions of service which can be vastly improved to the advantage of the employer, employed and the community at large.

In 1913 an adventurous group of domestic workers in Scotland issued a programme of reform, *viz*:

> A twelve-hour working day: half holiday once a week: fixed meal times: wages to be paid fortnightly (instead of monthly or quarterly): all public holidays: two hours out of each day for themselves: sanitary bedrooms: a graded scale of wages.

Readers may well ponder on the state of existence in which such a programme would bring relief.

Because domestic service has borne the mark of servitude, *lack of education* has been welcomed as a sign of the good servant. The more uned.cated, the less likely they were to "have ideas above their station in life". A woman of the suburbs once said to the writer, "If I had my way I would not allow any schooling for the domestic servant class; they would be better servants if they had never learnt to read or write—as it is they think they are as good as we are!" As a matter of fact it is just the lack of trained intelligence and an educated outlook applied to domestic affairs which has perpetuated the shocking waste, muddle and discontent in this occupation.

Labour women stand for a revolution in ideas on the subject of domestic service—to make it a well regulated industry, in which the social status of its workers will be equal to that of any other section of labour, an industry in which human energy will be conserved to minister to human needs, and really to make our homes places of rest and refreshment. The work of cooking and cleaning, etc., is honourable, necessary work, and if only the right relationship of mutual service and equality of status be established, it should provide worthy employment for a large body of educated women.

The most urgent reforms appear to be the regulation of the hours of work to a maximum eight-hour day, and the abolition of living in as a condition of employment; in cases where for mutual convenience board and lodging is given by the employers as part payment, the value of such accommodation should be stated in terms of money, to enable the worker to compare it with charges for accommodation outside the house. This knowledge would remove the suspicion that unfair advantage was being taken under the "Truck" system of payment.

Another necessary condition is that in her own time the worker's right to privacy and non-interference must be respected. Such a programme involves a radical change of attitude on the part of the average mistress. *The bell-ringing habit must be broken.* Human energy must not be wasted in running up and downstairs in obedience to the whims and fancies of idlers.

A great safeguard of the liberties and independence of the paid domestic will be found in a system of non-residential daily service. A memorandum issued by the Women's Industrial Council in January '918 outlines a practical scheme which deserves support and should certainly be widely discussed.

The scheme includes:

The establishment of domestic centres.

Daily workers, who will live either in hostels or in their own homes, to be supplied to households by the hour.

A Committee of Management to be attached to each centre, composed of representatives of employers and workers who will decide rates of pay, hours of work, holidays, etc. It is proposed to start with a minimum wage of 30s. for a forty-eight-hour week.

Domestic workers to be paid a fixed weekly wage by the Centre and all fees to be paid by the employers to the Manager.

Complaints about the conduct or inefficiency of the workers to be made to the Manager.

Domestic training courses to be established in connection with the centre; learners to be sent out in charge of skilled workers.

One essential condition of success for such a scheme would be sound trade-union organisation. The paid domestic workers must take their proper place with skilled and unskilled labour in the trade-union and Labour movements.

At a West Country Conference the future development of domestic work was being discussed: a trade-union comrade arose and impatiently dismissed the subject with "Why we do waste time discussing domestic service—we workers never have domestic service—we can't afford it!" He was promptly told by the housewives present that he got domestic service all right, *but he paid nothing for it*! The reply was very effective but not quite true—workpeople pay heavily in waste of time and energy and get the worst possible results, by adhering to a system of aggressive individualism long after communal effort has become possible.

The main problem of the unpaid house mother has its roots in defective housing conditions. As in this little book housing has a chapter to itself this point need not be elaborated here.

Co-operation is necessary to secure the freedom and development of the unpaid house mother. A secondary reason which is forcing co-operation is the need for national food economy. This will hasten the extensive development of the co-operative kitchen. Already busy women who are fortunate enough to be in reach of a well-managed communal kitchen wonder how they existed without it for so long—for it means not only release from the actual preparation and cooking of food, but also from the growing burden of shopping and the queue-horror.

It has been demonstrated by practical experiments that there will be a greater variety in the food, less waste and greater nourishment, by the use under co-operative methods of communal kitchens.

Co-operative wash-houses, electric power, central heating, co-operative nurseries and trained nurses for the wee babies, and Montessori or Kindergarten schools for the toddlers, are all aids to the simplification of domestic work possible in any national housing schemes.

The intolerably long working day of the average house mother can be reduced to about one third of the time taken up under the bad, old way. The house mother will then have leisure to bring her gifts to the common stock: her administrative capacity will no longer be confined to the little house: it may be available for the local administrative bodies and for the legislative chamber. She will be able to render social service of a high order by companioning her children. Housework under the new conditions will not be a drudgery but a pride and joy.

It may be said that working women do not desire to take part in public life, and if the household duties can be done in a third of the time women will abuse their leisure. That argument has been used against every body of workers who have tried to reduce the working day. Why are so many house mothers dull and petty minded? Because they have had no time to cultivate their minds and to plan their lives on large, spacious lines; because they have become slaves to the household and in time even their own children think little of them except as the household drudge. The competent housewife may not want to act on public bodies as men act today, but she will be thorough in her cleaning up and she will find that in addition to her co-operative washing and cooking arrangements she must needs learn how to use other accessories of good laws impartially administered for the common wealth.

The fable of "one in charge of a lighthouse who gave to the poor in the cabins the oil of the mighty lanterns that served to illumine the sea" is especially one for housewives. "The humblest mother who allows her whole life to be crushed, saddened, absorbed by the less important of her motherly duties, is giving her oil to the poor; and her children will suffer the whole of their lives from there not having been in the soul of their mother the radiance it might have acquired."

When women have reached this large social consciousness there will be such home building as the world has never known, and it is towards this goal that the women of the Labour Party have set their will.

4

from *Working-Class Wives*

MARGERY SPRING RICE

The day's work

"I believe myself that one of the biggest difficulties our mothers have is our husbands do not realise we ever need any leisure time. My life for many years consisted of being penned in a kitchen nine feet square, every fourteen months a baby, as I had five babies in five years at first, until what with the struggle to live and no leisure I used to feel I was just a machine, until I had my first breakdown, and as dark as it was and as hard as it was it gave me the freedom and privilege of having an hour's fresh air. And so I truly know this is the lot of many a poor mother. I know my third baby had rickets, but what could I do, I was expecting another little one and already had a baby three years of age and one two years. So many of our men think we should not go out until the children are grown up. We do not want to be neglecting the home but we do feel we like to have a little look around the shops, or if we go to the clinic we can just have a few minutes. . . . It isn't the men are unkind. It is the old idea we should always be at home."

Not many of the women go into such detail as this about the trials of their lives, but the record given of hours spent at work, the size of the family, the inability to pay for any help outside, the inconvenience of the house, the lack of adequate utensils and of decent clothes—let alone any small household or personal luxury— yields a picture in which monotony, loneliness, discouragement and sordid hard work are the main features—a picture of almost unredeemed drabness. It is not that all of the women are unhappy as the writer of the above letter manifestly is. Taken as a whole, their vitality must be prodigious, for, in spite of every possible embarrassment, life goes on undiminished in bulk, even if with a lessening vigour and enjoyment. Happiness, like health, can suffer an almost unperceived lowering of standard, which results in a pathetic gratitude for what might be called negative mercies, the respite for an hour a day, for instance, from the laboriousness of the other eleven, twelve or thirteen; the help that a kind husband will "occasionally give on washing days, when he comes home from work", the relief when a major disaster which threatened one of the children (in the case of a woman in Leeds whose eldest son lost one eye in an accident and was threatened with the loss of the other) was "miraculously overcome". . . .

For the majority of the 1,250 women under review the ordinary routine seems to be as follows. Most of them get up at 6.30. If their husband and/or sons are miners, or bakers, or on any nightshift, they may have to get up at 4 (possibly earlier), make breakfast for those members of the family, and then, if they feel disposed to further sleep, go back to bed for another hour's rest. The same woman who does this has probably got a young child or even a baby, who wakes up early, and sleeping in the same room will in no case give his mother much peace after 6 a.m. If there is a suckling baby as well, (and it must be remembered that the woman who has had seven or eight children before the age of thirty-five has never been without a tiny baby or very young child,) she will have had to nurse him at least as late as 10 the night before. There are many complaints of children who for some reason or other disturb the night's rest. Her bed is shared not only by her husband but, in all probability, by one *at least* of her young family. Sleeplessness is not often spoken of in this investigation, because it is not considered an ailment, but it is quite clear that a good night's rest in a well-aired, quiet room and in a comfortable, well-covered bed, is practically unknown to the majority of these mothers. A woman can become accustomed to very little sleep just as she can to very little food.

When once she is up there is no rest at all till after dinner. She is on her legs the whole time. She has to get her husband off to work, the children washed, dressed and fed and sent to school. If she has a large family, even if she has only the average family of this whole group, four or five children, she is probably very poor and therefore lives in a very bad house, or a house extremely inadequately fitted for her needs. Her washing up will not only therefore be heavy, but it may have to be done under the worst conditions. She may have to go down (or up) two or three flights of stairs to get her water, and again to empty it away. She may have to heat it on the open fire, and she may have to be looking after the baby and the toddler at the same time. When this is done, she must clean the house. If she has the average family, the rooms are very "full of beds", and this will make her cleaning much more difficult than if she had twice the number of rooms with half the amount of furniture in each. She lacks the utensils too; and lacking any means to get hot water except by the kettle on the fire, she will be as careful as possible not to waste a drop. The schoolchildren will be back for their dinner soon after 12, so she must begin her cooking in good time. Great difficulties confront her here. She has not got more than one or two saucepans and a frying-pan, and so even if she is fortunate in having some proper sort of cooking stove, it is impossible to cook a dinner as it should be cooked, slowly and with the vegetables separately; hence the ubiquitous stew, with or without the remains of the Sunday meat according to the day of the week. She has nowhere to store food, or if there is cupboard room, it is inevitably in the only living-room and probably next to the fireplace. Conditions may be so bad in this respect that she must go out in the middle of her morning's work to buy for dinner. This has the advantage of giving her and the baby a breath of fresh air during the morning; otherwise, unless there is a garden or yard, the baby, like herself, is penned up in the nine-foot-square kitchen during the whole morning.

Dinner may last from 12 till 3. Her husband or a child at work may have quite different hours from the schoolchildren, and it is quite usual to hear this comment. Very often she does not sit down herself to meals. The serving of five or six other people demands so much jumping up and down that she finds it easier to take her meals standing. If she is nursing a baby, she will sit down for that, and in this way "gets more rest". She does this after the children have returned to school. Sometimes the heat and stuffiness of the kitchen in which she has spent all or most of her morning takes her off her food, and she does not feel inclined to eat at all, or only a bite when the others have all finished and gone away. Then comes the same process of washing up, only a little more difficult because dinner is a greasier meal than breakfast. After that, with luck at 2 or 2.30 but sometimes much later, if dinner for any reason has had to go on longer, she can tidy herself up and REST, or GO OUT or SIT DOWN.

Leisure is a comparative term. Anything which is slightly less arduous or gives a change of scene or occupation from the active hard work of the eight hours for which she has already been up is leisure. Sometimes, perhaps once a week, perhaps only once a month, the change will be a real one. She may go to the Welfare Centre with baby, or to the recreation ground with the two small children, or to see her sister or friend in the next street, but most times the children don't give her the opportunity for this sort of leisure, for there is sewing and mending and knitting to be done for them; and besides there is always the shopping to be done, and if she possibly can, she does like to rest her legs a bit and sit down. So unless there is some necessity to go out, she would rather on most days stay indoors. And she may not have any clothes to go out in, in which case the schoolchildren will do the shopping after school hours. (Clothes are a great difficulty, "practically an impossibility".)

Then comes tea, first the children's and then her husband's, when he comes home from work; and by the time that is all over and washed up it is time the children began to go to bed. If she is a good manager she will get them all into bed by 8, perhaps even earlier, and then at last, at last, "a little peace and quietude!" She sits down again, after having been twelve or fourteen hours at work, mostly on her feet (and this means *standing* about, not *walking*), and perhaps she then has a "quiet talk with hubby", or listens to the wireless, "our one luxury". Perhaps her husband reads the paper to her. She has got a lot of sewing to do, so she doesn't read much to herself, and she doesn't go out because she can't leave the children unless her husband undertakes to keep house for one evening a week, while she goes to the pictures or for a walk. There is no money to spare anyhow for the pictures, or very seldom. She may or may not have a bite of supper with her husband, cocoa and bread and butter, or possibly a bit of fried fish. And so to bed—to her share of the bed, mostly at about 10.30 or 11.

This is the way that she spends six days out of seven, Sundays included, although Sunday may bring a slightly different arrangement of her problems because the shops are shut, the children and husband are at home. If she has been able to train her family well, and has got a good husband, they will relieve her of a little of the Sunday work, but it must be remembered that the husband is the breadwinner and must have his rest—and the children are young and will have their play. With luck, however, the mother will get "a nice quiet read on Sundays"—or a pleasant walk, or a visit to or from a friend; sometimes, if she is disposed that way, a quiet hour in church or chapel. But for her the seventh day is washing day, the day of extra labour, of extra discomfort and strain. At all times and in all circumstances it is arduous, but if she is living in the conditions in which thousands of mothers live, having to fetch water from the bottom floor of a four-storied house or from 100–200 yards or even a quarter of a mile along the village street; if she has nowhere to dry the clothes (and these include such bedclothes as there may be) except in the kitchen in which she is cooking and the family is eating, the added tension together with the extra physical exertion, the discomfort of the house as well as the aching back, make it the really dark day of the week. There is no avoidance of it. Even if she could raise the money to send the washing out—she hasn't got the second set of clothes or bed coverings which this necessitates. The bed clothes have to be used again, possibly on the same day as washing.

There is also no avoidance of the other great labour which is superimposed on the ordinary round, the labour of childbearing. The work will have to be done in the same way for those nine months before the baby comes and for the two or three months after she is about again but still not feeling "quite herself". The baby will probably be born in the bed which has already been described, the bed shared by other members of the family, and in the room of the use of which, even if she can get the bed to herself for a week, she cannot possibly deprive the family of more than a few hours. It is out of the question, she thinks, to go to hospital, and to leave her husband and children either to fend for themselves—or to the care of a stranger, or of an already overworked but friendly neighbour. Even if she is in bed, she is at least in her own home; and can direct operations, even perhaps doing some of the "smaller" jobs herself—like drying crockery, ironing,* and of course the eternal mending. How is it possible that she should stay in bed for long enough to regain her full physical strength, the strength that has been taxed not only in the actual labour of childbirth, but in six or seven of the preceding months, when every household duty has been more difficult to accomplish and has involved a far greater strain than it does when she is in her "normal" health? If she is sensible, she will have got help from the Clinic, extra milk if she is very poor, and tonics and, perhaps, if she is fortunate enough to live in an enlightened municipality, a good meal once a day for herself. But her scene and her work will not have changed, and unless she goes into hospital for the con-

---

*The writer found one woman sitting up in bed three days after the birth of her sixth baby ironing on a tray across her knees; the iron was handed to her by a neighbour who was washing up the dinner.

finement, it cannot bring that rest and comfort which she needs and deserves, but only extra difficulties for everyone in the family and very often serious ill-health for herself.

So the days, the weeks, the months, the years go on. There may be a break for an hour or two in the month when she attends some Guild or Women's Institute meeting. Once a year there may be a day's outing; but a holiday in the sense of going away from home, eating food she has not herself cooked, sleeping in another bed, living in a different scene, meeting other people and doing the things she can never do at home—this has been unheard of since the family arrived. She cannot go without the family, and there can be no question of taking them too. Possibly the children are somehow or other got into the country for a few days in the summer, if they live in the town; but it is without mother, unless she will go hop-picking, taking the small children with her. But it is only a very, very few who get the chance of even this "holiday". There is—again for the very few—another possibility of a holiday— convalescence. If the mother has been "really ill" she may be sent away by the hospital or under some insurance scheme, or by the Salvation Army or by one of the agencies whose merciful function it is to procure this kind of intermission for the woman whose strength has at last given way. She is sent away . . . away from her home, away from the smell of inferior and inadequately prepared food, away from the noise and worry of her family, away to the sea, for a fortnight or even three weeks. It may be that she is too ill to get much active enjoyment out of it, but oh, the blessedness of the rest, the good food, the comfortable bed, the difference of scene for her eyes, the glorious feeling of having nothing to do. "As dark as it was and as hard as it was, it gave me the privilege of having an hour's fresh air."

But if illness has been so severe as to merit this magnificent atonement, it has meant months probably of crippling in-disposition which has added enormously to the burden of work, and robbed it of all that potential satisfaction that can be found in the fulfilment of her task. She has had to let things slide, and she has slipped back so far that it will take months and months to catch up again even to her old standard of order and efficiency. This, in her eyes, is probably the worst disaster than can happen—her own illness. Other disasters are bound to come in the ordinary course of family life; the sickness of a child—the unemployment of her husband—the care of an old and perhaps tiresome grandparent.

But if she can keep fit, she will meet the extra burden. She may even voluntarily adopt another child, whose parents are dead; or she will augment the family income by going out to work herself, somehow or other squeezing her own housework into shorter hours. It may be a little less efficient, but the compensation is that she has a little more money for food, and can get better cooking utensils. At whatever cost of labour and effort a little more money is what she really wants; that is the magic which unties the Gordian knot. But there is little opportunity for this, and the poorer she is, the more difficult it is to arrange things in her own home so as to make it possible to leave it for even a couple of hours a day. Where it *must* be done, as in the case of a widow, or a woman with an invalid husband, the strain is nearly always almost insupportable.

Naturally there are some who seem to get more out of life than others; but almost without exception it is those women who have very few children, one, two or at the most three, and who for this or some other reason are in much better financial circumstances, who are able to get more real rest and change of scene and to employ their leisure in some way which suggests an interest in outside things. But there are not more than half a dozen who speak of politics, literary interests, study of any sort or music. The cinema is very rarely mentioned, and many women say that they have *never* been to the pictures. A few who live in the country speak of walking and gardening; others of going to chapel or church on Sundays. An overwhelming proportion say that they spend their "leisure" in sewing and doing other household jobs, slightly different from the ordinary work of cooking and house-cleaning.

The subject of husbands could form a thesis by itself. They are not very often specifically mentioned in the answers to this interrogatory, except in regard to their occupation and the money with which they provide their wives for housekeeping. But when a man adds to the embarrassments of life by bad temper or drunkenness, or is exasperatingly impatient with the wife's ill-health or unsympathetic with her difficulties, he generally appears in the list of her grievances directly or by implication. It is more often the visitor than the wife who makes special note of him. Equally, great solicitude for or sympathy with his wife is specially commended in a husband. Many instances are given of the husband carrying heavy tubs or coals for his wife—keeping watch over the children one evening a week, so that she can go out—reading aloud to her—or—if she is really ill—looking after her with great care, as far as his occupation allows. But the impression given in general of the attitude of the husbands in this enquiry is that of the quotation at the head of this chapter:—"our husbands do not realise we ever need any leisure". With the best will in the world, it is difficult for a man to visualise his wife's day—the loneliness, the embarrassments of her work, the struggle to spend every penny of his money to the best advantage. In most cases he can count upon her devoted service to himself and to their children—and he feels instinctively that her affection gives a pleasant flavour to her work which is absent from his own—and that she is fortunate in not being under the orders of an employer, and subject to regulations of time and speed of work etc. etc. If he is unemployed and therefore spends more time at home, the additional worry for both of them will take precedence of all other difficulties, and if he then notices the harassing conditions of her life, he will attribute them largely to this cause. Besides, the unemployed man can and does generally give his wife some help in the housework, which does much to lighten her physical burden, although it is little compensation for the additional mental worry.

Note is sometimes made in the women's accounts of the help given to them by the older of their schoolchildren. It is very usual to find mention of a child being kept back from school to do some of the work that the mother is too ill to do. Only a few mothers speak of training their children to help in the house as part of a regular routine—but this is probably less rare than it appears to be. It must be realised, however, that any help that a child under twelve can give costs so much in supervision and probably worry for a careful mother, that she feels it is easier to send the child out of the way and get on with the job herself. This may be a short-sighted policy, but it is easily forgiven in the woman who has no time to organise or plan.

It may be said that, even granting that there is no exaggeration in the above account of the working-class mother's life, there is no ground for giving special consideration to her case as apart from that of the father and the children; that their lot is just as hard as hers, and that the want from which she suffers is equally severe for them. That in many respects this is so, cannot be denied; but it is abundantly clear from the accounts given by the women themselves in this investigation that they are subject to many hardships from which circumstance or they themselves protect their families. To begin with, the working mother is almost entirely cut off from contact with the world outside her house. She eats, sleeps, "rests", on the scene of her labour, and her labour is entirely solitary. However arduous or unpleasant the man's work has been, the hours of it are limited and he then leaves not only the work itself but the place of it behind him for fourteen or sixteen hours out of every twenty-four. Even if he cannot *rest* in this time, he changes his occupation and his surroundings. If he is blessed with a capable hard-working wife, his home will represent to him a place of ease and quiet after an eight- or ten-hour day spent in hard, perhaps dangerous toil. He will have had ample opportunity for talking with his fellows, of hearing about the greater world, of widening his horizon. The children have equally either been out at work or at school, where for many hours of the day they have lived in airy, well-lighted rooms, with ample space for movement and for play. They too have met and talked with their fellows, and whatever the deprivations of their home, they go there to find that someone else has prepared their food, mended their clothes, and generally put things in order. Naturally they suffer, as the father does too, from the poverty of the home, the lack of sufficient food and clothes and warmth and comfort, but it is undoubtedly true that even in these respects the mother will be the first to go without. Her husband *must* be fed, as upon him depends the first of all necessities, money. The children must or will be fed, and the school will if necessary supplement. Equally husband and children must be clothed, not only fairly warmly but for school or work fairly decently. She need not be; she need not even go out, so it is not *absolutely* necessary for her to have an outdoor coat. And lastly, whatever the emotional compensations, whatever her devotion, her family creates her labour, and tightens the bonds that tie her to the lonely and narrow sphere of "home". The happiness that she often finds in her relationship of wife and mother is as miraculous as it is compensatory.

Much might be done even without dealing with the basic evil of poverty and without disintegrating the sacred edifice of the home, to introduce some ease into the lives of these women and so to lighten their work that they would have time to rest, to make contacts with the outer world, and to enjoy some at least of those cultural and recreative pursuits which would release them spiritually as well as physically from their present slavery. First of all, domestic and household training. As the Essex woman, quoted at the head of the preceding chapter, writes further on in her description of her life: "Never having been trained to housework, I find it very difficult to run my home efficiently—very small allowance prevents purchase of many labour-saving devices." If this is said of housework, how much oftener can it be said of more skilled work such as cooking and household management. Very few of these women know how to make *the best* of their slender resources by the wise expenditure either of money or of time. Better housing with equipment designed *to the very special needs of the woman who does all her own work* and every opportunity, if not compulsion to learn her trade would immediately release her from much of her present bondage. As to the lack of labour-saving devices, she might with gentle persuasion be induced to make use of certain communal amenities where these are too expensive to install in her individual house. Communal wash-houses, bake-houses, sewing rooms with good machines, should all be within easy reach of her home, for her use for a minute charge which would be less than she spends in individual firing at home; they would mean an immense saving of time and therefore indirectly of money expended in the attempt to do an expert job without the proper tools. This would also serve the very desirable purpose of bringing her in the course of her daily work into contact with other women doing the same job, and she would no longer have to find out for herself the better ways of doing things. And she should have also not too far from her home a club to which at any time in the week she can go to seek rest and companionship, cultural and recreative occupation and a blessed change of scene. If her work has been eased in the ways suggested above, she will find time for this, just as somehow now, she sometimes finds time for the weekly visit to the welfare centre with her babies. Here she could read, educate herself, talk to other women, listen, if she wanted to, to lectures, and get advice and help on any problem that worried her. Here too she should be able to bring her husband or friends for games or "socials"; but it should be *her* club, designed above all to meet *her* needs and to bring her enjoyment in whatever form she sought it. And lastly, she should have a holiday "with pay" once a year. She should be able for a week or a fortnight completely to stop work. Someone else must cook and clean and mend and bend not only for her husband and children but for herself. There is absolutely nothing revolutionary in any of these suggestions. It is as clear as day that even in the difficult question of finance they will save so much in sickness, hospital expenses and all the bolstering activities for which at present the nation is so heavily taxed, that they would very soon become self-supporting and be entirely free from that flavour of charity which is rightly so distasteful to the millions whose first wish is to be independent and to be enabled of themselves to lead the lives of human beings.

5

The Politics of Housework

PAT MAINARDI

"Though women do not complain of the power of husbands, each complains of her own husband, or of the husbands of her friends. It is the same in all other cases of servitude; at least in the commencement of the emancipatory movement. The serfs did not at first complain of the power of their lords, but only of their tyranny."

—John Stuart Mill, *On the Subjugation of Women*

Liberated women—very different from Women's Liberation! The first signals all kinds of goodies, to warm the hearts (not to mention other parts) of the most radical men. The other signals—*housework*. The first brings sex without marriage, sex before marriage, cosy housekeeping arrangements ("You see, I'm living with this chick") and the self-content of knowing that you're not the kind of man who wants a doormat instead of a woman. That will come later.

On the other hand is Women's Liberation—and housework. What? You say this is all trivial? Wonderful! That's what I thought. It seems perfectly reasonable. We both had careers, both had to work a couple of days a week to earn enough to live on. So why shouldn't we share the housework? So I suggested it to my mate and he agreed—most men are too hip to turn you down flat. You're right, he said. It's only fair.

Then an interesting thing happened. I can only explain it by stating that we women have been brainwashed more than even we can imagine. Probably too many years of seeing media-women coming over their shiny waxed floors or breaking down over their dirty shirt collars. Men have no such conditioning. They recognise the essential fact of housework right from the very beginning. Which is that it stinks.

Here's my list of dirty chores: buying groceries, carting them home and putting them away; cooking meals and washing dishes and pots; doing the laundry; digging out the place when things get out of control; washing floors. The list could go on but the sheer necessities are bad enough. All of us have to do these jobs, or get someone else to do them for us. The longer my husband contemplated these chores, the more repulsed he became, and so proceeded the change from the normally sweet considerate Dr Jekyll in to the crafty Mr Hyde who would stop at nothing to avoid the horrors of—housework. As he felt himself backed into a corner laden with dirty dishes, brooms, mops, and reeking garbage, his front teeth grew longer and pointier, his fingernails haggled and his eyes grew wild. Housework trivial? Not on your life! Just try to share the burden.

So ensued a dialogue that's been going on for several years. Here are some of the high points:

"I don't mind sharing the housework, but I don't do it very well. We should each do the things we're best at."
Meaning: Unfortunately I'm no good at things like washing dishes or cooking. What I do best is a little light carpentry, changing light bulbs, moving furniture. (How often do you move furniture?)
Also meaning: Historically the lower classes (Blacks and women) have had hundreds of years doing menial jobs. It would be a waste of manpower to train someone else to do them now.
Also meaning: I don't like the dull stupid boring jobs, so you should do them.

"I don't mind sharing the work, but you'll have to show me how to do it."
Meaning: I ask a lot of questions and you'll have to show me everything, every time I do it because I don't remember so good. Also, don't try to sit down and read while I'm doing my jobs because I'm going to annoy hell out of you until it's easier to do them yourself.

"We used to be so happy!" (Said whenever it was his turn to do something.)
Meaning: I used to be so happy.
Meaning: Life without housework is bliss. No quarrel here. Perfect agreement.

"We have different standards, and why should I have to work to your standards. That's unfair."

Meaning: If I begin to get bugged by the dirt and crap, I will say, "This place sure is a sty", or "How can anyone live like this?" and wait for your reactions. I know that all women have a sore called *guilt over a messy house*, or housework is ultimately my responsibility. If I rub this sore long and hard enough it'll bleed and you'll do the work. I can outwait you.

Also meaning: I can provoke innumerable scenes over the housework issue. Eventually, doing all the housework yourself will be less painful to you than trying to get me to do half.

"I've got nothing against sharing the housework, but you can't make me do it on your schedule."

Meaning: Passive resistance. I'll do it when I damn well please, if at all. If my job is doing dishes, it's easier to do them once a week. If taking out laundry, once a month. If washing the floors, once a year. If you don't like it, do it yourself oftener, and then I won't do it at all.

"I hate it more than you. You don't mind it so much."

Meaning: Housework is shitwork. It's the worst crap I'ver ever done. It's degrading and humiliating for someone of my intelligence to do it. But for someone of your intelligence. . . .

"Housework is too trivial to even talk about."

Meaning: It's even more trivial to do. Housework is beneath my status. My purpose in life is to deal with matters of significance. Yours is to deal with matters of insignificance. You should do the housework.

"In animal societies, wolves, for example, the top animal is usually a male even where he is not chosen for brute strength but on the basis of cunning and intelligence. Isn't that interesting?"

Meaning: I have historical psychological anthropological and biological justification for keeping you down. How can you ask the top wolf to be equal?

"Women's Liberation isn't really a political movement."

Meaning: The Revolution is coming too close to home.

Also meaning: I am only interested in how I am oppressed, not how I oppress others. Therefore the war, the draft and the university are political. Women's Liberation is not.

"Man's accomplishments have always depended on getting help from other people, mostly women. What great man would have accomplished what he did if he had to do his own housework?"

Meaning: Oppression is built into the system and I as the white American male receive the benefits of this system. I don't want to give them up.

Postscript

Participatory democracy begins at home. If you are planning to implement your politics there are certain things to remember.

1. He is feeling it more than you. He's losing some leisure and you're gaining it. The measure of your oppression is his resistance.

2. Most men are not accustomed to doing monotonous, repetitive work which never issues in any lasting let alone important achievement. This is why they would rather repair a cabinet than wash dishes. If human endeavours are like a pyramid with man's highest achievements at the top, then keeping oneself alive is at the bottom. Men have always had servants (you) to take care of this bottom stratum of life while he has confined his efforts to the rarefied upper regions. It is thus ironic when they ask of women: "Where are your great painters, statesmen, etc." Mrs Matisse ran a millinery shop so he could paint. Mrs Martin Luther King kept his house and raised his babies.

3. It is a traumatising experience for someone who has always thought of himself as being against any oppression or exploitation of one human being by another to realise that in his daily life he has been accepting and implementing (and benefiting from) this exploitation: that his rationalisation is little different from that of the racist who says "Niggers don't feel pain" (women don't mind doing the shitwork), and that the oldest form of oppression in history has been the oppression of 50 per cent of the population by the other 50 per cent.

4. Arm yourself with some knowledge of the psychology of oppressed peoples everywhere and a few facts about the animal kingdom. I admit playing top wolf or who runs the gorillas is silly but as a last resort men bring it up all the time. Talk about bees. If you feel really hostile, bring up the sex life of spiders. After sex, she bites off his head. The psychology of oppressed peoples is not silly. Blacks, women, and immigrants have all employed the same psychological mechanisms to survive. Admiring the oppressor,

glorifying the oppressor, wanting to be like the oppressor, wanting the oppressor to like them.

5. In a sense all men everywhere are slightly schizoid—divorced from the reality of maintaining life. This makes it easier for them to play games with it. It is almost a cliché that women feel greater grief at sending a son off to war or losing him to that war because they bore him, suckled him, and raised him. The men who foment those wars did none of those things and have a more superficial estimate of the worth of human life. One hour a day is a low estimate of the amount of time one has to spend "keeping" oneself. By foisting this off on others, man has seven hours a week—one working day—more to play with his mind and not his human needs. Over the course of generations it is easy to see whence evolved the horrifying abstractions of modern life.

6. With the death of each form of oppression, life changes and new forms evolve. English aristocrats at the turn of the century were horrified at the idea of enfranchising working men, were sure that it signalled the death of civilisation and a return to barbarism. Some working men even fell for this line. Similarly with the minimum wage, abolition of slavery, and female suffrage. Life changes but it goes on. Don't fall for any crap about the death of everything if men take a turn at the dishes. They will imply that you are holding back the Revolution (their Revolution). But you are advancing it.

7. Keep checking up. Periodically consider who's actually doing the jobs. These things have a way of backsliding so that a year later once again the woman is doing everything. Use timesheets if necessary. Also bear in mind what the worst jobs are, namely the ones that have to be done every day or several times a day. Also the ones that are dirty—it's more pleasant to pick up books, newspapers, etc., than to wash dishes. Alternate the bad jobs. It's the daily grind that gets you down. Also make sure that you don't have the responsibility for the housework with occasional help from him. "I'll cook dinner for you tonight" implies that it's really your job and isn't he a nice guy to do some of it for you.

8. Most men had a bachelor life during which they did not starve or become encrusted with crud or buried under the litter. There is a taboo that says that women mustn't strain themselves in the presence of men—we haul around fifty pounds of groceries if we have to but aren't allowed to open a jar if there is someone around to do it for us. The reverse side of the coin is that men aren't

supposed to be able to take care of themselves without a woman. Both are excuses for making women do the housework.

9. Beware of the double whammy. He won't do the little things he always did because you're now a "Liberated Woman", right? Of course, he won't do anything else either. . . . I was just finishing this when my husband came in and asked what I was doing. Writing a paper on housework. *Housework*? he said. Housework? Oh, my God, how trivial can you get. A paper on housework.

6

from *The Housewife*

SUZANNE GAIL

I married as soon as I graduated, explicitly anti-domestic, and bent on proving to myself that it was possible to combine marriage (an intense personal relationship mainly, but also a family much later) with unprejudiced exploration of literary values often remote from healthy-mindedness, hygiene and a stable society focused on the family. . . .

We had a flat which accumulated fluffy dust balls ankle-deep till a parental invasion was expected. Then we spent a few hours together making it respectable in order to avoid intrusive criticisms.

Carl was conceived unexpectedly that year, and the summer before he was born we moved to another flat. This was a great, rambling old place which we shared with an eccentric poetical colleague. He used to empty his pipe into my buckets of soaking nappies, and leave his part of the flat open to mating couples when he was away. I was shaken out of my cavalier attitude to housework. The baby immediately caught enteritis, and I was shattered by guilt when the doctor attributed this to the dirty flat. The housework proved enormously difficult in itself, partly because I was still tired, partly because the place was so large and dilapidated. I was humbled by the discovery that what I had considered work fit only for fools was beyond my capacity. Worst of all, Joe, who had regarded my non-domestication with complete tolerance, suddenly found the dirt and untidiness depressing, and begat status yearnings. As a man with a wife, a son and a salary for the uncongenial job foisted on him by Carl's appearance, he wanted a clean shirt every day, not just as something practical, but as his *right*. We were jolted out of our self-sufficiency, and reverted desperately for a while to Mummy's and Daddy's standards. If Joe was indignant when the dinner was burnt, I felt he had every right to regard me as a failure. And I sterilised everything that came remotely into contact with Carl, becoming deeply involved in germs. This provoked some passably hysterical scenes with our unfortunate poet, who held a generous communistic view of flannels and tooth-brushes.

The following autumn Joe got a university post, and we moved to the flat we are in now. . . .

I have long since passed the point where control of the housework seemed unattainable, and Carl as he grows older requires fewer and fewer elementary attentions. But I realised recently that I have developed an absurd cyclical pattern which stretches over a period of one or two months. I work up to a point where every room is in so organised a state that it requires only a few touches every morning to keep it perfectly clean and tidy (by my standards). Even the occasional job like dusting books or cleaning the cooker are done, and I move briskly from room to room in quite the efficient manner. The hearth is not only brushed after I've laid the fire—it is wiped and polished. As I work evangelical hymn-jingles from my carefully obliterated past well up in my mind. But I cannot achieve that degree of irony. It would be hubris, and the walls might fall in if I started chanting,

I'm H—A—P—P—Y.

Perhaps this stage lasts a week or two. Joe has his clean shirt every day *and* clean underwear; Carl is bathed several times. Then suddenly I flop. Every gesture requires an effort of will. The flat quickly sinks into chaos, dishes are washed under the tap as they are needed, and the airing cupboard stinks of urine because I have dried Carl's pants out instead of washing them. On Sunday evening I pick over the litter on the bedroom floor to find Joe's clothes to wash for Monday. The dinner comes out of tins, and far from presenting a clean hearth, the fire doesn't even get lit. Worst of all, that oasis in the afternoon when Carl is asleep and I can at last get down to my books, I waste destructively by going to bed. I have usually reached that point of tiredness where it takes some moments of fumbling to fix a plug in its socket, and there is an area of buzzing and shimmering between me and what I am trying to do, so I sleep. But my dreams are of the things I am trying to forget; static dreams, like a nauseating plateful of steaming sprouts.

What seems most undermining is that housework is anathema to concentration and intensity. Joe tells me I am freer than he is—I can do things in my own time without pressure from anybody. But that seems to me poor compensation for the sameness of jobs that require perhaps less than a quarter of one's mental awareness, while leaving the rest incapable of being occupied elsewhere. When something happens to stimulate me to my former awareness—an enjoyable social occasion, or the tutorials which I still give once a fortnight in the university—I feel I have come back to life; I am ashamed to admit that quite frequently I come home afterwards in a mood of savage rejection. I intended of course to carry on with my thesis quite as if nothing had happened after having Carl. I wanted him very much once I was pregnant, but expected him to play a limited role whose boundaries I was going to set. Alas! Long after I had pulled myself out of the morass of the first few months, come to look on Carl as something other than a cataclysm, and worked myself into a fever pitch of busyness to get everything necessary done first (I used to run to the shops), I was still not getting my thesis written. Two substantial chapters were already done, I was amassing ample material for a third—it was a genuinely interesting subject—and there, except for one joyous week last summer when they were both away, it still stands. I began to feel guilty about this failure too, because I had been so overweeningly confident in my ability to look after a baby, do the housework, and write a thesis, that I was still drawing a research scholarship. When it became obvious that I really was not capable of getting the thesis written in the circumstances, I had out of honesty to resign the money. My self-respect began to rot away. Step by step I dropped all the small rituals of vanity, and for a while it was a great effort even to bath. . . .

I let the flat get dirty when I am depressed, and the dirt depresses me further, even though I do not consider myself immoral for slipping into that state. Yet even this is not simply true; my happiest moods may coincide with the worst disorder. Then I am absorbed in thoughts of something else, and no longer notice my surroundings. Even when the flat is at its best it seems slightly sordid; we can't afford the spatial escape a car would give us, and mental "escape" has to do instead.

My hair-style is also an indication of the mood I am in. I grew it long one period when I was feeling resigned to this female role. Shortly after I had Carl I cropped my hair down to about an inch all over. It was a rejection of femininity because the dependency feeling pleasantly aroused by pregnancy, far from disappearing after giving birth as I had expected, intensified beyond all bearable limits. Feeling motherly seemed to be the last thing I would ever find time for, and an enormous chasm opened between me pregnant, and me with a deflated belly, my hands immersed in filthy nappies. I would not be so crudely symbolical with my hair now. I have achieved a measure of true independence within myself in the teeth of the last two years, and feel no need to flaunt it in the face of men. It is there, and does not need their recognition to exist. It was never a burden to me to be a woman before I had Carl. Feminists had seemed to me to be tilting at windmills; women who allowed men to rule them did so from their own free choice. I felt that I had proved myself the intellectual equal of men, and maintained my femininity as well. But afterwards I quite lost my sense of identity; for weeks it was an effort to speak. And when I again became conscious of myself as other than a thing, it was in a state of rebellion which I had to clamp down firmly because of Carl. I also grew very thin, and I still do not menstruate. This self-imposed penance, or this disgust at my subservience, had repercussions on all of us, some of which have still to be worked out. In a sense it is a triumph and a release not to menstruate. I have my sexual self intact with almost no danger of being called to account for it by pregnancy. But it seems that now I can achieve nothing unequivocally. I should hate Carl to be an only child; I know too well what it means to inflict that on him. But treatment of amenorrhoea is lengthy, and success uncertain. Meanwhile the time when I shall no longer be housebound recedes into the distant future.

My most obvious way back to feeling creative is to write the thesis, and I think I shall soon be able to tackle it again. The practical problem of libraries is minor compared with the fear I have felt of not being able to concentrate in the same way as before. It is not only mental concentration that is sapped by baby care and housework, it is personality concentration as well. A baby demands the whole of you. Before I had him I could turn away from everybody, into myself or my books, if I needed to; it was on this basis that I had resources and kept myself balanced. But I remain turned towards Carl even when he is asleep. At first this was a terrible burden. Now I bear it lightly, but not so lightly that I have felt safe so far in resuming the thesis in the odd periods of free time I have. . . .

Perhaps this seems to be an aside from "work", but Carl and housework are so closely interwoven that I cannot mention one without the other. This is especially true since I could never consider the possibility of staying at home as a housewife, even part-time, if I had no child to humanise the work for me. Office or factory work seems more annihilating because even less of me would be involved, but if I were given the choice between that or housework I would rather be out working in any conditions. My feelings of satisfaction or happiness are never connected with the housework, and are often in strict opposition to it, because Carl's vivacity and lawlessness oppose the reign of order and hygiene. I have of course received such a specialised education, voluntarily, that I would have to undergo a radical character change in order to fit the new mould adequately. That is a possibility, but one I have rejected. The other possibility, which I sought urgently for a long while, is to have other babies; I would then be so engrossed in the work entailed that I would not have time for thoughts of freedom till I emerged on the other side, maybe. But I have explained how this has not come about. I am not a bad mother most of the time, and might be a much better one in social conditions which did not try to integrate two hostile activities, but I am an incurably bad houseworker because I cannot pretend it is an essential, personalised task. Joe's work is much more necessary—we all live on it. Housework is housework, whoever does it. . . .

The mornings are always my worst time—the day stretches ahead in dreary sameness, with no possibility of anything unexpected; I would rather listen to anything or nothing than Housewives' Choice. The thought of all those millions of women performing exactly the same gestures as me, enclosed in their little circular activities, and perhaps with no desire or possibility of ever escaping, depresses me more than I can say. By the evening I am battered down to size, and Roundabout and Playtime, which are much younger programmes anyway, afford a very welcome relief.

When the housework was still new, I used to take a little pleasure in finding ways of doing the jobs quicker and better. But it is an exhaustible subject of interest, as you can tell by the way I keep veering off it. Now I am simply bent on eliminating as many tasks as possible. This is sensible to a certain extent. Joe did not notice the sheets were unironed last week, so it seems pointless to iron them any more—but it does cut the ground from under my feet. Another factor that undermines my interest is having to keep my mind on two things at once. I used to get very tense carrying on with a task while making sure Carl was not getting into trouble. I have overcome that by freeing the surface of my mind from thoughts altogether, leaving it swimming aimlessly so that it can be called into action by an alarming sound. This is a further loosening of concentration, and one that has to be practised for a distressingly large part of the day, often leaving me too empty for real concentration when the chance comes. And, as I said, any inclination I might have to take my work seriously is comically scotched by Carl himself, in his constructive moments as much as his destructive ones. Anything I do attracts his attention, so if I tidy a room he picks up the object as I put it down. Or if I clean windows on his level he comes after me, imitating my movements with his hands, and smearing what I have just done. Even if I give him a duster his fingers slip off; it is the movement he is intent on, not the sense of the gesture. I begin to feel hilariously unreal.

It is constantly niggling not only to be doing jobs that require so little valuable effort, but also jobs which are mainly concerned with simply keeping level with natural processes—cleaning jobs, whether of objects or for people, which once done are not done for good, and will have to be done all over again, just as if I have not already made the effort, the next day, or even within a few hours. There is something so negative about this role that society heaps entirely on to the shoulders of women, that of making sure things do not get dirty, and people do not get unhealthy. I want to believe in health as something basic, neutral, to assume that all the essentials are cared for, or at least will not magnify themselves into a full-time occupation. In my research I always felt at the end of a day's reading, writing or teaching that I had somehow added to life, enriched my experience, moved forward in a quite tangible sense. . . .

Life that does not move forward seems to me to stagnate, and in this sense I cannot help seeing Carl as a parasite. He can move forward to the time when he will no longer need me only on the understanding that I am prepared to stand still and grow older quietly, without too much fuss. My life slips away uncharted precisely when I am most eager to find out what I am capable of. I sit crouched in a chair, feeling all that useless and unwanted power suppressed inside me. I neither feel I have married the wrong man, nor that I don't want Carl, but I often wish that I had not had such confidence in my ability to ignore the established meaning of marriage, and had waited a few years longer before marrying. Sometimes I want to stretch out my arms to bring the whole imprisoning structure of home and family crashing around me, annihilating me with the rest. This is the only possibility, unreal as it is, that presents itself vividly to me. To walk out is never a real, live image, although I am curious to know how much of me would be left if I did. This, all round me, is my only creation so far, however incomplete and shoddily achieved; my split function goes too deep to be resolved by such a gesture.

Can you imagine what would happen to a man who was suddenly uprooted from a job in which he placed the meaning of his life, and delegated to a mindless task, in performing which he was also cut off fairly completely from the people who shared his interests? I think most of the men I know would disintegrate completely. (The maternal "instinct" is a comfortable male myth; a woman can only give freely if she is in a position where she does not feel deprived herself.) This is only a small example, but after two years of the sights and smells of a baby, Joe still refuses to change a nappy, except once a fortnight when I am literally not there to do it. He plays with Carl better than I, because the responsibility is not in terms of his own personal success. But chores are a different matter . . .

The way the family is structured leads inevitably to tyranny, against all one's clearsightedness and efforts to avoid it. Financial and patriarchal tyranny in Joe, however discreet its expression, is a reality, and it drives me to tyrannise over Carl. Then Joe will often reassert justice—by siding quite rightly with Carl against me. I would not believe a girl who claimed this had not happened to some extent in her family, because I know how hard we have struggled to avoid it.

Housework in these circumstances also constitutes an outright attack on femininity. It suddenly becomes a problem to keep slim, an impossibility to look attractive all the time. . . .

As in everything else, men's viewpoints prevail, so there are no new nursery schools being built. And there are so few state places that, in this town at least, you have to put the baby's name down by the time he is six months old. I have managed to get Carl into a private nursery school in a few months' time, afternoons only; some of those afternoons I shall spend teaching to pay for it, and I hope there will be some left for writing my thesis. He was sociable enough to spend half days at school months ago. . . .

I know many of his frustrations could be sorted out by a good nursery class, where he was given something constructive to do, and more company of his own age than I can arrange at the moment.

It would obviously be beneficial to Carl not to have to live with me so much. Perhaps it is unfair of me to blacken other more adaptable women with my dirt, but I feel it should be more widely recognised that it is in the very nature of a mother's position, in our society, to avenge her own frustrations on a small, helpless child; whether this takes the form of tyranny, or of smothering affection that asks the child to be a substitute for all she has missed. . . .

There are odd moments exquisitely satisfying in themselves, moments when I identify myself with Carl's discoveries. I suddenly see into his mind as if it were my own. One day he bent down to scratch a pale spot on the pavement with his fingernail, to find out if it was raised or level. Maybe without my book knowledge I would not have noticed, or not realised what he wanted to know. Or I can anticipate his discoveries; he looks at a toy vehicle sideways, and I ask him how many wheels it has. He answers two, so I turn it upside down for him to see all four.

In postscript, it is obvious that Carl is quite the best thing that has ever happened to me. And Joe isn't a tyrant.

7

Women and the Family

JAN WILLIAMS, HAZEL TWORT and ANN BACHELLI

This paper has been written by three women, each with two kids. We talked and wrote together as a group. We are oppressed and have been from the moment we were born. Our families have squashed us into roles because our mothers wanted daughters in their own image, and our fathers wanted daughters like their submissive wives. We each had a *girlhood* instead of a childhood and are only now beginning to be conscious of what that means in terms of what we are now. Now we feel we are martyrs. Martyrdom that has, over the years of being housewives and mothers, become almost enjoyable. The family exists on martyrdom. This is generally getting less but only since we have glimpsed how we live from outside. We have found it extremely difficult to look at ourselves—as through a window—and most of all it has been a sheer impossibility to imagine ourselves being involved in change of any sort. Our window on the world is looked through with our hands in the sink and we've begun to *hate that sink and all it implies—so begins our consciousness*. We need to work, work is a dignity, or should be, we know that most work is not, but at least at worst it involves you with other people, ideas and a struggle. Women are still told that they are oppressed because of capitalism: get rid of that and it'll all be all right. But this serves no purpose at all to women who don't feel part of anything, it *just pushes them further away from ever feeling anything*. The oppression every woman suffers is deeply in her, she first has to realise this and then to fight it—with other women helping. Men will not generally help with this, they need passive, ignorant, decorative women. We are, therefore, talking about that 65 per cent of women who do not work and who are presumably housewives.

The "family", as it is experienced, is the woman and the children *in* the house, the flat or the room and the man who comes and goes. The space that the family occupies is essential to its own image of itself, its own way of living, its self-expression. The woman who goes out to work goes out of her family if only for that period of time: however drab the work routine, children are temporarily forgotten, housework ignored. *In the home* the woman is *in the family*, and the two are disturbingly synonymous. Housework cannot be separated from children, nor the children from the four walls, the food you cook, the shopping you do, the clothes you wear. How you, the house, the children, *look* may not be how they are, but reflects what you want them to be. It is not just that every pop-psychologist's "mum" lives in a *Woman's Own* dreamhouse, where the material solution to any problem is immediately on hand; it is that in our society being a mother is being a housewife: the security of the family is the stability of the walls—the image of the family home is the image of the family, but not in any simple way. The folk-lore has many permutations—from happy secure family in new semi, to poor but happy slum dwellers, to the "broken home" of the "juvenile delinquent" who comes from both.

There is little to be said about housework on its own. An endless routine, it creates its own high moments of achievement and satisfaction so as to evade not monotony—the feature of many jobs—but *futility*. The bolt you tighten on the factory floor vanishes to be replaced by another: but the clean kitchen floor is tomorrow's dirty floor and the clean floor of the day after that. The appropriate symbol for housework (and for housework *alone*) is not the interminable conveyor-belt but a compulsive circle like a pet mouse in its cage spinning round on its exercise wheel, unable to get off. Into this one inserts one's own saving peaks: "happiness is the bathroom scrubbed down". But even the glorious end of today's chores is not even an anti-climax as there *is* no real *climax*—there is nothing to fill the "joyful moment". But the routine is never quite routine, so the vacuum in one's mind is never vacuous enough to be filled. "Housework is a worm eating away at one's ideas." Like a fever dream it goes on and on, until you desperately hope that it can all be achieved at one blow. You lay the breakfast the night before, you have even been known to light the gas under the kettle for tomorrow's tea, wishing that by breakfast time everything could be over with—by 8 a.m. the children washed, teeth-cleaned and ready for bed, tucked-up, *the end*.

And yet there is nothing tangible to force you to do it. A job is compulsory: either you go or you don't have a job. The pressures of housework are more insidious: neighbours criticise and compare; grandmothers hand on standards; within you and without you is your mother's voice, criticising and directing. Their overriding criterion is cleanliness: a dirty house is a disintegrating person. The compulsion to housework, then, is not economic or legal: it is moral and personal. And the housewife sees it in moral and personal terms. Hence her description of this structure of her oppression assumes querulous and complaining tones, the tones of a private neurosis to express a social fact—the imposed isolation of her work. For emancipated women to attack the complaint and ignore the whole socialising force which produces it simply reinforces the position.

Like every other form of social activity, every other aspect of social relationships, housework cannot be pinned down to a neat descriptive formula. The more we examine it, the more aspects it reveals, and the more we become aware of its contradictions and paradoxes. Isolated, the only adult in a private house, the housewife is yet crowded, by the emotional and physical demands of her family, by the unseen pressures of society. But although isolated, the housewife is never alone: her domain is the kitchen, the most communal room, and even the possibility of sleeping alone is denied her. To have the right to sleep alone is essential. People in permanent relationships do not do this. A woman needs time alone—after a day of being a public servant to the rest of the family, of giving out all the time, of being open to all demands— and in ordinary families the only time of the day this feeling of aloneness is possible is during the few moments before she goes to sleep after getting into bed. To then have to touch, caress, console yet another person is too much. The hatred of the man and sex begins—it is the beginning of such sayings as, "Oh, God, he wants his rights again," or the husband saying: "You can't have a headache every night." So that eventually she has no identity, no specificity, no privacy—she is defined by the demands of others. The only escape is the daydream, turning-in-on-oneself is the only way out. It is a journey from a body which is always being touched—the mother must always allow herself to be open to physical contact— to an area which cannot be touched, to an area of total privacy, where one's body is one's own again. Ironically, housework is often seen as being self-determined labour—"your time is your own". In fact, in order to "keep up", in order to be "a good housewife", one has to work to a pre-determined routine. The "freedom" of the housewife is in fact the denial of her right to a job. Even the division work/place of work, leisure/home does not apply to the housewife: her place of work is also the place of leisure and further it is her work which provides the basis of other people's leisure.

The "rationalisation" of housework is held out as a future prospect—better technical equipment means less work. But even if this different equipment were made easily available to all classes, the situation of the housewife would be essentially unchanged, and problems would remain. Indeed some would be exacerbated. The only social world most housewives have is the shopping centre—hence their "irrational" tendency to shop every day rather than once a week. Deprived of this they would lose one way of keeping up their morale. Being literally housebound, afraid of leaving the house and being seen is a typical woman's syndrome. Developments in technology on their own cannot change women's position in the home. We must be quite clear about this.

Unless we can discuss through the implications of the role of the housewife—the *institution* of the housewife, if you like—and work out the reasons why this institution survives so tenaciously, we will be unable to combat the various levels of oppression. Moreover, it is not enough simply to command women out to work—particularly since we all know that means that women usually end up with two jobs, one monotonous, the other futile.

We would like at this point to make clear that we do hold our children very dear. We love them passionately and care deeply about them. We feel it is because of this, or at least with this as one of the main reasons, that we have become immersed in working for the liberation of women.

Women are brought up for marriage and motherhood. The essential time spent in this is five years—five out of a lifetime of seventy years and more. The discrepancy between the time spent and the importance given to it is understandable—the human infant *does* need much care and attention. But from the viewpoint of the woman the discrepancy is absurd. Her whole life seems to be one long "before" and "after". Children go on being children beyond their first five years, in fact often until they produce the grandchildren which can replace them in their mother's eyes. But what does being a mother mean? In modern mythology it means a consistent being, untouched by the moods which the child exhibits, always forgiving, understanding, and certainly never violent or moody. The tyranny of consistency undermines both mother—she must never give way to anger or even to sudden affection—and child—whatever it does the superior adult can cope. It sets in motion a circular pattern. Consistency eventually means monotony; inconsistency leads to guilt; both cover suppressed feelings which can erupt into violence—which itself once more produces guilt and the struggle for the elusive and magical consistency. The smooth, unruffled exterior is simultaneously a masking of and a cause of conflict. Modern notions of the perfect and well-adjusted mother must be questioned and challenged. It may well be that they are designed not only to produce a compliant child, but also to produce the mother who, by turning a serene and contented face to the world, gives it an alibi for ignoring her problem.

Guilt and anxiety always weave their way through one's happiness. The guilt of giving birth is endorsed by the constant notion that you are responsible for the child's personality. The first months of a baby's life are full of difficulties—the lack of sleep, the fear (particularly with the first child) that you are not doing the right thing, the appalling ignorance and one's amateur status. The only answer to these problems appears to be total dedication to the child. Furthermore, this dedication can be seen as an investment in the child's future—at least one might prevent future neuroses. Even more, your anxiety can cover up feelings of violence and hatred towards your child. The mother of the battered baby acts out the fantasies of many mothers. And however anti-authoritarian the mother hopes to be in the future, or for that matter in the present, she still wants the children to do what she wants them to do.

For some families, one route out of the problem of the all-embracing mother and the pressures upon her has been a shifting of roles. The father has entered more into the life of the child. But this shifting of roles has also been a subtle reversal of roles. Instead of the comforting mother, whose ultimate threat was always "I'll tell your father", and the punitive father, the father has become the source of amusement, and the mother has remained the person ultimately responsible for the child's psychological and emotional future. Although the roles have changed, the ultimate responsibility has remained unchanged.

For this reason we should not be misled into thinking that the simple extension of woman into the man's role and the man into the woman's is the solution of the problem. Man as mother as well as man as house-slave is no answer. Obviously men can, and should, (and in rare cases do) perform domestic tasks and bring up families. This is not the point at issue. In the end the demand for complete reversal is the demand to extend oppression—understandable, but leading to a dead end. Our perspective must be different.

The demand for communal living must be understood in this way. The commune offers obvious advantages—at the minimum it helps to spread the load, to share work and thus to allow us time which is really free. But we must be careful not to turn it into an extended family, turned in on itself, where all are enclosed in increasing domesticity.

We must also be aware of its limitations. Living communally can only change the lives of the people in the community. It can help people to become less obsessed about their possessions and help them to regard their children in a less possessive way. It could help people out economically and offer them a less competitive home environment. It can free women a little to pursue their own work by sharing the practicalities of daily living. What it cannot do is be anything more than an individual solution to an individual's neuroses. The causes of these neuroses will still be present and real to all around her and thereby to her. Living in a commune must not be envisaged as a resolution of the housewife problem. The crucial point is that however women live in this society, their militant work must be governed by the imperative need to rouse the consciousness of their silent, submerged sisters. Women must realise the deadly effects of their passivity and overcome them by working together for their liberation.

8

The Political Economy of Women's Liberation

MARGARET BENSTON

"The position of women rests, as everything in our complex society, on an economic base."

—Eleanor Marx and Edward Aveling

The "woman question" is generally ignored in analyses of the class structure of society. This is so because, on the one hand, classes are generally defined by their relation to the means of production and, on the other hand, women are not supposed to have any unique relation to the means of production. The category seems instead to cut across all classes; one speaks of working-class women, middle-class women, etc. The status of women is clearly inferior to that of men,[1] but analysis of this condition usually falls into discussing socialisation, psychology, interpersonal relations, or the role of marriage as a social institution.[2] Are these, however, the primary factors? In arguing that the roots of the secondary status of women are in fact economic, it can be shown that women as a group do indeed have a definite relation to the means of production and that this is different from that of men. The personal and psychological factors then follow from this special relation to production, and a change in the latter will be a necessary (but not sufficient) condition for changing the former.[3] If this special relation of women to production is accepted, the analysis of the situation of woman fits naturally into a class analysis of society.

The starting point for discussion of classes in a capitalist society is the distinction between those who own the means of production and those who sell their labour power for a wage. As Ernest Mandel says:

> The proletarian condition is, in a nutshell, the lack of access to the means of production or means of subsistence which, in a society of generalised commodity production, forces the proletarian to sell his labour power. In exchange for this labour power he receives a wage which then enables him to acquire the means of consumption necessary for satisfying his own needs and those of his family.

> This is the structural definition of wage earner, the proletarian. From it necessarily flows a certain relationship to his work, to the products of his work, and to his overall situation in society, which can be summarised by the catchword alienation. But there does not follow from this structural definition any necessary conclusions as to the level of his consumption . . . the extent of his needs, or the degree to which he can satisfy them.[4]

We lack a corresponding structural definition of women. What is needed first is not a complete examination of the symptoms of the secondary status of women, but instead a statement of the material conditions in capitalist (and other) societies which define the group "women". Upon these conditions are built the specific super-structures which we know. An interesting passage from Mandel points the way to such a definition:

> The commodity . . . is a product created to be exchanged on the market, as opposed to one which has been made for direct consumption. *Every commodity must have both a use-value and an exchange-value*.
>
> It must have a use-value or else nobody would buy it. . . . A commodity without a use-value to anyone would consequently be unsalable, would constitute useless production, would have no exchange-value precisely because it had no use-value.
>
> On the other hand, every product which has use-value does not necessarily have exchange-value. It has an exchange-value only to the extent that the society itself, in which the commodity is produced, is founded on exchange, is a society where exchange is a common practice. . . .
>
> In capitalist society, commodity production, the production of exchange-values, has reached its greatest development. It is the first society in human history where the major part of production consists of commodities. It is not true, however, that all production under capitalism is commodity production. Two classes of products still remain simple use-value.
>
> The first group consists of all things produced by the peasantry for its own consumption, everything directly consumed on the farms where it is produced. . . .
>
> The second group of products in capitalist society which are not commodities but remain simple use-value consists of all things produced in the home. Despite the fact that considerable human labour goes into this type of household production, it still remains a production of use-values and not of commodities. Every time a soup is made or a button sewn on a garment, it constitutes production, but it is not production for the market.

> The appearance of commodity production and its subsequent regularisation and generalisation have radically transformed the way men labour and how they organise society.[5]

What Mandel may not have noticed is that his last paragraph is precisely correct. The appearance of commodity production has indeed transformed the way that *men* labour. As he points out, most household labour in capitalist society (and in the existing socialist societies, for that matter) remains in the pre-market stage. This is the work which is reserved for women and it is in this fact that we can find the basis for a definition of women.

In sheer quantity, household labour, including child care, constitutes a huge amount of socially necessary production. Nevertheless, in a society based on commodity production, it is not usually considered "real work" since it is outside of trade and the market-place. It is pre-capitalist in a very real sense. This assignment of household work as the function of a special category, "women", means that this group *does* stand in a different relation to production from the group "men". We will tentatively define women, then, as that group of people who are responsible for the production of simple use-values in those activities associated with the home and family.

Since men carry no responsibility for such production, the difference between the two groups lies here. Notice that women are not excluded from commodity production. Their participation in wage labour occurs but, as a group, they have no structural responsibility in this area and such participation is ordinarily regarded as transient. Men, on the other hand, are responsible for commodity production; they are not, in principle, given any role in household labour. For example, when they do participate in household production, it is regarded as more than simply exceptional; it is demoralising, emasculating, even harmful to health. (A story on the front page of the *Vancouver Sun* in January 1969 reported that men in Britain were having their health endangered because they had to do too much housework!)

The material basis for the inferior status of women is to be found in just this definition of women. In a society in which money determines value, women are a group who work outside the money economy. Their work is not worth money, is therefore valueless, is therefore not even real work. And women themselves, who do this valueless work, can hardly be expected to be worth as much as men, who work for money. In structural terms, the closest thing to the condition of women is the condition of others who are or were also outside of commodity production, i.e., serfs and peasants.

In her recent paper on women, Juliet Mitchell introduces the subject as follows: "In advanced industrial society, women's work is only marginal to the total economy. Yet it is through work that man changes natural conditions and thereby produces society. Until there is a revolution in production, the labour situation will prescribe women's situation within the world of men."[6] The statement of the marginality of women's work is an unanalysed recognition that the work women do is *different* from the work that men do. Such work is not marginal, however; it is just not wage labour and so is not counted. She even says later in the same article, "Domestic labour, even today, is enormous if quantified in terms of productive labour." She gives some figures to illustrate: In Sweden, 2,340 million hours a year are spent by women in housework compared with 1,290 million hours spent by women in industry. And the Chase Manhattan Bank estimates a woman's overall work week at 99.6 hours.

However, Mitchell gives little emphasis to the basic economic factors (in fact she condemns most Marxists for being "overly economist") and moves on hastily to superstructural factors, because she notices that "the advent of industrialisation has not so far freed women". What she fails to see is that no society has thus far industrialised housework. Engels points out that the "first premise for the emancipation of women is the reintroduction of the entire female sex into public industry. . . . And this has become possible not only as a result of modern large-scale industry, which not only permits the participation of women in production in large numbers, but actually calls for it and, moreover, strives to convert private domestic work also into a public industry."[7] And later in the same passage: "Here we see already that the emancipation of women and their equality with men are impossible and must remain so as long as women are excluded from socially productive work and restricted to housework, which is private." What Mitchell has not taken into account is that the problem is not simply one of getting women into *existing* industrial production but the more complex one of converting private production of household work into public production.

For most North Americans, domestic work as "public production" brings immediate images of a Brave New World or of a vast institution—a cross between a home for orphans and an army barracks—where we would all be forced to live. For this reason, it is probably just as well to outline here, schematically and simplistically, the nature of industrialisation.

A pre-industrial production unit is one in which production is small-scale and reduplicative: i.e., there are a great number of little units, each complete and just like all the others. Ordinarily such production units are in some way kin-based and they are multipurpose, fulfilling religious, recreational, educational, and sexual functions along with the economic function. In such a situation, desirable attributes of an individual, those which give prestige, are judged by more than purely economic criteria: for example, among approved character traits are proper behaviour to kin or readiness to fulfil obligations.

Such production is originally not for exchange. But if exchange of commodities becomes important enough, then increased efficiency of production becomes necessary. Such efficiency is provided by the transition to industrialised production which involves the elimination of the kin-based production unit. A large-scale, non-reduplicative production unit is substituted which has only one function, the economic one, and where prestige or status is attained by economic skills. Production is rationalised, made vastly more efficient, and becomes more and more public—part of an integrated social network. An enormous expansion of man's productive potential takes place. Under capitalism such social productive forces are utilised almost exclusively for private profit. These can be thought of as *capitalised* forms of production.

If we apply the above to housework and child rearing, it is evident that each family, each household, constitutes an individual production unit, a pre-industrial entity, in the same way that peasant farmers or cottage weavers constitute pre-industrial production units. The main features are clear, with the reduplicative, kin-based, private nature of the work being the most important. (It is interesting to notice the other features: the multipurpose functions of the family, the fact that desirable attributes for women do not centre on economic powers, etc.) The rationalisation of production effected by a transition to large-scale production has not taken place in this area.

Industrialisation is, in itself, a great force for human good; exploitation and dehumanisation go with capitalism and not necessarily with industrialisation. To advocate the conversion of private domestic labour into a public industry under capitalism is quite a different thing from advocating such conversion in a socialist society. In the latter case the forces of production would operate for human welfare, not private profit, and the result should be liberation, not dehumanisation. In this case we can speak of *socialised* forms of production.

These definitions are not meant to be technical but rather to differentiate between two important aspects of industrialisation. Thus the fear of the barracks-like result of introducing house-keeping into the public economy is most realistic under capitalism. With socialised production and the removal of the profit motive and its attendant alienated labour, there is no reason why, in *an industrialised society*, industrialisation of housework should not result in better production, i.e., better food, more comfortable surroundings, more intelligent and loving child-care, etc., than in the present nuclear family.

The argument is often advanced that, under neocapitalism, the work in the home has been much reduced. Even if this is true, it is not structurally relevant. Except for the very rich, who can hire someone to do it, there is for most women an irreducible minimum of necessary labour involved in caring for home, husband, and children. For a married woman without children this irreducible minimum of work probably takes fifteen to twenty hours a week; for a woman with small children the minimum is probably seventy or eighty hours a week.[8] (There is some resistance to regarding child-rearing as a job. That labour is involved, i.e., the production of use-value, can be clearly seen when exchange-value is also involved—when the work is done by baby-sitters, nurses, child-care centres, or teachers. An economist has already pointed out the paradox that if a man marries his housekeeper, he reduces the national income, since the money he gives her is no longer counted as wages.) The reduction of housework to the minimums given is also expensive; for low-income families more labour is required. In any case, household work remains structurally the same—a matter of private production.

One function of the family, the one taught to us in school and the one which is popularly accepted, is the satisfaction of emotional needs: the needs for closeness, community, and warm secure relationships. This society provides few other ways of satisfying such needs; for example, work relationships or friendships are not expected to be nearly as important as a man-woman-with-children relationship. Even other ties of kinship are increasingly secondary.

This function of the family is important in stabilising it so that it can fulfil the second, purely economic, function discussed above. The wage-earner, the husband-father, whose earnings support himself, also "pays for" the labour done by the mother-wife and supports the children. The wages of a man buy the labour of two people. The crucial importance of this second function of the family can be seen when the family unit breaks down in divorce. The continuation of the economic function is the major concern where children are involved; the man must continue to pay for the labour of the woman. His wage is very often insufficient to enable him to support a second family. In this case his emotional needs are sacrificed to the necessity to support his ex-wife and children. That is, when there is a conflict the economic function of the family very often takes precedence over the emotional one. And this in a society which teaches that the major function of the family is the satisfaction of emotional needs. [9]

As an economic unit, the nuclear family is a valuable stabilising force in capitalist society. Since the production which is done in the home is paid for by the husband-father's earnings, his ability to withhold his labour from the market is much reduced. Even his flexibility in changing jobs is limited. The woman, denied an active place in the market, has little control over the conditions that govern her life. Her economic dependence is reflected in emotional dependence, passivity, and other "typical" female personality traits. She is conservative, fearful, supportive of the status quo.

Furthermore, the structure of this family is such that it is an ideal consumption unit. But this fact, which is widely noted in Women's Liberation literature, should not be taken to mean that this is its primary function. If the above analysis is correct, the family should be seen primarily as a production unit for housework and child-rearing. *Everyone* in capitalist society is a consumer; the structure of the family simply means that it is particularly well suited to encourage consumption. Women in particular *are* good consumers; this follows naturally from their responsibility for matters in the home. Also, the inferior status of women, their general lack of a strong sense of worth and identity, make them more exploitable than men and hence better consumers.

The history of women in the industrialised sector of the economy has depended simply on the labour needs of that sector. Women function as a massive reserve army of labour. When labour is scarce (early industrialisation, the two world wars, etc.) then women form an important part of the labour force. When there is less demand for labour (as now under neocapitalism) women become a surplus labour force—but one for which their husbands and not society are economically responsible. The "cult of the home" makes its reappearance during times of labour surplus and is used to channel women out of the market economy. This is relatively easy since the pervading ideology ensures that no one, man or woman, takes women's participation in the labour force very seriously. Women's real work, we are taught, is in the home; this holds whether or not they are married, single, or the heads of households.

At all times household work is the responsibility of women. When they are working outside the home they must somehow manage to get both outside job and housework done (or they supervise a substitute for the housework). Women, particularly married women with children, who work outside the home simply do two jobs; their participation in the labour force is only allowed if they continue to fulfil their first responsibility in the home. This is particularly evident in countries like Russia and those in Eastern Europe where expanded opportunities for women in the labour force have not brought about a corresponding expansion in their liberty. Equal access to jobs outside the home, while one of the preconditions for women's liberation, will not in itself be sufficient to give equality for women; as long as work in the home remains a matter of private production and is the responsibility of women, they will simply carry a double work-load.

A second prerequisite for women's liberation which follows from the above analysis is the conversion of the work now done in the home as private production into work to be done in the public economy. To be more specific, this means that child-rearing should no longer be the responsibility solely of the parents. Society must begin to take responsibility for children; the economic dependence of women and children on the husband-father must be ended. The other work that goes on in the home must also be changed— communal eating places and laundries for example. When such work is moved into the public sector, then the material basis for discrimination against women will be gone.

These are only preconditions. The idea of the inferior status of women is deeply rooted in the society and will take a great deal of effort to eradicate. But once the structures which produce and support that idea are changed then, and only then, can we hope to make progress. It is possible, for example, that a change to communal eating places would simply mean that women are moved from a home kitchen to a communal one. This *would* be an advance, to be sure, particularly in a socialist society where work would not have the inherently exploitative nature it does now. Once women are freed from private production in the home, it will probably be very difficult to maintain for any long period of time a rigid definition of jobs by sex. This illustrates the interrelation between the two preconditions given above: true equality in job opportunity is probably impossible without freedom from housework, and the industrialisation of housework is unlikely unless women are leaving the home for jobs.

The changes in production necessary to get women out of the home might seem to be, in theory, possible under capitalism. One of the sources of women's liberation movements may be the fact that alternative capitalised forms of home production now exist. Day care is available, even if inadequate and perhaps expensive; convenience foods, home delivery of meals, and take-out meals are widespread; laundries and cleaners offer bulk rates. However, cost usually prohibits a complete dependence on such facilities, and they are not available everywhere, even in North America. These should probably then be regarded as embryonic forms rather than completed structures. However, they clearly stand as alternatives to the present system of getting such work done. Particularly in North America, where the growth of "service industries" is important in maintaining the growth of the economy, the contradictions between the alternatives and the need to keep women in the home will grow.

The need to keep women in the home arises from two major aspects of the present system. First, the amount of unpaid labour performed by women is very large and very profitable to those who own the means of production. To pay women for their work, even at minimum wage scales, would imply a massive redistribution of wealth. At present, the support of a family is a hidden tax on the wage earner—his wage buys the labour power of two people. And second, there is the problem of whether the economy can expand enough to put all women to work as a part of the normally employed labour force. The war economy has been adequate to draw women partially into the economy but not adequate to establish a need for all or most of them. If it is argued that the jobs created by the industrialisation of housework will create this need, then one can counter by pointing to (1) the strong economic forces operating for the status quo and against capitalisation discussed above, and (2) the fact that the present service industries, which somewhat counter these forces, have not been able to keep up with the growth of the labour force as presently constituted. The present trends in the service industries simply create "under-employment" in the home; they do not create new jobs for women. So long as this situation exists, women remain a very convenient and elastic part of the industrial reserve army. Their incorporation into the labour force on terms of equality—which would create pressure for capitalisation of housework—is possible only with an economic expansion so far achieved by neocapitalism only under conditions of full-scale war mobilisation.

In addition, such structural changes imply the complete breakdown of the present nuclear family. The stabilising consuming functions of the family, plus the ability of the cult of the home to keep women out of the labour market, serve neocapitalism too well to be easily dispensed with. And, on a less fundamental level, even if these necessary changes in the nature of household production were achieved under capitalism it would have the unpleasant consequence of including *all* human relations in the cash nexus. The atomisation and isolation of people in Western society is already sufficiently advanced to make it doubtful if such complete psychic isolation could be tolerated. It is likely in fact that one of the major negative emotional responses to women's liberation movements may be exactly such a fear. If this is the case, then possible alternatives—cooperatives, the kibbutz, etc.—can be cited to show that psychic needs for community and warmth can in fact be better satisfied if other structures are substituted for the nuclear family.

At best the change to capitalisation of housework would only give women the same limited freedom given most men in capitalist society. This does not mean, however, that women should wait to demand freedom from discrimination. There *is* a material basis for women's status; we are not merely discriminated against, we are exploited. At present, our unpaid labour in the home is necessary if the entire system is to function. Pressure created by women who challenge their role will reduce the effectiveness of this exploitation. In addition, such challenges will impede the functioning of the family and may make the channelling of women out of the labour force less effective. All of these will hopefully make quicker the transition to a society in which the necessary structural changes in production can actually be made. That such a transition will require a revolution I have no doubt; our task is to make sure that revolutionary changes in the society do in fact end women's oppression.

NOTES

1. Marlene Dixon, "Secondary Social Status of Women".
2. The biological argument is, of course, the first one used, but it is not usually taken seriously by socialist writers. Margaret Mead's *Sex and Temperament* is an early statement of the importance of culture instead of biology.
3. This applies to the group or category as a whole. Women as individuals can and do free themselves from their socialisation to a great degree (and they can even come to terms with the economic situation in favourable cases), but the majority of women have no chance to do so.
4. Ernest Mandel, "Workers Under Neocapitalism", paper delivered at Simon Fraser University. (Available through the Department of Political Science, Sociology and Anthropology, Simon Fraser University, Burnaby, B.C., Canada.)
5. Ernest Mandel, *An Introduction to Marxist Economic Theory* (New York, Merit Publishers, 1967), pp. 10–11.
6. Juliet Mitchell, "Women: The Longest Revolution", in *New Left Review*, December 1966.
7. Frederick Engels, *Origin of the Family, Private Property and the State* (Moscow, Progress Publishers, 1968), Chapter IX, p. 158. The anthropological evidence known to Engels indicated primitive woman's dominance over man. Modern anthropology disputes this dominance but provides evidence for a more nearly equal position of women in the matrilineal societies used by Engels as examples. The arguments in this work of Engels do not require the former dominance of women but merely their former equality, and so the conclusions remain unchanged.
8. Such figures can easily be estimated. For example, a married woman without children is expected each week to cook and wash up (10 hours), clean house (4 hours), do laundry (1 hour), and shop for food (1 hour). The figures are *minimum* times required each week for such work. The total, 16 hours, is probably unrealistically low; even so, it is close to half of a regular work week. A mother with young children must spend at least six or seven days a week working close to 12 hours.
9. For evidence of such teaching, see any high-school text on the family.

9

Women's Work is Never Done
PEGGY MORTON

> *"A socialist who is not a feminist lacks breadth. A feminist who is not a socialist lacks strategy."*
> —Quoted in Radical America, "Women in the Socialist Party"

There has been a great deal of debate in Women's Liberation over the past few years about the function of the family in capitalist society. Discussion has generally focused on the role of the family as the primary unit of socialisation: the family is the basic unit in which authoritarian personality structures are formed, particularly the development of authoritarian relationships between parents and children and between men and women; the family is necessary to the maintenance of sexual repression in that sexuality is allowed legitimate expression only within the confines of the marriage institution; through the family men can give vent to the feelings of frustration, anger and resentment that are the products of alienated labour, and can act out the powerlessness which they experience in work by dominating the other members of the family; and within the family little girls learn what is expected of them and how they should act.[1]

This theoretical work has provided important insights and understanding of the ways in which the family oppresses women, and the functions of the family in alleviating tensions created within the society. It has also forced the English-Canadian new left to deal with the questions of cultural, sexual and psychological oppression. But we have neglected to deal with the family as an economic unit, and as a result the question of women and the family has been divorced from our understanding of advanced capitalism, and has failed to develop an understanding of the dialectic between the economic and psychological functions of the family. Women's Liberation becomes an afterthought; women are viewed as one more minority group along with black people, Indians and perhaps students who are recognised as oppressed. Women are not, however, a minority group; they are one half of the human race. This repressive tolerance toward the question of women only further retards real analysis. Until this liberalism is smashed the pre-conditions for socialist men and women making alliances or working together in the development of a class analysis cannot exist, nor will the women's liberation movement succeed in developing revolutionary strategy.

Women themselves have been guilty of this "minority group" approach. The analogy between the oppression of black people and the oppression of women is common in women's liberation groups, and does serve as a way of forcing men to take seriously both the psychological and the economic oppression of women, and to expose the ways in which the culture does not recognise, in very fundamental ways, the existence of women.[2] But too often analogy passes for analysis, and when you try to build strategy out of analogy you are in trouble. These analogies often contain an inherent chauvinism both toward black people and toward women. Marlene Dixon states in her article "Why Women's Liberation?":

> In fact, women are as trapped in their false consciousness as were the mass of black people twenty years ago, and for much the same reason.

She goes on to say:

> Yet the greatest obstacle facing those who would organize women remains women's belief in their own inferiority. Just as all subject populations are controlled by their acceptance of the rightness of their own status, so women remain subject because they believe in the rightness of their own oppression.[3]

It is true, as Dixon points out, that one way the ruling class tries to control people is to mutilate their identities. But our task as organisers is not to tell women that they are oppressed but first to understand the ways in which people rebel every day against their oppression, to understand the mechanism by which this rebellion is co-opted and contained, how people are kept separate so that they see their oppression as individual and not sex and class oppression, and to provide revolutionary theory and practice which can give rise to new forms of struggle against that oppression. The greatest obstacle is not "false consciousness" but not knowing how to fight the family system, as for blacks the greatest obstacle was not knowing how to fight the racist system. Revolutionary movements are born out of the consciousness that people already have of their oppression and the transformation of individual understanding through collective action which produces a higher level of consciousness. It is our own chauvinism toward other women that keeps us from understanding how much women already understand about their own oppression.

A second problem with much of both the psychological and economic analysis of women's oppression is that it often has been developed out of the need to *justify* the importance of women's liberation rather than as a serious attempt to lay the basis for an understanding of the relationship of women to the capitalist system and a basis for strategy. Dixon mentions the "invisible participants" (movement men) in her article in *Radical America*, and she is right, but the problem goes even deeper. Even socialist women in Women's Liberation do not yet see analysis as a tool for the development of *strategy*, but only as a tool for increasing our individual and collective *understanding* of our oppression. This encourages a real liberalism among us about the way we look at the oppression of women, because lack of strategy means we don't have to act and so "analysis" serves instead to focus on our individual lives and the hope of changing them.

Most of the writing on the economics of women's liberation and the family have fallen into this trap. "Consumerism" has been such a bugaboo. Take, for example, this passage on women as consumers:

> The $16 billion a year advertising industry has swollen since the end of World War Two, paralleling women's mass exodus from productive labour to the home or the bottom rung of the labour force. The frustrating, boring, essentially passive and self-denying aspects of females' present roles probably make them "natural" consumers and suckers for ads. Yet, the advertising industry consciously and purposefully plants the idea in women that the road to fulfilment, to happiness, to overcoming obstacles to catching and keeping a man lies in greater and greater consumption. After all, the business of advertising is to sell and females make up to 75 per cent of all consumer decisions. More important, it is women who consume most of the "wasteful" products of an over-productive economy—with the exception of military waste—the ever-changing cosmetics, the latest in patterned, scented fancy paper products, decorator extension phones, lovely flowered plastic boxes of margarine, the final word in any of the fifty brands of soap powder.[4]

In this analysis the growth of the advertising industry is tied to the "mass exodus" of women from the labour market to the home—

while in fact, 42 per cent of women over 14 were in the labour force in the US and 32 per cent in Canada in 1968. Women are portrayed as rather stupid, malleable creatures easily manipulated by the big, bad advertising man. But the writers of the paper have themselves fallen prey to the myths of the advertising men—the myth, for example, that women make all the decisions about buying in the family, the myth that there is real choice in the market-place (the 50 brands of soap are made by a few large companies), and the myth that women's work—buying and preparing food for their families, buying clothing and making the purchases that sustain their families from day to day is somehow pleasurable consumption and not work or production. And the whole picture is based on an incredible ignorance of the lives of working-class women and a false picture of North American affluence. Wasteful consumption by the middle class is only one way in which surplus is disposed of. Working-class families spend most of their income on essentials— food, shelter, transportation, clothing, medical care, insurance and taxes.

Waste in capitalist society is related not just to consumption, or even primarily to consumption, but to the structure of production. The system is not going to collapse if we stop buying genital deodorants and lipsticks. Moreover, the basis of wasteful consumption under capitalism rests in the fact that people have very little choice about how they spend their money, and this cannot be explained by a neo-Freudian emphasis on psychic manipulation. Ellen Willis, in an excellent paper on consumerism has noted:

The locus of the oppression resides in the *production* function: people have no control over what commodities are produced (or services performed), in what amounts, under what conditions, or how they are distributed. Corporations make these decisions solely for their own profit. It is more profitable to provide luxuries for the affluent (or, for that matter for the poor, on exploitative instalment plans) than to produce and make available food, housing, medical care, education, recreational and cultural facilities according to the needs and desires of the people. We can accept the goods offered to us or reject them, but we cannot determine their quality or change the system's priorities. In a truly human society, in which all people have personal autonomy, control over the means of production and equal access to goods and services, consumption will be all the more enjoyable because we will not have to endure shoddy goods at exploitative prices by means of dishonest advertising.

As it is, the profusion of commodities is a genuine and powerful compensation for oppression. It is a bribe, but like all bribes, it offers concrete benefits, in the average American's case, a degree of physical comfort unparalleled in history. Under present conditions, people are preoccupied with consumer goods not because they are brainwashed but because buying is the one pleasurable activity not only permitted but actively encouraged by the power structure. The pleasure of eating an ice-cream cone may be small compared to the pleasure of meaningful autonomous work, but the former is easily available and the latter is not. A poor family would undoubtedly rather have a decent apartment than a new TV, but since they are unlikely to get the apartment, what is to be gained by not getting the TV?[5]

Willis also points out that the "consumerism" syndrome is symptomatic of an elitist and individualistic approach to the oppression of women. The only strategy that can come from this analysis is an individualist response—moral exhortation not to buy products, and not to objectify oneself. This serves to reinforce the feelings of superiority that middle-class radicals too often have toward working-class people with their "plastic" existence and their "materialist values", and suggests that we who do not wear bras and buy genital deodorants are morally superior to other women who do.

It would be more useful to look at advertising as a form of social control, as capitalist art, to understand the ways in which advertisers turn revolt against the system into propaganda for the system, than to look at it in what are essentially bourgeois psychological terms. This would allow us to look at the problem of consciousness dialectically. In other words, we would come to understand more clearly the anger and anxieties that women feel which all mechanisms of social control, including advertising, work to transform from dissent into assent. For example, the "revolution" in women's underwear—a new bra which looks like "no-bra" costs even more than the old kind.

What defines women? Or does Lady Astor oppress her garbageman?

Maggie Benston's paper "The Political Economy of Women's Liberation" is very important as one of the first arguments that we must analyse the role of women in the family from the point of view of production rather than consumption. Benston argues that because the work of women in the home is based not on commodity production, which in capitalist society is the only kind of production considered to be real work, but on the production of use-values without exchange-values, that the work that women perform is not considered to be real and valid work, and that therefore women are defined as inferior to men.

> The material basis for the inferior status of women is to be found in just this definition of work. In a society where money determines value, women are a group who work outside the money economy. Their work is not worth money, is therefore valueless, is therefore not even real work. And women themselves who do this valueless work, can hardly be expected to be worth as much as men, who work for money. [6]

Benston thus sees the family, and women's production role within the family, as the material basis for the oppression of women. This argument is significant not only in that it rejects the idea that the family is primarily a unit of consumption, but because it challenges the view that the only *economic* basis to the oppression of women is the super-exploitation of women in the labour market. Those who argue that the economic oppression of women exists only within the workplace conclude that therefore women need not organise either separately or differently from men, and that there is no need for an autonomous women's movement. And even marxist women's liberationists often envisage organising working women in the same terms as if they were organising men, using the same analysis and the same strategy.

In this view, male supremacy is seen primarily as an attitude, (male chauvinism) an attitude conveniently used by the capitalists to further exploit women. If male supremacy is primarily an attitude, then the problem of male supremacy is one that can and will be dealt with after the seizure of state power. In its grossest form this analysis implies that women cannot be liberated until after the revolution, and that the abolition of wage slavery will also abolish the oppression of women, with cultural hangovers that will be dealt with by the "cultural revolution".

If male supremacy is not attitudinal but structural, then no understanding of the economic base is possible without understanding male supremacy and how it maintains the hegemony of the ruling class. Only when we understand the actual divisions within the working class which exist on the basis of sex, race, nationality, status, skill level, etc., not as attitudes which people can be exhorted to change but manifestations of contradictions, can we begin to understand the potential basis for unity of the working class.

Benston correctly situates the oppression of women as stemming from their role in the family and correctly argues that real contradictions exist for women as women, and not only on the basis of their class position. Because of this, many of us have accepted her arguments with a certain sense of relief that we have "solved" the problem of this class position of women. Clearly her paper was not meant to provide a complete analysis and should not be faulted for failing to solve questions it did not set out to solve. But there are very serious problems within the structure of Benston's argument.

The chief problem is that it does not provide any basis on which strategy for a women's movement can be based. What does it mean to say that women have a unique relationship to the means of production and are therefore a class? We know that despite this common relationship to production in the home women are nevertheless objectively, socially, culturally and economically defined, and subjectively define themselves, through the class position of their husband or their family and/or the class position derived from work outside the home. We know that upper-class women gain very real privileges from their class position which override the oppression which they experience as women. Although it is not Benston's intent to say that a bourgeois woman has more in common with her maid than with her husband, that conclusion could be drawn from the argument as it stands.

Secondly, to define women through their work as unpaid household labourers does not help us to understand how to organise women. The logical conclusion would be that women should be organised around their relationship to production, i.e. organised around their work in the home. Yet the isolation of housewives, which is an important aspect of their oppression, is also a great barrier to their organisation. Historically, women have begun to organise not when they were tied to the home, but when they entered the labour market.

There are some areas where this analysis does bear fruit. The demand to socialise the care of children through day-care centres must clearly be part of our strategy. Another possibility is the demand for housing which does not isolate people in family units but provides space for people to live in other arrangements. With facilities for day-care, areas for children to play, common areas for women who are forced to live a prison-like existence in the privacy of their own homes, and communal eating facilities to relieve women of the task of preparing food daily for their families. But within a capitalist society, unless these demands are tied in with an attack on the private ownership of the means of production, the logical solution would be the capitalisation, not the socialisation of household labour. And probably women would be hired at low wages to perform these services. We need to integrate the demand for the socialisation of household labour with the demand for the socialisation of labour outside the home.

A third problem with Benston's analysis is that it is static not dialectic, and does not provide the framework for understanding the changing nature of the family as an economic institution. As John and Mickey Rowntree point out,[7] women do not play a peripheral role in the labour force, and the numbers of women working outside the home are growing very significantly. The sense in which women's role in the labour force is peripheral is that women's position in the family is used to facilitate the use of women as a reserve army of labour, to pay women half what men are paid, but women's work in the labour force is peripheral neither to the women's lives nor to the capitalist class. In Canada, the percentage of all women 14 years of age and over in the labour force has risen from 23.4 per cent in 1953 to 34.5 per cent in 1968, while the percentage of men has declined from 82.9 per cent to 77 per cent[8] (because of earlier retirement and longer periods of schooling). At the same time, more women are also attending school.

One, two, three, many contradictions

We need an analysis of the family that will help us understand how and why these changes are taking place. I have been arguing that very little of the analysis of women's oppression that we have done in Women's Liberation has been strategic analysis, and that the way we look at women's oppression reflects both the inner-directedness of the women's movement and our desire to prove to ourselves and to men that we are Marxists, that we have an economic analysis, and so on. We must now begin to examine the specific material and historical conditions out of which the present Women's Liberation movement has arisen, and the contradictions which women experience that are increasing women's consciousness. Strategy is a question of the correct handling of contradictions. We must understand both the contradictions between women's role in the family and their role in the labour force, and the contradictions that exist within the family in the various roles which the family is expected to perform under capitalism.

The essence of the position I want to argue in this paper is as follows: (a) as Benston argues, the primary material basis of women's oppression lies in the family system; (b) that particular structural changes are taking place in capitalism that affect and change the role of the family, are causing a crisis in the family system, and are raising the consciousness of women about their oppression; (c) that the key to understanding these changes is to see the family as a unit whose function is the *maintenance of and reproduction of labour power*, i.e. that the structure of the family is determined by the needs of the economic system, at any given time, for a certain kind of labour power; (d) that this conception of the family allows us to look at women's public (work in the labour force) and private (work in the family) roles in an integrated way. The position of women in the labour force will be determined by (i) the needs of the family system, i.e. what the family needs to do in order to carry out the functions required of it, and (ii) by the general needs of the economy for specific kinds of labour power; (e) strategy must be based on an understanding of the contradictions within the family, contradictions which are created by the needs that the family has to fulfil, of the contradictions within the work-force (contradictions between the social nature of production and the capitalist organisation of work), and the contradictions created by the dual roles of women—work in the home and work in capitalist production. This paper will try to deal with the contradictions within the family, and the contradictions between public and private roles.

We are taught to view the family as a sacrosanct institution, as the foundation-stone of society and as constant and never-changing. As Juliet Mitchell says:

> Like woman herself, the family appears as a natural object, but it is actually a cultural creation. There is nothing inevitable about the form or role of the family any more than there is about the character or role of women. It is the function of ideology to present these given social types as aspects of nature herself. [9]

Particularly in times of social upheaval, the family is extolled as the "greatest good", whether it be the *Kinder, Kirche, Kuche* of the

Nazis or the togetherness preached in Amerika. Because the family is so clearly important in maintaining social stability, many women's liberationists see the family as the "linch-pin" of the capitalist system, and see their major task as the destruction of the family. The problem with this view is that it tends to become totally idealist—a declaration of war on the *ideology* of the family system and not its substance. Instead our task is to formulate strategy from an understanding of the contradictions in the family system. To do this we must understand how the family has developed in different stages of capitalism as the requirements for the maintenance and reproduction of labour power change. When Benston analyses the oppression of women in terms of their productive role being that of unpaid household labourers, she is analysing only one part of the maintenance and reproduction of labour power. Through this definition we can examine the size of families encouraged, the socialisation of children in the home and in educational institutions, the working place of women in or out of the home and the role of the wife in giving psychological support and playing a "tension-management" role for her husband. In short, we can study the economic, social, ideological and psychological functions of the family in an integrated way.

By "reproduction of labour power" we mean simply that the task of the family is to maintain the present work force and provide the next generation of workers, fitted with the requisite skills and values necessary for them to be productive members of the work force. When we talk about the evolution of the family under capitalism, we have to understand both the changes in the family among the proletariat, and the changes that come from the increasing proletarianisation of the labour force engaged in agriculture, and the consequent urbanisation of the society.

The pre-capitalist family functioned (as does the farm family in capitalist society) as an integrated economic unit; men, women and children took part in production: work in the fields, the cottage industry, and production for the use of the family. There was a division of labour between men and women, but in essence all production took place within the family. We should not idealise the pre-capitalist family, for there was much brutality in the old system—the oppression of women, harsh ideas about the raising of children, and a culture that reflected the limitations of peasant life. But the family also served as a structure for the expression and fulfilment of simple human emotional needs.

The family in the first stages of capitalism

For those who became the urban proletariat, this was ruthlessly swept away with the coming of industry. The function of the family in the reproduction of labour power was reduced to the most primitive level. Instead of skilled artisans, the factories required only a steady flow of workers who required little or no training, learned what they needed on the job, and who were easily replaceable. Numbers were of primary importance, and the conditions under which people lived were irrelevant to the needs of capital. The labour of women and children took on a new importance.

> In so far as machinery dispenses with muscular power, it becomes a means of employing labourers of slight muscular strength and those whose bodily development is incomplete, but whose limbs are all the more supple . . . The labour of women and children was therefore the first thing sought by the capitalists who used machinery. That mighty substitute for labour and labourers was forthwith changed into a means for increasing the number of wage-labourers, by enrolling under the direct sway of capital every member of the workman's family, without distinction of age or sex. Compulsory work for the capitalist usurped the place, not only of children's play, but also of free labour in the home within moderate limits for the support of the family. . . . The value of labour power was determined not only by the labour time necessary to maintain the individual adult labourer, but also by that necessary to maintain his family. Machinery, by throwing every member of that family onto the labour market depreciates the power of the man . . . In order that the family may live, four people must now, *not only labour but expend surplus labour for the capitalist*.[10]

The consequence was a drastic increase in the exploitation of child labour in Britain in the period 1780–1840. Even small children worked 12–18 hour days, death from over-work was common, and despite a series of Factory Acts which made provisions for the education of child labourers, the education was almost always mythical. When teachers were provided, they were themselves often illiterate. The report on Public Health, London, 1864, documents that in industrial districts infant mortality was as high as one death in four in the first year of life, as compared to one in ten in non-industrial districts. As many as half the children died in the first five years of life in the industrial slums—not because of a lack of medical knowledge, but because of the conditions under which the urban proletariat were forced to live. Girls who had worked in the mills since early childhood had a characteristic deformation of the pelvic bones which made for difficult births; women worked until the last week of pregnancy and would return to the mills soon after giving birth for fear of losing their jobs; children were left with those too young or too old to work, were given opiates to quiet them, and often died from malnutrition resulting from the absence of the mother and the lack of suitable food.[11]

In other words, in the stage of primitive accumulation of capital, the need of capitalism for a steady flow of cheap and unskilled labour primarily determined the structure of the family. In contrast, the prevailing ideology of the middle classes continued to idealise the family, and this ideology was used in turn to prepare the working class for the new drudgery. The repressive Victorian morality, brought to the working class through the Wesleyan sects, clamped down harder on the freedom of women, and perpetrated the ideology of hard work and discipline. The Victorian concept of the family was both a reflection of the bourgeois family, based on private property, and an ideal representing a status to which the proletarian would like to rise. Marx retorted:

> Abolition of the family! Even the most radical flare up at this infamous proposal of the Communists.
>
> On what foundation is the present family, the bourgeois family, based? On capital, or private gain. In its completely developed form this family exists only among the bourgeoisie. But this state of things finds its complement in the practical absence of the family among the proletarians, and in public prostitution . . . The bourgeois clap-trap about the family and education, about the hallowed correlation of parent and child, become all the more disgusting, the more, by the action of Modern Industry, all family ties among the proletarians are torn asunder and their children transformed into simple articles of commerce and instruments of labour.
>
> But you communists would introduce community of women, scream the whole bourgeois chorus.
>
> The bourgeois sees in his wife a mere instrument of production. He hears that the instruments of production are to be exploited in common, and naturally, can come to no other conclusion than that the lot of being common to all will likewise fall to the woman.
>
> He has not even a suspicion that the real point aimed at is to do away with the status of women as mere instruments of production.[12]

A similar pattern emerges for groups within advanced capitalism who serve as a reserve army of unskilled labour. During slavery, the black family was systematically broken up and destroyed, and in many ways has never been reinstated. Because black people have been used as a reserve army of unskilled labour, there has been no need for a family structure that would ensure that the children received education and skills. And direct oppression and repression (racism) eliminated the need for more subtle social control through the socialisation process in the family. Often the women were the breadwinners because they were the only ones who could find jobs, and when there were no jobs the welfare system further discouraged the maintenance of the family by making it more difficult to get welfare if the man was around.

In North America, conditions were initially the same as in pre-capitalist Europe. The settling of the continent required the family structure, initially in an even stronger form than in Europe, given the absence of other developed institutions to meet social and psychological needs. Industrial workers did experience conditions similar to those of Europe in the early stages of capitalist development. But, in Europe and in North America, the evolution of capitalism called for a restructuring of the family.

The constant need of each capitalist to increase the productivity of his enterprise in order to remain competitive was secured both by increasing the level of exploitation of the workers, and by the continual introduction of new, more complex and more efficient productive apparatus (machinery). Thus a new kind of worker was required as the production process became more complex—workers who could read instructions and blueprints, equipped with skills that required considerable training. As the need for skilled labour increases the labour of women and children tends to be replaced by that of men. Workers involve a capital investment and therefore it makes more sense to employ those who can work steadily throughout their lives.

At the same time, the growth of trade unions and the increasing revolutionary consciousness of the working class forced the ruling class to meet some of their demands or face full-scale revolt. The rise in material standards of living accommodated both the need to restrain militancy, to provide a standard of living that would allow for the education of children as skilled workers, and the need for consumers to provide new markets for the goods produced. The abolition of child labour and the introduction of compulsory education were required by the need for a skilled labour force.

Reproduction of labour power in advanced capitalism

Marx noted in a discussion of the way in which the value of labour power is determined, that it was determined by the costs of "the working time necessary for its production", and also by the costs of those necessities "required by future (substitute) power, i.e. the labourers' children. Likewise included in the sum total are the costs necessitated by learning the skill and dexterity required for a given branch of labour-cost, which, however, are insignificant in so far as ordinary labour power is concerned".[13]

The transformation in the costs of educating and training the new generation of workers is fundamental to the changes that have taken place and are still taking place in the family structure. A fundamental law of capitalism is the need for constant expansion. Automation is required for the survival of the system. Workers are needed who are not only highly skilled but who have been trained to learn new skills. Profits depend more and more on the efficient organisation of work and on the self-discipline of the workers rather than simply on speed-ups and other direct forms of increasing the exploitation of the workers. The family is therefore important both to shoulder the burden of the costs of education, and to carry out the repressive socialisation of children. The family must raise children who have internalised hierarchical social relations, who will discipline themselves and work efficiently without constant supervision. The family also serves to repress the natural sexuality of its members. This is an essential process if people are to work at jobs which turn them into machines for eight or more hours a day. Women are responsible for implementing most of this socialisation.

The pressure to stay in school and the growth in post-secondary education, which serves both to train skilled workers and managers and to absorb surplus manpower that cannot be employed, means that the earnings of married women begin to replace the earnings of unmarried children. In 1951, married women were only 8.9 per cent of the labour force; by 1965, 18.5 per cent of all workers were married women. In contrast, there has been a decline in the number of unmarried children in the labour force—from 20.7 per cent of the labour force in 1951, to 17.2 per cent in 1965. As young people tend more to move away from home when they start to earn money, fewer families have the income of older children to help make ends meet. And besides not having these extra wages, the family must often pay for tuition for the children's education.

The second paycheck often makes the difference between poverty and keeping your head above water. A study of data from the 1961 census found that only 43 per cent of non-farm families had only one wage-earner. In 37 per cent of all non-farm families, the wives had earned income, and in 20 per cent income had been contributed by unmarried children. As the percentage of working women has risen from 28.7 per cent in 1961 to 34.4 per cent in 1968, the percentage of families having income from wives would now be still larger. In 1965, the average income for families with one paycheck coming in was $5,626, for families with two wage earners it was $6,784, and for families where three or more people were working, $9,166.[14] Obviously much of the "affluence" of working-class, and even many "middle-class" families depends on the wages of women.

In this situation, the mother is at one and the same time indispensable to the family (as an economic structure) and totally purposeless at the same time. Women are indispensable to the maintenance of the family where the children are coerced into remaining at school, supported by their parents or prone to unemployment if they have left school at an early age. They are superfluous because the children who they are supposed to mother are old enough to take care of themselves, resentful of parental authority and rebelling against the system's enforcement of control over their lives. The institution of the family makes a lot more sense when the job of the mother entails the care of children who really do need care.

> The family group then consists of a woman of forty-five wiping the noses of her graduate school children. Of course this stereotype applies directly only to the upper class and middle classes, but it is the world view of the ruling class which has hegemony over the media of mass communications and hence forms the ideal type.[15]

The pressure to finish high school and the growth of community colleges for the children of the working class makes this picture more real for the working class as well. The mother role must be maintained because her work is necessary to the family unit and because the family unit itself is economically essential.

The schizophrenia of living through other people becomes even more pronounced as those whom one is supposed to live through rebel and demand their autonomy. It is little wonder that the largest group of "speed freaks" are women in their forties and fifties, or that one half of the hospital beds were taken up by victims of mental-emotional disease, many of these middle aged women. The majority of these suffer from schizophrenia, a disease of advanced capitalism which is rooted in the nuclear family.[16]

> Such a breakdown in normal social relations indicates the stress brought to bear on the so-called private sector. To put this another way, it shows the extent to which the social, psychic, and economic costs of maintaining the labour force are exacted from people through the family.[17]

The changes in the kind of labour needed are also reflected in the decline in the size of families. For a rural family, large numbers of children are taken for granted—lots of children mean more hands to do chores as well as more mouths to feed, and since food and housing are not such a major cost on a farm as in the city, large families are not a liability but are valued for the sense of security and companionship they provide. In the early stages of capitalism, large numbers of workers were needed and so large families were not discouraged. Even though large families meant hardships for working-class urban families, the old social patterns were slow to change.

The high cost of housing, food, clothing, education and the easier access to birth control have all produced a tendency toward smaller families. And because urbanisation is a quite recent phenomenon, the gap between cultural values and economic necessity means that the trend to smaller families is more recent still.

Only 40 per cent of the Canadian population was living in towns and cities in 1911; in 1961 almost 70 per cent of the population was urban, with only 10 per cent of the labour force engaged in agricultural production. Much of this change has taken place quite recently. The rate of urbanisation since 1945 has been higher than that between the first and second world wars.[18] And the mechanisation of agriculture and the transfer from family farms to agri-business is still being completed in many parts of the country.

The demands that women are now making for birth control and abortion will eventually be met because they do not threaten the basic needs of the system. But we should see this as our first victory, not as proof that these demands are "reformist" and that we should not organise around them. And the general reluctance of the ruling class to grant these demands should also make us aware of their double-edged nature. On the one hand, the family itself could function better if birth control and abortion on demand were readily available to all classes. On the other hand, the existence of the family itself is threatened by the introduction of measures which will further legitimise and make possible sex outside the institution of marriage. As women have fewer children, to define themselves primarily as mothers will make less and less sense, and a whole Pandora's box is opened. Also, part of the rationale for the exclusion of women from so many jobs requiring training disappears when women are capable of determining when they wish to have children.

The trend to smaller families is both a reflection of the family's need for the wages of women, and a further cause of the increases in the numbers of working women. A study of the family in Chicago in 1927 showed that in those families studied, the average period when one or more children were under the age of 16 was 23 years, and the average period when one or more children was under 7 was 14 years. Smaller families make it more possible for women to remain out of the labour market while the children are small and return when they are in school.[19] This is precisely the pattern that is developing.

For young people themselves, the changes in the kind of labour power required also have an effect on the formation of families, how soon those who marry have children and whether the young wives work. Prolonged schooling has reduced the percentage of men 14 and over in the labour force from 82.9 per cent in 1953 to 77 per cent in 1968. In 1953, 51.7 per cent of males 14–19 were in the labour force, in 1968, only 39.1 per cent. Similarly, only 84.3 per cent of males 20–24 were in the labour force in 1968 as compared to 92.9 per cent in 1953.[20]

For those who quit school, the picture is often bleak. Men 14–19 experience unemployment rates double the average unemployment for all men, and men 20–24 are also much more likely to be unemployed than older workers. With unemployment now at the level of 6.5 per cent in Canada and still growing, unemployment for males 14–19 is probably now running close to 15 per cent. (The unemployment rates for women are considerably lower than those for men, but this has more to do with biased collection of statistics than with actual unemployment.) And even university graduates are finding jobs hard to get, and often when they do get jobs, particularly women, they are not doing the work they were trained to do. For those who are working, there is an increasing gap between the wages paid to young workers and older workers. Young workers, male and female, are more concentrated in two sectors. The first area is the one in which employment is declining, especially primary industry where their unskilled labour is being supplanted by increased automation, and in the construction industry, where pre-fab and new methods mean less labour is required. The second area of concentration is in low paid sectors like retail sales and clerical work.

Compare this situation with that after World War II which produced the baby boom. The baby boom was caused by a rise in the proportion of married women, not by women having larger numbers of children. It has been estimated that in Canada 90 per cent of the increase was due to increases in the numbers of married women, and about 10 per cent to higher fertility rates in individual women.[21]

One reason for the increases in the numbers of married women was that women were thrown out of the jobs that had fallen to them during the war in sectors that were usually reserved for men. Just as important were the "opportunities" for young male workers. Low birth rates during the depression meant that young workers were in short supply. The economy was in a period of boom and expansion of imperialism. Jobs were in good supply in heavy industry, and the average earnings for young workers were quite close to those of older workers. The demand for labour encouraged immigration on a large scale and brought many rural youths to the cities. Many young people were alone in the city, uprooted from their communities and families. In the absence of the kind of youth culture that now provides some alternatives to marriage, there were natural reasons why young people married and started their own families.

The 70s, in contrast, will see a period of rising unemployment, wage freezes, coercion of youth to stay in school and increasing distance between the wages of younger and older workers. In 1961 constant dollars,* the average wages of a male wage earner 35–44 rose $1481 between 1951 and 1961, while those of men 20–24 rose only $520 and those 14–19 rose only $20.[22] So not only the cultural

---

*Constant dollars purport to measure the real purchasing power of the dollar; in fact, inflation has made wage gains much less than statistics indicate.

but the economic situation makes the stable family of the 50s an unlikely model for the 70s. Young people who do marry find that they desperately need the wages of the wife—58 per cent of women 20–24 were working in 1968, a rise of 10 per cent from 1960. If there is a male in the family he is considered the head whether or not he supports the family. In those cases where the "family head" was under 25, women contributed about one quarter of the total income for those families in 1965. Given the low wages paid to women, this indicates a high number of young working wives.

The trend to early marriage has abated and fertility rates have hit an all-time low. More sexual freedom outside marriage, the availability of birth control and the economic situation will probably mean that the trend to low birth rates that has been going on since 1959 will continue. Birth-control pills clearly had an effect here. Births went down 2.7 per cent in 1964, 7.6 per cent in 1965 and 7.7 per cent in 1966, the years when pills first began to be widely available.[23]

Women as producers

It is clear that the way in which the family is evolving creates new contradictions that produce a higher level of consciousness of their oppression among women. But we cannot understand the contradictions within the family system unless we understand more clearly the other half of the coin, the situation of women in the labour force. For the same structural changes in capitalism which affect the family also affect women in their role as wage labourers, and the contradictions between these two roles are an important source of the new consciousness.

Therefore we need to be more precise about "super-exploitation" of women workers. Women's liberationists have argued correctly that women are overly exploited both in the sense that women who have jobs outside the home work not eight but sixteen hours a day for the capitalist, both to maintain and reproduce the working class and also to be members of the labour force. In addition, women are paid only about half the wages that a man would receive. But we have treated this moralistically, to prove that women are more oppressed than men, rather than to analyse the structure of women's employment. A vulgar marxist analysis of the "super-exploitation" of women is often put forward: because of the system of male supremacy the bosses are able to squeeze more profits out of their workers by employing women at low wages. And we are not clear about the implications of this analysis for strategy. Some women will argue that Women's Liberation should see its task as organising women into unions to demand higher wages and better working conditions. Others will argue that imperialism allows the ruling class to "buy off" the workers in the developed nations with higher wages, that the workers in the highly developed nations live "off the backs of the Third World" and that wage demands are only demands for a bigger slice of the imperialist pie and have no revolutionary potential.

Questions about the importance of wage demands cannot be argued in the abstract. On the one hand, any demand short of the overthrow of capitalism is a "reformist" demand, on the other hand, we know that the present trade union movement bargains only over the price at which workers will sell their labour power and not about the system of wage-slavery itself. Do we want to organise women into the present male-dominated, sell-out unions, and in Canada into American controlled unions? Yet we know that no organising in the workplace can neglect the real needs of the people, which means especially for women, the fact that meagre paychecks cannot provide the essentials of life. And the possibility of economic independence is a precondition for women conceiving of their own autonomy and independence.

But we must also understand the specifics of the importance of women in the labour force if we are to be clearer about the importance of unions and wage demands. In those sectors of industry at the highest stage of capitalist development (a very high degree of monopolisation and automation, huge investments in plant and equipment, etc.) the investment in variable capital (chiefly labour power) as opposed to constant capital (plants, machinery, raw materials, repayment of loans) is very small.[24] The need to control wages is not an absolute. For example, in Sarnia, Ontario, which has the highest average wages of any city in Canada, one of the largest corporations, Imperial Oil, which is non-unionised, pays very high wages and sets the standard for union contracts in other plants. Clearly, Imperial Oil sees its interest, not just in keeping wages down, but in keeping the unions out and therefore maintaining stability, avoiding strikes and so on. In addition, in the highly monopolised industries in the goods-producing sectors, higher wages are passed on to the consumer in the form of higher prices and do not affect profits. Even here, there are conditions when higher wages will be fought most bitterly—for example, at the present moment, the government is insistent on keeping wages down to check inflation (though it is doubtful whether wage freezes have the intended effect). But generally, in these industries, wage demands do not pose a very serious threat to the interests of the capitalist class.

In contrast, the type of industry where women are concentrated tends to be labour-intensive rather than capital-intensive, and wages form a relatively higher percentage of total costs. In manufacturing firms employing more than 20 people (which make up 91 per cent of all manufacturing firms) 24.2 per cent of the workers are women. But women constitute 75 per cent of all clothing workers, 65 per cent of workers in knitting mills, and 51 per cent in leather products.[25] (About 70 per cent of all women workers are in the textile, clothing and related industries, in food and beverages, or in electrical apparatus and supplies.) Average weekly wages and salaries for clothing and related industries were, for September 1969, $78 in clothing and knitting mills, and $81 in leather products, as compared to $139 in chemicals, and $133 in non-metallic metal products, where women were 22 per cent and 11 per cent of the total workers respectively. (These figures are calculated before deductions, include overtime, bonuses, and the salaries of managerial personnel and are therefore much higher than real wages in these sectors.) These are also the industries with the lowest rate of automation. One measure of the degree of automation is to compare figures for the "total value added per worker" from raw material to finished product, since a worker who uses mainly his own labour will be much less "productive" than one who works at a job which utilises a lot of machinery.

Clothing, textile and related industries realise only about half the overall average in total value added per worker and less than a third of that of the highest—the coal, petroleum and chemical industries.[26] The low wages of women in these sectors (and thus the lower wages of male workers as well) are not simply a matter of the capitalist making higher profits from employing women at low wages. Equal wages in this sector would not just mean less profit for the capitalist, but a transformation of the industry. (In textiles, it might force automation, or it might mean that the industry would not survive in competition with textile industry in the Third World.)

Moreover, within industries employing many women where average wages are high (like electrical products, where women are 31 per cent of all workers, and average wages and salaries are $132 a week), women generally work at labour-intensive jobs like assembling and packaging where low wages are important in keeping costs down and profits up.

Most women are not employed in manufacturing, but in the service or non-goods-producing sector. The employment of large numbers of women in the industrialised service sector is part of a general tendency for employment to grow fastest in this sector. In Canada, as early as 1961, the percentage of trade and service workers in the labour force (40.6 per cent) equalled that in direct production of goods (manufacturing 23.4 per cent, construction 7.3 per cent and agriculture 10.1 per cent). The Economic Council of Canada states:

> Average employment for Canada's goods-producing industries—that is—combined employment in manufacturing, construction, utilities, forestry, fishing and mining—was actually no higher in 1968 than it was in 1966. All of the growth in employment took place in the service industries. Thus, there was a significant further shift in the employment structure towards increasingly service-oriented economic activities. *In particular, two thirds of the net increase in jobs in 1967 was in the non-commercial service sector of the economy*, (mainly education, health and public administration). We expect that employment will continue to rise more rapidly in services than in other sectors of the economy. [27]

These figures are all the more amazing given the very high growth rate of the Canadian labour force, which is growing faster than that of any western nation, by about 250,000 a year (total labour force just under 8 million). Of projected growth to 1980, over 40 per cent of the net increase is expected to be women, and in fact the female labour force has been growing faster than projected. [28] It seems that even given this high growth in the number of women workers, more women are looking for work than can find jobs. The growth would be even higher if more jobs were available.

The growth in employment in the services and the lack of this growth in the goods-producing sector does not mean, as we have said before, that productivity is not increasing in the goods-producing sector. On the contrary, because constant investment in new machinery raises the productivity of each worker, growth in employment is slow. Automation is taking place in some service industries, like banks and insurance companies, but generally, automation cannot produce the same increases in productivity as in the goods-producing sector, and many jobs simply cannot be automated.

Not only is the service sector growing, but the jobs within it are becoming more industrialised and thus more amenable to organisation. Growth in this sector means both the creation of (a) more "professional and technical" or "new working-class" jobs, which are reasonably well-paid, and potentially creative; which require a considerable degree of training and education (such as teachers, technicians, nurses, engineers); and some of which are proletarian in character, and (b) a whole sector of jobs which are badly paid, in which the work is uncreative and unrewarding (although sometimes potentially creative) and where working conditions are very bad—store clerks, hospital workers, waitresses, clerks in government bureaucracies, etc; and which require little training.

A growing number of these jobs are in the state service sector. The growth of the state sector is one way in which the capitalist class acts to control the market for goods and thus guarantee its investment—a necessity when investment in plant and equipment is so large. State spending on military, space and other such programmes helps provide such a guaranteed market. In addition, the corporations increasingly expect the state to subsidise both the building of the infrastructure needed for industrial expansion (roads, railways, hydro-power, etc.) and the indirect costs of production (education, social welfare, research and development, social management). Often the state is expected to provide the initial investment for the development of new industry. Thus more and more jobs depend on government employment, either directly, or indirectly, through government contracts to industry. The demands on the state are creating a crisis of major proportions in state finance, both in Canada and the US.

. . . Once this tendency toward the socialisation of indirect costs of production gets underway, it is obvious that the corporations will not accept large increases in taxation to finance it. If they were to pay the taxes needed to cover all these costs, there would in fact be no "socialisation". They would continue to pay for them privately but instead of doing so directly, they would do so indirectly through their taxes (and pay for the administration of these payments too). Instead of lessening the burden such a solution would in fact increase it. So there is an inevitable institutionalised resistance of the corporations and the capitalist class to increasing taxes up to the point where they would make possible a functional public service capable of satisfying the needs of the entire population. For this reason, it is probable that the gap between the wages of public employees and that of private workers in the United States (and Canada) will remain, and that the trend toward radicalisation of public employees—both increase unionisation and even possible political radicalisation—will continue.[29]

The expansion of state employment also heightens the tendency to permanent inflation (large numbers of workers who are not producing goods for consumption by other wage-earners means that there is more purchasing power than goods available). The state is forced to freeze wages and cut back on employment in periods when inflation "gets out of hand". (The first thing that happened in the Canadian government's anti-inflation campaign was the lay-off of civil servants.)

Large numbers of women work as public employees. When we say that women are used as a reserve army of labour (as, for example, black people in the U.S. are used as a reserve army of labour) we are not talking about a group of workers that are peripheral to the economy, but a group which is central to the maintenance of labour-intensive manufacturing, and service and state sectors where low wages are a priority. Even in the professional and technical sphere, where wages are highest for women, the average wages are over $1,000 a year less than those of male production workers and only in the service sector, a field where many women are employed, do men make less than the average for women in the highest field.

The unionisation of women workers, which is already beginning to take place in previously unionised sectors, will clearly be a blow to the stability of the capitalist system. The vast majority of women workers have jobs which are, by any sensible definition, "working-class". Only about 15 per cent of all women workers are professionals, and about 85 per cent of these are found in those professions already beginning to unionise—nurses and teachers. Very few women have managerial jobs, and the vast majority are wage-earners.[30]

Sisters, let's get it together

Clearly women workers are in a strategic position: the emphasis on exclusion of women from jobs rather than the development of a strategy to organise working women has held back the women's movement. But we should not conclude that we can "bring down the system" by making wage demands and working for the unionisation of women workers. Our revolutionary potential lies in the fact that most working women are both oppressed as women and exploited as workers; our strategy must reflect this duality. The demands of women strike both at an institution which is central to the system—the family, and at sectors of the economy which are ill-provided to meet even traditional demands of the labour movement. Because organisers in the past have refused to organise women as women, women have been viewed as "unorganisable" because they have little time, work in sectors that are hard to organise, and they move in and out of the labour force. For example, all the structural reasons that make the textile industry the most exploitative, also make it harder to organise there—the workers can easily be replaced, the low investment in plant and equipment mean that management can hold out longer against strikes, the plants are small, and so on. Similarly, many women in the service sector are hard to organise in the traditional way because they work in such small establishments—waitresses, store clerks, etc. A strategy of workplace organising alone cannot overcome these problems, but as we develop an analysis of the oppression of women, we can turn these same factors into a basis for organising and an integral part of our strategy.

I have argued that the importance of the family as an economic unit, the importance of the cheap labour supply that women provide means that the system must act to retain the family system. The breakdown of the family, besides meaning that women will demand jobs that don't exist, will make the struggle for equal access to jobs, equal pay, day care, maternity leave, job security, etc., the object of even more militant struggles. At the present time, one family in ten has a woman as its sole supporter. Neither the state nor the sectors where women work will easily be able to meet the needs of women who must support themselves and often their children.

Yet most people, especially the working class, will continue to hold onto the family as the only place where basic emotional needs for love, support and companionship can be met at all, and because there are no alternatives, as things stand, most women can't, and don't want to go it alone. If our cry is "destroy the family", the women's movement will be contained within a small sector of professional and younger women without families. The masses of women will not relate to women's liberation because it is not relating to their needs. What we must do instead, is to begin to organise around demands which provide the precondition for autonomy for women—economic independence. This struggle will, in fact, heighten the contradictions within the family system.

At the same time, we must not fall prey to the chauvinism and arrogance that assumes that working-class women are capable of being organised around only economic issues, and that they have no consciousness of their oppression as women and no yearnings for freedom and independence. Issues like birth control both meet direct needs that women have and allow us to talk about repressive sexuality and its functions in capitalist society. Day care strikes at the privatisation of the individual within the family and provides an exemplary form of communal care of children and other communal forms, while meeting a direct need that women have. Material demands raise the possibility of economic independence. The clear male domination of the present unions makes it that much easier to talk about rank-and-file caucuses (women's caucuses) or new unions to replace those controlled by male, sell-out leadership. Laws against abortion, and the oppressive treatment of women in hospitals, and the high cost of medical care even under medicare allow us to talk about socialised medicine, and to raise demands for community controlled clinics. Many women work not only for money but to escape the isolation of their homes, and because they want to have an identity based upon what *they* do. Thus the lack of creative work is a real and bitter disappointment when they do take a job. In workplace organising we can respond to this consciousness by talking about the potential of creative work in a society not directed to profit-making and by raising demands for workers' control.

The issues which we have talked about for a long time must now be raised as public demands by the women's movement, and we must think strategically about how they should be posed. For example, many women's liberation groups have organised day-care centres, which have helped us to develop theory and practice in anti-authoritarian child raising, and are therefore important, but have served the needs of only a few women. We must begin a public campaign about day care, but we must think through, in a concrete way, how our demands can best serve women and how they can be posed to raise consciousness. Do we want, for example, to demand care for children at the mother's work place? This would make the point that child care should be a responsibility of the society, and not of individual parents (provided it were free), and these demands would also raise new demands about control over work and the work process. On the other hand, day care in the work place would reinforce the idea that it is the mother, not both parents, who share responsibility to care for children, and it would mean that mothers would have to take their children with them to work, without even a few moments to themselves.[31]

These questions are academic until the women's movement begins to take seriously the fact that it is a product of objective conditions that are moving all women to greater consciousness of their oppression, and begins seriously to organise among the masses of women. The point to be made is not that we should have all the answers before we begin, but that only if we analyse women's situations a whole, if we formulate strategy based on the real needs of women and the real contradictions that exist, can we hope to build a revolutionary movement of women. Do it!

NOTES

1. For example, see Limpus, *Sexual Repression and the Family* (reprinted by NEFP), R. D. Laing, *The Politics of the Family*, and *The Self and Others*, and Wilhelm Reich, *The Function of the Orgasm, The Sexual Revolution* etc. (most of Reich's best work has been suppressed and never been translated into English) and the use of Talcott Parson's work on the family. Several papers on the psychological aspects of the family are in preparation by women in Toronto.

2. I wonder how long we will have to read articles by "revolutionaries" who assume that all readers and all movement people are white, male and middle-class. Cf. articles in a recent *Ramparts* by Jerry Rubin on the Conspiracy and the article on Chuck Berry: I have never had a crew-cut nor do I "ball chicks".

3. Marlene Dixon, "Why Women's Liberation?", *Ramparts*, December 1969.

4. "A Woman is a Sometimes Thing", by Evie Goldfield, Sue Munaker and Naomi Weisstein, reprinted in *The New Left*, Pricilla Long, ed.

5. Ellen Willis, *Consumerism*.

6. Margaret Benston, "The Political Economy of Women", *Monthly Review*, September 1969.

7. Mickey and John Rowntree, "More on the Political Economy of

Women", *Monthly Review*, January 1970.

8. All statistics on labour force participation etc. are from the Dominion Bureau of Statistics.

9. Juliet Mitchell, "The Longest Revolution", *New Left Review*, no. 40, November and December 1966, also available as a REP reprint.

10. Marx, *Capital*, Part LV, Ch. 15, Section 3, Machinery and Modern Industry.

11. See E. P. Thompson, *The Making of the English Working Class*, for a great deal of useful material on the family in the industrial revolution in Britain.

12. Marx and Engels, *The Communist Manifesto*.

13. Marx, "The Buying and Selling of Labour Power", *Capital*, Vol. 1, Ch. 6.

14. Jenny Podoluk, *Incomes of Canadians*, DBS 1968.

15. Heather Jon Maroney and Peggy Morton, *Women's Liberation, An Introductory Paper*.

16. See the work of R. D. Laing.

17. Heather Jon Maroney and Peggy Morton, op. cit.

18. Jenny Podoluk, op. cit.

19. *Annals of the American Political Science Association*, 1927 (a useful anthology of articles on women).

20. Dominion of Bureau of Statistics.

21. Jenny Podoluk, op. cit.

22. Wolfgang Illing, *Population, Family, Household and Labour Force Growth to 1980*, Economic Council of Canada, September 1967.

23. Illing, op. cit.

24. Dick Howard, "French New Working-Class Theories", in *Radical America*, April 1969, (available from Hogtown Press in Canada).

25. *Employment and Average Weekly Wages and Salaries*, DBS, September 1969.

26. *Survey of Manufacturers*, Canada (annual survey).

27. Economic Council of Canada, *Sixth Annual Report*, 1968.

28. Illing, op. cit.

29. Ernest Mandel, "Where is America Going?", in *New Left Review*, No. 54, March and April 1969; also reprinted in *Leviathan*.

30. See Helge Sanders, "Red Kindergartens", in *Radical America*, February 1970.

31. Dick Howard, op. cit.

10

from *The Dialectic of Sex*

SHULAMITH FIRESTONE

The Ultimate Revolution
(Structural imperatives)

. . . We have seen how women, biologically distinguished from men, are culturally distinguished from "human". Nature produced the fundamental inequality—half the human race must bear and rear the children of all of them—which was later consolidated, institutionalised, in the interests of men. Reproduction of the species cost women dearly, not only emotionally, psychologically, culturally but even in strictly material (physical) terms: before recent methods of contraception, continuous childbirth led to constant "female trouble", early ageing, and death. Women were the slave class that maintained the species in order to free the other half for the business of the world—admittedly often its drudge aspects, but certainly all its creative aspects as well.

This natural division of labour was continued only at great cultural sacrifice: men and women developed only half of themselves, at the expense of the other half. . . .

I submit then, that the first demand for any alternative system must be:

(1) *The freeing of women from the tyranny of their reproductive biology by every means available, and the diffusion of the childbearing and childrearing role to the society as a whole, men as well as women.* . . .

Our second demand will come also as a basic contradiction to the family, this time the family as an *economic* unit:

(2) *The full self-determination, including economic independence, of both women and children.* To achieve this goal would require fundamental changes in our social and economic structure. This is why we must talk about a feminist socialism: in the immediate future, under capitalism, there could be at best a token integration of women into the labour force. For women have been found exceedingly useful and cheap as a transient, often

highly skilled labour supply,[1] not to mention the economic value of their traditional function, the reproduction and rearing of the next generation of children, a job for which they are now patronised (literally and thus figuratively) rather than paid. But whether or not officially recognised, these are essential economic functions. Women, in this present capacity, are the very foundation of the economic superstructure, vital to its existence.[2] The paeans to self-sacrificing motherhood have a basis in reality: Mom *is* vital to the American way of life, considerably more than apple pie. She is an institution without which the system really *would* fall apart. In official capitalist terms, the bill for her economic services[3] might run as high as one-fifth of the gross national product. But payment is not the answer. To pay her, as is often discussed seriously in Sweden, is a reform that does not challenge the basic division of labour and thus could never eradicate the disastrous psychological and cultural consequences of that division of labour. . . .

NOTES

1. Most bosses would fail badly had they to take over their secretaries' job, or do without them. I know several secretaries who sign without a thought their bosses' names to their own (often brilliant) solutions. The skills of college women especially would cost a fortune reckoned in material terms of male labour.

2. Margaret Benston ("The Political Economy of Women's Liberation"), in attempting to show that women's oppression is indeed economic—though previous economic analysis has been incorrect—distinguishes between the male superstructure economy based on *commodity* production (capitalist ownership of the means of production, and wage labour), and the pre-industrial reduplicative economy of the family, production for immediate *use*. Because the latter is not part of the *official* contemporary economy, its function at the basis of that economy is often overlooked. Talk of drafting women into the superstructure commodity economy fails to deal with the tremendous amount of necessary production of the traditional kind now performed by women without pay: Who will do it?

3. The Chase Manhattan Bank estimates a woman's over-all domestic work week at 99.6 hours. Margaret Benston gives her minimal estimate for a *childless* married woman at 16 hours, close to half of a regular work week; a *mother* must spend at least six or seven days a week working close to 12 hours.

11

The Carrot, the Stick and the Movement

SHEILA ROWBOTHAM

This is not a detailed review of all the points in Selma James's pamphlet "Women, the Unions and Work". Instead I want to take up some of the more general questions she raises.

Selma is preoccupied with several forms of co-option: unions are presented as continually nobbling workers, and capitalists co-opt both workers and Women's Liberation, while left groups lie in wait for women's liberators.

I'm not going to deal with the last kind of nobbling as I think it's better discussed out loud with very specific examples. Vague accusations only create an atmosphere of political paranoia and a reds-under-the-bed mentality which I am sure is very far from what Selma intends and only benefits the ruling class.

As for the co-option of unions, the working class and possibly of Women's Liberation too, it would be absurd to deny that these have not gone on and are not going on, or might not go on. The point is, how can we most effectively stop this process?

Selma keeps coming up with a series of scapegoats to explain failures and partial successes. This is all very well if we want to work off some rhetorical rage. But it doesn't help us to see how capitalism works and understand how to change it. The scapegoats serve as decoys. As long as we chase them we miss the social reality which brought them into being.

She says the unions fragment the working class, "into those who have wages and those who don't". In fact such a division was created by capitalism. The factory system finally removed production from the home and brought the working class under the wage system. The growth of modern unions has come from this concentration of the labour force in the factory.

The work discipline of the factory which kept the machines running regularly was, and still is, bitterly resented by workers. It takes hours, days, years out of their lives. The employer takes a large part of what workers produce in the form of profits.

In resistance to the exploitation of their labour in this way workers have combined to raise the sum they can get out of the surplus they produce. Capitalism has thus made it possible for workers to create organisations to defend themselves on a scale that was impossible before.

Now although this kind of organising is limited to the wage bargain, it still constitutes a threat to the absolute control the employing class has over what the workers produce and the time they spend at work. It also makes possible the class pride and confidence workers gain through solidarity in strike action. The union organisation is necessary in order to prevent isolation of particular groups of workers.

Ever since the unions have been made legal the employers have tried alternately to use the carrot and the stick. The carrot has been the co-option Selma notes. The stick has been the use of the state and the laws in the interests of private capital. The only effective weapon against this has been the continual creation of rank-and-file pressure and organisation. The shop steward movement is the obvious example; the movement for workers' control, another.

But this does not make the union structure unnecessary. If we only say women should organise where they work, how do women on strike get support from other workers? How do they get strike pay?

If we are really serious about challenging male domination in the unions, we should start by organising Women's Liberation groups at work and in union branches. Not as *alternatives* to unions but as a way of making industrial organisation both more effective against capitalism and more democratic, to go beyond the economic basis of the wage bargain. Women's liberation groups are places where women can develop trust for each other as women. But working-class women need class solidarity with men too.

Both feminism and the Women's Liberation movement have come, like the unions, out of particular historical situations in capitalist society. The early feminist movement's origin was the economic, social and political helplessness of middle-class women who were excluded from production.

The main theme of this kind of feminism was for equal rights of jobs, before the law and for the vote. But Selma does them a disservice by saying they invited women to vote and be free. Many socialist feminists in the early twentieth century saw the vote as a necessary reform but by no means the answer to the oppression of women.

It is very important that we try to understand what kind of

changes in capitalism have produced our own movement. Selma picks out one important factor, the potential use of educated female labour in middle management at lower rates of pay than men. She sees this as a way in which the women's movement could be co-opted. But the way she presents this very real danger is confusing in the same way as is her analysis of the role of the unions in capitalism.

It was not the women's movement which produced the girls coming out of university as she implies. Higher education for women is a result of the need for a more educated labour force and of feminist agitation. It is of course still restricted mainly to middle-class girls and is also not equal to men. None the less, the concentration of girls in universitites which resulted from post-war expansion, meant that middle-class girls were shuffled into one of the most developed points of capitalism only to confront more clearly the underprivilege of their sexual future.

We came up with a terrible bump against the block between educational promise and practical reality.

We were not the only ones to be affected by changes in modern capitalism. The growth of welfare and the direct intervention of the state in the reproduction of the labour force have not only come about as a result of working-class pressure. They also serve the long-term needs of capitalism for a relatively healthy and intelligent, if subservient, labour force.

Fortunately this combination has proved dodgy again for capitalism and has created new ways of bargaining with the state, like the Claimants' Union.

It has also made the nature of our upbringing in the family, our education, our sexual relations, our feelings towards our parents and children, and the work women do in the family in reproducing the labour force, into vital political questions. It is very important that we organise against capitalism at all the points where it reproduces itself.

However this does not mean that we throw the baby out with the bath water (to use a bad image). We should not dismiss effective organisation at the point of production.

Selma's analysis disregards the significance of what has been an interrupted but long-term trend in this century, the absorption of married women into the labour force. Capitalism has landed itself in the awkward position of depending on women's work in two places at once, at home and in industry.

It has tried of course to have it both ways, and force women to do two jobs. This process pre-dated the emergence of women's liberation. It was not a result of it, as the Italian article Selma quotes implies:

"Capital itself is seizing upon the same impetus which created a movement—the rejection by millions of women of women's traditional place—to recompose the workforce with increasing numbers of women."

In fact, this recomposition was well under way in the USA and in parts of Europe in the 1950s when the propaganda about women being in the home was strongest and when Women's Liberation was being thought about only by tiny groups of women, among them, Selma in America and Simone de Beauvoir in France.

I am not saying that movements are the automatic response to crude economic facts or that consciousness does not change society, but that in reacting against this distortion in marxism, Selma lands us in another one.

Because she does not see movements and ideas as coming out of social reality as well as transforming it, she misses the contradictory forces which bring us to conscious resistance. This has a serious strategic consequence, because it means she emphasises organisation at home, around the reproduction of the labour force, at the expense of organisation at the point of production.

Simply because some boneheaded marxist men have been dozy enough to stress only economic organising doesn't mean that we have to rush off in the opposite direction.

The importance of Women's Liberation is precisely that it makes it possible to cut through the separation between home and work, production and consumption, wage earner and dependant, man and woman, which has always helped to make capitalism stable. That is why working-class women are such an important group— their class and sex situation makes the connection *necessary*.

It's no good making a demand like paying people to do housework. This does not socialise housework. It merely confirms the isolation of the houseworker, in her, or less likely in his, nuclear home. It does not connect those who are responsible for the reproduction of the work force to wage workers in commodity production.

Implicit in Selma's pamphlet is an analogy between women and the underdeveloped economies. The Italian article she quotes touches on this, and on the danger of struggling against women's specific oppression only to reach "another degree of capitalistic control and regimentation". This is a very real danger and I think it's a pity she hasn't tried really to disentangle what this under-development of ours involves and how this relates to the dominant form of production in capitalism and to the dominance of men in our culture.

This confusion means she falls into the opposite trap. Instead of simply getting capitalism to rationalise itself, she tends to idealise the symptoms of our weakness in capitalism. Absenteeism may be a gesture of revolt, but I don't see how we can stop the Tories cheating us out of equal pay if we never turn up for work.

We must be careful in asserting an alternative to male domination that we stress our possible strengths, not our existing vulnerability.

Many of Selma's demands are based on the desire most of us feel to find a short cut out of capitalism. Of course we are opposed to price rises, but it is a problem when we try to take long-term effective action against them. Of course we would like to work less. But this demand would get many employers laughing up their sleeves at the moment.

This is why the men and women who are demanding the right to work have a more realistic idea of making a demand which can be organised round in a decaying capitalist economy. To say we want to work less confuses the present situation with a future socialist society and misses out the struggle in between.

There is no short cut out of capitalism, no amount of wishing and willing and demanding in the air will make the grotesque old monster pack his bags and go quietly off to some remote desert island for a quiet retirement.

The disentangling of the non- or sub-capitalist elements in our predicament is one of the most crucial theoretical and practical tasks ahead of us. The danger of exposing women more completely to capitalism mentioned in the Italian article quoted by Selma is very real.

Capital itself has whittled away at patriarchal authority, which is based on the ownership of women's persons by men and rooted in the family as an economic unit of production.

Patriarchy, however, has survived though in a distorted form into capitalism. Like other "backward", i.e. non-capitalist, forms of ownership and production, it owes its survival to the manner in which it serves capital. Capitalism is thus continually eating away at the sub-capitalist remnants which feed it.

It is not clear whether capitalism could continue without patriarchy and the special oppression of women. It is certainly very difficult to imagine capitalism without male domination. But it would be rash of us to imagine that the struggle against male domination *alone* is sufficient to end capitalism. Our success will depend on the strength of other movements against imperialism, racism and class exploitation, and on our ability to unite with them.

Our task is to make a strategy which will guard our autonomy but to make alliances with other movements of the oppressed, which will devise means of continuously breaking down the divisions capitalism has forced between us, and which neither idealises underdevelopment nor exposes us to more systematic exploitation. The difficulties are tremendous. But it is our only chance of victory.

12

When is a Wage not a Wage?

CAROLINE FREEMAN

In the women's movement we find a deep ambivalence towards housework, that labour we all know so well, and from the inside, as demanding and tedious in ways peculiarly its own. As women we cannot be indifferent to it. We are supposed to dedicate ourselves to its claims, and thus it threatens us whether we accept it or reject it.

We want housework recognised as hard work. We want social recognition of the time and sweat it involves to take forms more tangible than sentimental clichés about the woman's place behind every successful man and ensuring the present and future well-being of his children. But together with this resentment against those who spurn us for clearing up after them, we find that in the women's movement we too reject housework. We see it as unacceptable, as wasteful and limiting in itself, not just because the situation of dependence in which it is usually done destroys or taints all its possible satisfactions. "Wages for Housework" sounds such an exciting slogan because at first sight it seems to offer a solution, but I shall argue that while it reproduces our contradictory reactions to housework it cannot overcome them, because it does not allow us to understand the real contradictions in housework itself.

Wages for housework has usually been counterposed to the demand for "socialisation". In fact its supporters, or some of them, have in common with those who want to go straight for "socialisation" that they want to make housework *like other work* (under capitalism). It must no longer be an expression of the adequacy or inadequacy of our *personal* relations, but a job done for remuneration which represents the *public*, social recognition of the social necessity of this work. The idea is that if housework were waged it would no longer be seen as the destiny of women in particular. It would become a job which, like other jobs, people could choose because it appealed to them, or, more often, because it seemed the lesser evil. Only when this had been achieved could housework be distanced from the concept of womanhood, and hed its element of emotional servicing . . . so runs the argument.

But the two crucial terms here, "wages" and "housework", have implications we have not yet begun to explore. Our first task is to ask what these terms mean.

Mariarosa Dalla Costa, Selma James and others have argued that housework is socially productive work. The woman as mother produces the labour force of the future, and as housewife maintains the labour power of her husband. Since this unpaid work is essential to capitalism and thus to the system of relations within which surplus value is produced, they argue that it produces surplus value in its own right and is thus productive in the marxist sense. Thus the housewife is a worker like another except that she is unpaid. The main element present in the situation of the wage worker and absent in that of the housewife is the wage, so wages are seen as the key to the transformation of housework. If housework were waged the housewife would no longer be excluded from the sphere of social production, and the other characteristic features of housework—its isolation, its technological backwardness—could be overcome by houseworkers if they had the power and independence a wage of their own would give them.

The first defect of this argument is its misrepresentation of the marxist concept of "productive". The designation of housework as "unproductive" is taken as a slur, instead of as a technical concept allowing us to describe the relation between housework and capital. The productive/unproductive distinction does have implications for the sorts of struggle appropriate for different sorts of workers, but it does not *evaluate* their work. Bearing children and bringing them up does, indeed, produce labour power, but not surplus value—which is crucial if the term "productive" is to be correctly applied in the specific sense it bears in marxism. Child care does not become productive in this sense by virtue of the child's possible future production of surplus value. Similarly, keeping a working husband going makes it possible for him to produce surplus value, but does not itself directly produce it. Certainly the woman's unpaid work means that the *man* can produce more surplus value, for it is his labour power which creates *value* in the marxist sense.

This whole argument, important as it is, has become something of a diversion. The productive/unproductive distinction in marxism is not used to drive a wedge between those who work inside the home and those who work outside it, since many of the latter, many of the very husbands we are talking about, are themselves unproductive workers. The difference between housewives and waged unproductive workers is that the housewife does not offer her labour power for sale on the market. Housework could not be transformed into productive work by the simple addition of the wage into the privatised setting in which housework is done.

When Selma James calls the home a factory she is indulging in a sleight of hand which has the effect of confusing the issue. If the house *were* a factory the lines of struggle would be relatively clear. We are concerned precisely with the differences between the house and the factory, differences which mean that women are isolated from each other and from wage workers, and are deprived of any direct leverage and bargaining power in the sphere of production. The setting in which housework is done is not the house as a physical structure, it is the home-as-family, and women are separated from each other not just by bricks and mortar, but by the sacrosanct privacy of family life.

The work which women do in the home and family has important similarity to the work of some unproductive workers who *do* receive wages, such as university lecturers, clergymen, social workers and policemen. All of these groups work to contribute to the reproduction of the relations of production, to the system of ownership and of power which governs our lives, and its maintenance both by force and through its acceptance by those who live under it. The work women do in maintaining and reproducing labour power is crucial to this, and thus to advanced capitalism. It is unproductive work by its very nature, but none the less essential. The state trusts us to do a good job in producing a future workforce which will not only be physically capable of contributing, directly or indirectly, to the production of profit, but which will also find its own compensations or satisfactions in doing so; and, ironically, it can trust us to do this dirty work unsupervised, in the privacy of our own homes.

Housework would be unproductive whether it were waged or not. (The provision of domestic services as commodities we are not calling housework.) Certain of its most oppressive features would remain unchanged. While we still labour in the home and in the family, we shall never get a working day with defined limits—we shall never become the sort of worker who can at least try to put her work aside as she leaves the factory gates, however awful it is while she does it. Wages for housework could not undo the identification between housework and being available twenty-four hours a day by virtue of being a woman. If we had wages for housework we should be more like those workers outside the home who are expected to sell their commitment as an integral part of their labour power, so that work is constantly with them, at meals, at leisure, in bed. But these considerations do not rule out the possibility of a wage for housework, and it could be argued that they simply emphasise the need for tangible compensation. To find out if a wage for housework is what we want we must go on to ask what a wage is.

We often hear "money for women" used interchangeably with "wages for housework". Yet they're not the same thing. Wages are paid for the sale of labour power, which is then consumed in the service of the buyer, and *under his control*. The control need not be continuous, as it is when people work under the eye of a supervisor. It can be in the form of retrospective quality control or periodic inspections. If we ask the state to pay wages for housework, we are saying: it is in the interests of capitalist society that we are maintaining and reproducing the workforce. Take your responsibility and pay us *for the work we are doing*. To ask for payment where the option remains of struggling to better the conditions of work and to control its nature might be progressive, but the demand of wages for housework would leave the family set up intact as the private arena in which the work is done. It would not overcome the isolation of individual workers, and they would be left to face the repercussions of increased state control in their original isolated condition. In this case a wage would not free us from these most oppressive features of housework, would not attack the notion that there is something inherently feminine about it, and would invite capital to control the family in formal and direct ways without undermining its ideological role in maintaining capitalist relations of production.

This argument was vehemently rejected at the workshop on "wages for housework" at the Bristol conference [1973]. Women said indignantly that the whole point had been missed, that once women were paid they could do much *less* housework, if any. Very well, but in that case the demand is not for *wages* for housework. You cannot on the one hand argue that women do productive work in the home and should be paid for this, and on the other hand that once they are paid they will be so independent that no one will be able to force them to do it. The women who argue like this are assuming that after wages for housework it will still be husband and children who complain if the work is not done, and that the wage will give them the strength to stand up against their families. Not at all. Once we make the state our employer, the state will do the policing. A wage is a lever which keeps the worker at home. If we want wages for housework, we must accept that it would be tied to *doing* housework.

One of the great potentialities of the slogan seems to be its capacity to unite women. Before we could mobilise on this basis we should have to spell it out. It is no good saying, as Selma James did at the Bristol conference, that it doesn't matter what you call it; a wage, a grant, a subsidy, an income . . . words do matter, as she knows very well, and in the case of Wages for Housework they are being used to cover up the weakness of the position. Let us look at a few of the difficulties.

An argument for Wages for Housework is that it would make housework into ''visible'' recognised work. Must the wage then recognise, by quantitative differences, the vast difference children make? To pay everyone the same however many children they had, *or* to pay them according to the number of children, would be divisive. Should single women be paid for doing their own housework? One of the papers distributed by the ''Power of Women Collective'' was by a single woman who explained that if there were wages for housework she wouldn't have to go out to work. ''I could give up that shitty job and just begin to enjoy my time a bit. Women who do paid work outside the home could give that up.'' If women who work outside the home did as ''Helen'' wants, they would jettison along with their jobs the struggle for equal pay and conditions, and would strengthen the concept of ''women's work''. But the difficulties of applying the slogan to single women run deeper. If they are excluded, wages for housework must bolster up the family, since if the wage were made conditional on the performance of the work, anyone who wanted to leave their family would risk being financially penalised. But if single women are included, so must single men be, for all the same arguments apply to them.

We are caught in a cleft stick, since if we demand wages for housework for everyone, however much or how little they do, this becomes a different demand, which cannot serve the function of getting social recognition for housework—it becomes the demand for a minimum income for all. This demand is being put forward, of course, by people who are quite aware of its incompatibility with "Wages for Housework". It is not a demand for a wage, since it is not tied to work. It is a demand for a grant or income, and it would be ridiculous to pretend that such an income is a wage for the reproduction of labour power if it results in those who receive it no longer offering their labour power for sale. As it stands, this demand for a minimum income for all equal to an average wage cannot be taken up by socialists. Opting out of production is no basis for mass revolutionary struggle to change the relations of production and overthrow the capitalist state.

If we reject the slogan "Wages for Housework", what do we put in its place? There is no one answer.

We all know how underdeveloped, how limited are the sketchy embryonic forms or suggestions of socialisation of housework which we find under capitalism. Firstly there is the capitalisation of housework, which is not socialisation at all but is one step nearer it. This means the provision of various services by private enterprise: restaurants, laundrettes, nurseries etc., which at present few can afford to use often. Secondly there is the case where employers take over some of the work involved in maintaining and reproducing labour power, by providing showers, canteens, work clothes and so on. Crèches are rather different since they are usually a straightforward device for attracting a cheap workforce, but the other facilities (which have often still to be paid for) have been wrung from capital by the power of organised labour. Nevertheless their effect is often to tie the worker to his employer more effectively than could the wage on its own, as we see in the case of miners and their supposedly enviable colliery houses. A third form, and the nearest thing to socialisation of housework which we find under capitalism, is the assumption of responsibility by the state for the reproduction of the labour force and maintenance of workers, which exists only piecemeal in the remnants of the "welfare state" and the educational system. Most welfare benefits do not radically affect the status of housework within the family or the role of the women—in this category come family allowances, maternity benefits and so on, which are grants rather than steps in the direction of a wage. Certainly we should fight tooth and nail to keep and to increase these welfare pittances, but without any misconceptions about them.

In deciding how we should relate to these socialising tendencies I think we must distinguish between child care and the rest of housework, without forgetting that the latter is greatly increased where there are children. We want the state to provide public and free facilities for the care of children. This is of course double-edged. In capitalist society individuals' autonomy is largely restricted to the sphere of the family and to private lives in general, so socialisation of work done in this area seems to encroach on the few freedoms we have. Socialisation of education has not been "for the people"—is it right, then, to ask the state to assume responsibility for our children at an even younger age? However, the freedom we enjoy in the family is largely mythical, and even in its present form socialisation of education has been progressive. Such demands have to be part of a wider struggle for the control of the content of education and the administration of nursery care, which must in turn be part of the general struggle against capitalist ideology and the specific mechanisms for reproducing the relations of production.

As far as the rest of housework goes, we want to do as little of it as possible, and we want there to be as little of it as possible for anyone to do. We must aim to drive a wedge between the physical tasks of housework and the emotional servicing wives and mothers are expected to do *as women*. Even private enterprise can help us to do this. Once these services are taken out of the home they are done in a technologically more efficient way, and they offer much less scope for our supposed "fulfilment as women". It is true that it is still mainly women who do them. But once the mystique is taken from housework, once it is no longer the exclusive prerogative of wives, we shall have new strength in the old struggle against considering its equivalents outside the home as tasks particularly suited to women.

An actual catalogue of demands can only be abstract when it is presented without any analysis of the current situation, and it is just such an analysis (and the theoretical tools we need for it) that we must work towards. But it is still possible to indicate some of the implications of various sorts of demands.

If we demand wages for all men and all women workers that allow them to use restaurants etc. whenever they need to, this does not rule out campaigning for increased state responsibility for what is now housework, that is for *free* laundrettes and laundries, restaurants and so on. Whoever controls these services, whether it be private enterprise or the state, the individual family would still be the consumer, and it is the ideological work of the individual family that we are trying to undermine. Perhaps we don't sufficiently realise that the demands for equal pay and equal opportunity, which are often criticised, are part of the ideological struggle. The fight for equal pay is part of the fight to get the price of women's labour power calculated on the same basis as is that of men: in terms of the means of subsistence necessary to reproduce as well as to live. And the demand for equal opportunity, inadequate as it is, attacks the concept of women's work. Together they threaten the ideology of the family and the power relations within it just as much as does, for instance, the Women's Abortion and Contraception Campaign. The question we must ask is not whether these demands are co-optable, but whether the ways in which the system would have to be changed to meet them would help us break open the loving trap of the family.

"Wages for Housework" cannot fill the strategic and theoretical vacuum in the women's movement, but perhaps in the discussion around it we can begin the theoretical work without which we shall never overcome our practical weaknesses.

13

Oppressed Politics

ROS DELMAR

Selma James's paper [*Women, the Unions and Work*] reaches out to us as an authentic and desperate search for a way of understanding our movement, of bringing strands together, of looking for the traps we might unwittingly have fallen or be falling into. It is a call for action, and a cry of warning.

Full of intuitions of danger, and of the fear that we might wake up one day finding ourselves demoralised and broken, having been the political expression of women's desire for release from the oppressed and subordinated, intolerable lives that we live, but having pursued the desire for freedom down dark alleyways which have left us as oppressed as ever.

What comes over is the sense of urgency—the potential of our movement is being squandered—an anguished look at our politics, expressed with an energy which drives through all the confusions, contradictions, all those, in my view, profound errors, with which her paper is riddled.

What I am trying to do here is to present some alternative framework for the analysis of the women's movement, an alternative perspective on the problem of the relation of our movement to that of the working class. This means trying to go through some of the problems of the relationship of capitalism to sexism. For although there are points on which I am in agreement with Selma, I am in fundamental disagreement with her conclusions and with many of her theoretical positions.

The main consideration which prompts me to write a reply to "Women, the Unions and Work" is a political one. I looked at it from this point of view: if we won our four existing demands, I could envisage that we might find ourselves in struggle around the application in practice of those demands, but not against the principles they embody, that women should have control over their own reproductive powers and that discrimination against women in all spheres, schools, factories and so on, should be eliminated, but that the demand for wages for housework should be institutionalised as a category of paid wage-labour, and that in this way the housewife should be treated in the same way as any other wage labourer, seems to me to be thoroughly misconceived, and I will try to show why later on. In the long and the short term we would certainly be squandering our energy if we fought for demands which, if ever we won them, we would then find ourselves struggling against.

Then the way in which the demands are discussed, in terms of whether or not they are ultimately "co-optable" by the government, is profoundly depressing. The first consideration must always be the relation of demands to the needs of women and to the struggle of women against sexism.

Of course there is a real need of women to which this demand does correspond—the need for just a little more time, just a little more money, particularly in a situation of rising unemployment, rising prices, wages being forcibly kept down and so on. But it does not follow at all that housewives' wages is the solution we should put forward.

It seems clear to me that as a movement we are extremely weak in certain respects. We haven't yet solved the problem of how to create an information service, although that is the need we have felt from the beginning. It is not so much that we don't know what groups are doing—in our own city, in other towns and cities—even more important we have not yet worked out ways to communicate how we evaluate our experiences, what kinds of criteria we use in reflecting on and learning from our work.

We have no journal in which the ideas which we are developing can be expressed and debated, and have tended to turn for that to American journals. So that in a very real sense we are ignorant of our own movement.

The movement's energies are not being "squandered". To put it like that implies a direction, a controlling group. The situation is much more that the movement has a spontaneous dynamic, is in a sense out of our own control in that we have not yet learnt how to understand the movement.

How do we respond to this situation? One way is to try to impose a centralised direction. This solution became the politics of the Women's National Co-ordinating Committee, which we abolished last year at Skegness. Competing groups within the WNCC saw in it a potentially centralising body and tried to gain control over it and the movement.

The WNCC was abolished because it had signally failed to keep in touch with the politics of the developing movement, and prepared a conference the terms of which the majority at the conference rejected. These groups confused the politics of women's liberation with the politics of a committee. It was perhaps no coincidence that the contending groups were both the women's sections of male dominated left organisations.

Another way is to struggle for the acceptance of specific demands as a unificatory element of the movement. Thus, much of the debate around Selma's paper has centred around the demands spelt out at the end of her document, and specifically around that for the payment to housewives for their domestic work.

As a women's movement we have adopted three historic demands developed within socialist women's movements: equal pay, equal education and job opportunity, and 24-hour day nurseries. To these we have added one new demand: free abortion and contraception.

One thing about demands is that they certainly do give a kind of direction to the movement which power struggles in committees do not. The campaign for free abortion and contraception on demand, for example, has united on a practical level women with very different theories of women's oppression and women's liberation.

But one of the mistakes which can be made in that of summing up the objectives of the movement as the gaining of particular demands, i.e., to present the women's liberation movement as four campaigns, and to talk as if a society with free abortion and contraception on demand, equal education and job opportunity and 24-hour day nurseries would be a society within which women would be liberated rather than a society within which the *minimum preconditions* of our liberation from our present oppression would exist.

Another problem of demands is that part of their significance derives from the politics within which they are articulated. Thus, the demand for free abortion and contraception has one significance as a part of a strategy for liberating women; it has a totally different significance when it is the objective of a pressure group like the Family Planning Association, and we should be quite clear what that difference is.

Eugenics movements for population control will support the same demand as us, but their objective is totally different in that what we demand is the right of women to control their own reproductive capacities, and our objective should be to wrest the control of women's reproductive capacities from men and the state.

We must be clear that our development as a movement depends much more on the development of an understanding of the structures which oppress us as women and the strategy which we work out in order to overthrow this oppression. It depends much more on our ability to communicate to the mass of women on the basis of our specific critique of sexist and capitalist society, on building eventually a mass movement to overthrow sexism rather than the gaining of a specific demand.

It is striking that Selma James constantly talks about capitalism and never about sexism. However, she represents capitalism as if it were a self-determining and self-controlling institution. An example: "The government, acting in the interests of the capitalist class in general, has created unemployment in the hope that, instead of fighting for more pay and less work, we will be glad of the crumbs." This is in fact a psychological image of the government.

The point is that the government, however powerful it may be in capitalist Britain can no more control unemployment than it can control the sun and the moon. The impression which it tries to give us is that it can, and reassuring noises have been broadcast to this effect in all the mass media for the past five years.

Theorists, notably John Maynard Keynes in Britain, have been dedicated to the attempt to find methods of controlling employment and thus the labour market, but there is no reason at all to believe that they have yet discovered the secret.

Marx devoted his intellectual life to the discovery of the mechanisms of the capitalist economic system (mode of production) one of whose characteristics is that it is precisely anarchic (the anarchy of competition), and operates independently of the will of the capitalist.

It is only through the process of the transition through socialism to communism that a dominant class (i.e. the proletariat) learns how to control the laws of economy so that man governs the economy and not the other way round. Although the capitalist class is a powerful and dangerous enemy to all who struggle for liberation from all forms of oppression we must not ascribe to it magical qualities—that would be to believe its myth about itself.

In the present situation we can see that what is happening is out of the government's control—civil war in Ireland (or are we to believe that it created that in order to have somewhere to send the unemployed?), endless strikes, rising prices to the extent that even the Confederation of British Industry is asking the government to put an end to it, a return of female militancy, revolutionary groups even appearing in schools. From the government's point of view the situation must appear sometimes to be frighteningly out of control, rather than well in hand. We have no reason at all to believe that they knew it all along.

A similar confusion is revealed in these sentences: "This use of rebellion, to co-opt the most articulate minority for the purpose of developing capital . . . is not new and not confined to women. It is the overriding principle of capitalist development."

It is difficult to see the point of writing such nonsense in the name of marxism. The whole point about Marx was that he precisely demonstrated the way in which the overriding principle of capitalism is the extraction of surplus value, not the use of rebellion to co-opt articulate minorities (whatever those articulate minorities might think).

Sentences like these do not stand up to political analysis. When examined they reveal a curiously liberal centre. Who after all are being described as the "most articulate minority"? Women graduates. Doesn't this suggest the equation between "most articulate" and "most highly educated" which is so popular among the state functionaries who run this educational system? Surely from our point of view the "most articulate minority" are those women who express what the real condition of women is—and these will not necessarily be university graduates.

The women's liberation movement (and it is important to take this very seriously) represents "the most articulate minority". We must not accept the definitions given to us by this society that you need a degree in English before you can be considered articulate. This same curious liberalism can be found in the description of the indigenous ruling groups in ex-British colonies as "grateful outsiders". What, after all, are they grateful for? The chance to be cut in on the proceeds of the exploitation of their own people and their own country. They are only "grateful outsiders" to the extent that all quislings are. And when these peoples rise up against imperialism and its agents they will be swept away without a twinge of sympathy.

Of course, the fear that lies behind all this is the fear that we, the women's liberation movement, will be co-opted, and turned into an annexe of the capitalist system. And that this could be done through bribery.

But this fear of co-option seems to be a somewhat mysterious one. The idea is, indeed, clear enough—that capitalism will absorb the movement into itself and in this way kill it. But is this an adequate description of the process by which a movement can become a secondary aspect of bourgeois politics?

Within our own history—the history of English feminism—we have the example of the suffragettes, who although demonstrating great militancy and courage, in the end seem to have been an attempt to gain women entry into bourgeois politics.

How can we explain this?

The beginnings of some sort of answer can be found by looking at the main organising body of the suffragettes, the WPSU (Women's Political and Social Union). One outstanding feature of the WPSU was that it was totally undemocratic, to the point of mimicking a military organisation (the organisers were called "the General Staff", the main organiser was nicknamed "The General" and so on).

This small and powerful group of women which dominated the suffragette movement were absolutely determined to restrict the significance of the movement to the gaining of the demand for the vote. Their power came from the popularity of the demand, which, as militancy developed and the government became increasingly recalcitrant and repressive, gained the resonance of a symbol of female emancipation.

The decision was also made, early in the history of the WSPU, to link the fortunes of the women's movement to the governmental struggle between the Liberal and Conservative Parties: i.e. there was a determination within the women's movement, more, in the leadership of the movement, to link the women's movement to parliamentary manoeuvres.

This was itself accompanied by a parliamentary understanding of the significance of the demand. As a demand the right of women to political citizenship on the same terms as men is unexceptionable. As one demand in an articulated strategy for freeing women from their oppression it would certainly have its place. However, the strategic decision of the leadership of the movement was to limit its objectives to the gaining of that demand, and this signified the adoption and absorption of bourgeois politics by the movement.

That Christabel Pankhurst appeared on recruiting platforms for the government during the 1914–18 war is as unsurprising as the fact that before then those women, including notably Sylvia

Pankhurst, who wanted to link the fortunes of the women's movement to that of other oppressed and exploited groups were forced
out of the WPSU.

If we examine and analyse our own history we will find plenty of
reminders that the question of which kind of politics was to
dominate the women's movement was as much under discussion
then as it is now. And that there is much more to the failure of the
suffragettes, (as indeed there would be to our own) than "co-
option" by a fiendishly clever capitalist class.

It should also be added that the demand was never "co-opted".
The ruling class resisted female suffrage as long as it could, and the
battle was only won after a hard and courageous struggle by
thousands of women, many of whom went through the torture of
forcible feeding in prisons to win the vote for women.

Of course, there is always the possibility, reading through
Selma's paper, that co-opted stands for successful. From that point
of view it could be argued that female suffrage was "co-opted"
because it became law.

But this obliterates the reality of the struggle which was waged,
and of the message of that movement, which is that you only get
what you want by struggle, and that as long as you content yourself
with simply asking politely you are ignored. Of course capitalism
proved itself equal to the task of accommodating the female vote,
just as it accommodated to the working-class vote.

To understand that we need a political analysis of the theoretical
and political weaknesses and failures of the movement. Otherwise
we are left with the hardly satisfactory schema of the eternal goodie
fighting the eternal baddy who, mysteriously, always somehow
wins.

Perhaps the most enlightening confusion about what the term
"demand" is stretched to mean lies here: "ultimately the only
demand which is not co-optable is the armed population demanding the end to capitalism", which put simply means that the
bourgoisie will never lead a revolutionary struggle against
capitalism. Which is to be expected.

But why express it in such tortuous terms? Surely the whole
argument about "demands" and "co-options" stands in place of a
serious analysis of the problem of how it is that parties and
movements of revolutionary forces in society—the exploited and
oppressed—can be dominated by what is fundamentally a
bourgeois ideology. A conspiracy theory is inadequate to explain

that problem (for example, leaders always "sell out"). In *What is to be Done?* Lenin began an analysis of it.

The paragraph on Lenin really is incomprehensible. "We are told we must bring women to . . . 'trade-union consciousness'. This phrase is Lenin's and comes from a pamphlet called *What is to be Done?* In many ways . . . brilliant . . . but written in the early days . . . Lenin repudiated a good deal of what he wrote before these two revolutions" (1905, 1917).

We are left with the distinct impression that Lenin repudiated his particular conception of "trade-union consciousness" in later life, and that he would have endorsed that view were he alive today. The latter is such speculation as to be closed to discussion. As for the first claim, I believe that we have a lot to learn from Lenin's analysis of trade-union consciousness, never, to my knowledge, disowned by him.

In *What is to be Done?*, Lenin engaged in polemic with those who considered that trade-union struggle and trade-union consciousness (that is, the theoretical understanding of capitalism which comes from that struggle) were sufficient to the development of a revolutionary movement capable of overthrowing the state.

Lenin's argument was that this was not the case and that a revolutionary politics was needed which was capable of articulating the struggles of all the oppressed, not just the working class, for the overthrow of the state power. It was revolutionary political consciousness which was the need in the struggle, not trade-union consciousness.

More, Lenin argued that trade-union consciousness was a spontaneous product of capitalism, and, if left to its own spontaneity, would be dominated by bourgeois ideology, just as all modes of thinking spontaneously produced by capitalism are spontaneously dominated by those modes of thinking which are dominant in capitalist society—those of the bourgeoisie.

14

"The Housewife and her Labour under Capitalism"—a Critique

MARGARET COULSON, BRANKA MAGAŠ and HILARY WAINWRIGHT

The political significance of Wally Seccombe's analysis of domestic labour's relation to capital lies in his attempt to show the material basis for the strategic unity of the struggle to liberate women and the struggle for proletarian revolution.[1] Against those who view the family solely as an ideological institution of capitalist society, he argues that the labour performed within the family is an essential component of the material process of reproduction of capital. He is not the only author who has argued this point in recent years, but what singles out his attempt is that the thesis is spelt out rigorously and in some detail. However, Seccombe's concern to demonstrate the importance of housework for capitalism leads him, as we shall argue, into a contradictory position of asserting that housework produces value while at the same time being outside the rule of the law of value. Arguing that "sex relations and family relations have become capitalist relations in the bourgeois epoch",[2] he fails to understand the contradictory nature of female labour under capitalism and thus cannot identify the forces, both objective and subjective, that will drive housework out of history and liberate women. What we argue in the following pages is that the central feature of women's position under capitalism is not their role simply as domestic workers, but rather the fact that they are *both* domestic and wage labourers. It is this dual and contradictory role that imparts a specific dynamic to their situation. Without this contradiction, their position, however oppressive, would be essentially unproblematic. Further, we shall argue that while domestic labour is a necessary condition of reproduction of labour power, it does not contribute to its value or realise its own value when that commodity is sold on the market, because it is not in the marxist sense socially necessary labour. The consequences of this fact are by no means academic for proletarian women living in a society dominated by the law of value.

Women and production

Seccombe, like Benston[3] and Dalla Costa[4] before him, takes as his starting point the materialist premise that sexual subordination flows from the sexual division of labour, which under capitalism takes the extreme form of separation of the general economic process into a domestic and an industrial unit. All these three writers, at least for the purpose of their immediate analysis, assume that women and housewives are synonymous.[5] Seccombe writes: "With the advent of industrial capitalism, the general labour process was split into two discrete units: a domestic and an industrial unit . . . This split in the labour process had produced a split in the labour force roughly along sexual lines—women into the domestic unit, men into industry."[6] Of course, as a first step in the development of a theory of women's oppression, the identification of women and domestic labour is entirely valid: women's actual or anticipated domestic position is the main axis of their social determination. On the other hand, while Seccombe, like Benston and Dalla Costa, is aware of the importance of female wage labour for any politics of women's liberation, he too is unable to relate the two forms of women's labour in any coherent fashion.[7] Yet the coexistence of these two forms of female labour, actualised or only latent, is the historical contribution—however fundamentally limited—that capitalism has made towards women's liberation. The rift between the domestic and industrial units of production is closed in the life of those proletarian women who become also wage labourers. The role they perform in conditions of legal-economic dependence as domestic labourers has followed women into industry, reproducing the sexual division of labour on the larger terrain of socialised production, depressing their wages to a norm well below that of male labour, concentrating them within a narrow occupational range generally at the bottom of the job hierarchy and making them an easy prey for trade-union opportunism. Engels's optimism regarding the fate of the bourgeois family in the working class turned out to be premature: a whole historical epoch has separated the entry of women into production from the social organisation of housework.

On the other hand, as Seccombe describes so well, the generalisation of commodity production has turned the domestic unit into an oppressive backwater and the labour performed within it has become de-realised from the point of view not only of the capitalist but also of the domestic labourer herself: "the position of the domestic labourer relative to all but the lowest sectors of the proletariat has deteriorated".[8] But while arguing convincingly against Dalla Costa that "the effect of privatisation of domestic labour's relation to capital and its removal from the arena of surplus appropriation is that the law of value does not govern domestic labour",[9] Seccombe in fact makes only a limited advance over her theory because, among other things, he fails to consider the contradictory consequences of this separation or the effects it has on the consciousnes of women. The nature of housework's relation to capitalism, coupled with the latter's demand for female wage labour, makes the position of women much more explosive than Seccombe realises within the terms of his analysis. He is, therefore, not really able to show how, far from being able to find a peaceful solution to the problem of women's oppression, the growth and maturation of the capitalist system in reality only exacerbates it. The birth of the women's liberation movement in the sixties and the growing radicalisation of female industrial workers around this question in recent years[10] show the extent to which the unprecedented development of productive forces since the end of the Second World War has only helped to produce an unprecedented revolt by sections of women against their oppression. In order to understand the force and significance of this radicalisation of women, it is necessary first of all to re-evaluate the basis of Seccombe's analysis—his characterisation of housework as value-creating labour—and to examine in a more systematic fashion the indirect but powerful effects which the law of value has on domestic labour.

Does housework create value?

Seccombe's central thesis is that housework under capitalism exhibits a dual nature: on the one hand, it has no direct relation to capital, produces no surplus value and is therefore not governed by the law of value; on the other hand, it does create value, because it creates in part the commodity labour power which, when exchanged on the market for the wage, realises the value created by the housewife's labour also. Seccombe develops his argument in four stages. Firstly, the housewife's labour is a necessary labour, given that "the commodities which the wage purchases are not themselves in a finally consumable form at the point of purchase.

An additional labour—namely housework—is necessary in order to convert these commodities into regenerated labour." Secondly, in the course of this the housewife creates value, because "all labour produces value when it produces any part of a commodity that achieves equivalence in the market place with other commodities". Thirdly, "It matters not at all that the concrete conditions of domestic labour are privatised. The fact is that labour power as a commodity sold in the market place abstracts each of its labour components regardless of their private origins." Here a comparison is made between the housewife and the shoemaker, who are both engaged in private labour. Fourthly, housework "creates value equivalent to the 'production costs' of its maintenance".[11] Here a comparison is made between the domestic labourer and unproductive workers who render personal service, "such as cooks, seamstresses, etc.".

In fact, however, Seccombe's whole analysis of domestic labour under capitalism is based on an incorrect premise. It is not true that domestic labour creates value, and the arguments put forward by Seccombe to show that it does are fallacious. In the first place, while domestic labour, as Seccombe rightly says, is necessary labour—the working-class housewife is no parasite—it nevertheless does not create value at all, because its immediate products are use values and not commodities; they are not directed towards the market, but are for immediate consumption within the family. This at once differentiates the housewife's labour from that of a shoemaker: the forms of privatisation involved in their respective situations are of a quite different order.

In the second place, given that the housewife does not sell her labour power, the comparison between housewife and cook, etc. does not hold. In the passage quoted by Seccombe, Marx talks of the value of the labour of cooks, etc. only in the specific circumstances of these workers becoming wage-labourers. Thus, in marxist terms, by definition domestic labour has no value.

Thirdly, it is true that, as Seccombe brings out well, the working-class housewife contributes to the production of a commodity—labour power—the sale of which guarantees her existence (this she has in common with other proletarians) and through this process participates in social production and exchanges her labour for labour involved in the production of the means of her subsistence. But what mediates this participation and this exchange is not the market but the marriage contract: it is on the basis of the social relations of marriage and parenthood that the housewife's labour is related to social labour. Under capitalism, the market is the only mediator that allows different concrete labours, through the sale and exchange of the commodities they produce, to reach their equivalence and therefore become abstract social labour. The social conditions under which housework is performed prevent any such relation being formed, so that the conditions of the housewife's labour cannot be abstracted from, as Seccombe would argue. The fact that her labour is necessary does not turn it automatically into socially necessary labour in the sense used by Marx: the social relations of the family block any direct impact of the market, which alone provides conditions for the homogenisation of human labour under capitalism. Housework under capitalism therefore remains a specific labour to which the concept of abstract labour does not apply: it is this aspect which gives it its specific privatised character and which provides a material basis for the relative autonomy of women's oppression from the central axis of capitalist exploitation. Of course, the knowledge that she creates no value, that her labour has no value, is of little comfort to the working-class housewife, who often works round the clock to maintain herself and her family. But this cruel seeming absurdity has nothing to do with the intrinsic value of her labour, but with the absurdity of the capitalist system itself. To sum up, then, we cannot define domestic labour in terms of the labour theory of value, and can grasp its specificity only once we understand that this is the case. As we shall see, a purely structural analysis of housework under capitalism (such as Seccombe seeks to develop in NLR 83 or Jean Gardiner elsewhere in this issue) is not at all adequate; only an historical account of the modifications which it has undergone and continues to undergo can interrelate and explain what in Gardiner's article, for example, appear as discrete forces acting upon domestic labour.

Basis for unity

According to Seccombe, the fact that the housewife creates value provides a material basis for working-class unity. In rejecting the notion that domestic labour creates value, we by no means imply that the male worker and his wife have no common interest in the wage: indeed, the wage is often the most immediate focus of unity, since it represents their joint means of existence. The political implication of this is the strong tendency towards unity within the working-class family in the fight for higher wages and against the immediate ravages of inflation. The strength of this unity has been demonstrated again and again in the face of the most massive onslaughts of anti-strike propaganda. However, the strategic unity between the struggle for women's liberation and the proletarian class struggle transcends the immediate economic interests of working-class men and women and does not flow immediately from them.

Indeed, the immediate interest in the wage can take the wage labourer and his dependants in quite opposite directions. This was well illustrated recently in the course of a series of conflicts at the Cowley complex of British Leyland, the largest UK car manufacturer, in the spring of 1974. In the course of a dispute provoked by the management's attempt to victimise a militant shop steward—in order to weaken the workers' resistance to redundancies and a speed-up—the management and the bourgeois press were able to use resentment among the wives of some laid-off workers in a particular section of the factory to whip up an anti-strike campaign among the car workers' wives, in order to demoralise and disunite the strikers.[12] The existence of this weak flank within the Cowley working class was not simply a result of the atomisation of housewives; it was more crucially the result of a conflict between their immediate interest in having a wage coming into the household and the longer-term need to resist the management's strategy for introducing wage-cuts, redundancies and speed-ups (a need which produced its own short-term imperative—to prevent the victimisation).[13]

The conflict between immediate dependence on the wage and aims that can be achieved only at the risk of a struggle is, of course, inherent in the conditions of working-class existence under capitalism. This conflict is most acutely felt at the point of consumption, within the family. While advanced capitalism, through its extreme division of labour and consequent socialisation of that labour, unites the working class on the factory floor, it at the same time differentiates it internally through privatised organisation of distribution (according to labour) and hence of consumption. Sectional interests—as opposed to collective, strategic interests of the class as a whole—are then defended through trade-union activity. But the individual interest of a worker asserts itself first of at home. Family values and domestic virtues have, therefore, always been one of the chief ingredients of bourgeois ideology and propaganda. It is not accidental, for example, that the recent bid by Sir Keith Joseph to make himself the front-running right-wing candidate for the leadership of the Conservative Party was made in a speech which emphasised the need to rebuild the moral, as distinct from the material, fibre of British capitalism through (among other things, such as higher unemployment, stricter control of working-class births, etc.) ideological struggle to defend the family.

Seccombe is quite right, therefore, to emphasise that, under capitalism, whereas socialised production allows the possibility of collective action, privatised housework atomises the housewife's political potential. What he fails to mention, however, is that this "problem" of the housewife is a problem for the working class as a whole, in a much deeper sense than simply how to achieve conjunctural unity in action. The fact itself of collective consciousness, of course, by no means prevents workers from acting in a sectional fashion. One of the main reasons why the immediately felt interest of the housewife can and often does clash with the needs of the political or trade-union struggle is as a consequence of the short-term interests of male workers who, nine times out of ten, believe that these struggles have nothing to do with women in general and their wives and daughters in particular. Some of the Cowley workers, in the situation described above, when confronted with a co-ordinated offensive from their wives and employers, reacted with shouts of "Go home where you belong!" Sexism within the working class, as Seccombe points out, is based ultimately on the solid foundation of the man's control over the wage. Engels, in a striking analogy, once wrote that within the family the man is the bourgeois and his wife the proletarian. The history of working-class struggle is also a history of uphill struggle against more or less extreme forms of anti-feminism within the class itself.[14] Moreover, such attitudes are buttressed by the huge disparities between male and female wages, prospects for promotion, etc.—disparities whose divisive political consequences are often as valuable to the capitalist as their direct economic advantages.

The only way in which sectional interests can be suppressed and the collective interest of the class assert itself is, of course, through revolutionary politics. But before we discuss this central political question, we must first return to our initial thesis that the central feature of women's position under capitalism is the fact that th are *both* domestic and wage labourers, that the two aspects of their existence are by no means harmoniously related and that this dual and contradictory role generates the specific dynamic of their oppression. A key concomitant of this thesis is the recognition that capitalism, as we show below, is unable to transform radically, whether through extension of the market or of the welfare state, the privatised nature of domestic labour. While we are under no illusion that we already have a fully worked out theory of women's oppression and liberation, we can nevertheless, if we take this as our starting-point, begin to determine the main aspects of such a theory.

Capitalist housework

Any such theory of women's oppression must proceed from the historical specificity of bourgeois marriage and family and the nature of their stability under capitalism. What characterises domestic labour under capitalism is that it is a labour engaged in activities associated with consumption, that it is not mediated through the market and that it is inserted in a system in which consumption is separated from production through the intervention of the market. As long as production was of use values only, or production for the market was only a subsidiary element of general economic activity, production and consumption were fused within one labour process. Although women tended to be employed in some labour processes rather than others, the sexual division was more in terms of different concrete labours or stages of the labour process than in terms of men producing for the surplus while women produced for consumption. Women produced a surplus, i.e. goods over and above what was necessary for their maintenance, and the exchange between their labours and the labours of other members of the family was on the basis of marital or filial relations, dominated by the father or the husband. Nevertheless, their labour was visible and was seen by all as a necessary (though perhaps inferior) complement of the labour of the father or husband. The growth of the market, based on increasing differentiation of labour, took out of the family most production capable of generating a surplus. While domestic labour continued to participate in the social exchange, the nature of this participation now "de-realised" domestic labour. The marriage contract, previously based on the solid foundation of material production, has in conjunction with other capitalist relations become "voluntary" and therefore less stable. This is not to argue that the "freedom" of the marriage contract is of the same type as the "freedom" of the wage contract, but only to say that the family takes a new form under capitalism.

The instability of the bourgeois family is further aggravated by the demands of capital for female wage labour (which allows women to escape total economic dependence) and for more efficient reproduction of labour-power (which tends to change the scope and intensity of housekeeping). The continued existence of the bourgeois family, in spite of its fading lustre, has never been seriously challenged. But that family has nevertheless been undermined in a number of subsidiary ways. In the early history of capitalism, at the time of the first industrial revolution, the demand for labour was so high that at times and in certain places men, women and children all became wage labourers. For example, at the peak of the first industrial revolution, in many areas of Britain domestic work was commercialised, in a haphazard sort of way. Very young girls and old women were paid to look after children and clean the family house, while the mother was working in the mill or factory. The bond of property, even at the level of parental control of children's labour, was loosened. The disappearance of privatised housework coincided with high instability of the family in the working class. This was also a time of great misery for the proletariat, which showed in the "poor quality" of the labour force and in high infant mortality. However, increasing mechanisation of the productive process reduced the demand for labour and, coupled with the raising of the real wage, allowed for a partially spontaneous and partially encouraged regeneration of the bourgeois family in the working class. At the other end of capitalism's historical spectrum, in contemporary Sweden, high demand for female labour (due among other factors to the small size of the population and to the lack of an agricultural reserve labour force) has resulted in the extension of socialised services into the area traditionally reserved for domestic labour, in a way that has provided fuel for social-democratic dreams of a peaceful, gradual elimination of female oppression.

Impact of the law of value

It is clear from these examples that the history of housework under capitalism is by no means one of gradual stagnation, as implied by

Seccombe. One of the main ways in which the effects of the law of value have disturbed the apparent tranquillity of the domestic domain has been the need for women as industrial workers. (Though it should not be forgotten that housewives constitute only one among several reserve sources of labour in phases of capitalist expansion. In much of post-war Western Europe, for example, migrant labour has been of at least as great importance. Failure to understand this can lead to an exaggeration of the potential effects on domestic labour of economic fluctuations under capitalism.) Because housework is a specific labour, the tempo and organisation of which is not in a radical degree affected by the law of value, it has a significant degree of elasticity that gives scope for capital in its expansive phases to utilise the labourers involved more productively.[15] This has explosive consequences for women's position under capitalism. It widens the possibility of economic independence for women, without making this fully or permanently achievable; it shortens the time available for domestic work, without providing an alternative basis for it; it breaks down the isolation of women, without lightening the burden of her private responsibilities. The birth of the women's liberation movement and the increasing militancy of women workers reflect the tensions generated by the operation of the law of value on social relations that are not fully capitalistic.

The second channel of capital's influence on the domestic labour process, and the only one considered by Seccombe, is what the latter describes as the "constant infusion of new technology into the household via commodity production".[16] While he is quite right to emphasise the essential limitations of this influence, he makes the common mistake of trivialising its importance. Yet the technological revolution in the kitchens of the working class has contributed to the rationalisation of domestic labour and allowed women that modicum of extra time, that minimal improvement in the drudgery of everyday life, that has so clearly helped stimulate the new resolution on the part of many women to fight their oppression. The reduced intensity of labour necessary at home has made it easier for women to seek independent means of economic and social existence and apply themselves more energetically to trade-union and other activities.

The third crucial way in which the law of value affects the scope and intensity of domestic labour is through the taking over, by capitalist enterprises or the bourgeois state, of many of the until recently traditional duties of the housewife. The feeding, housing, cleaning, education and childcare of the vast army of the proletariat concentrated in the cities of advanced capitalist countries transcend the potential of the traditional organisation of reproduction of labour power in the family. Semi-processed foods, expanded and rationalised shopping facilities, dry-cleaning and laundering services, nurseries and child-minding agencies, cheap cafés and restaurants, factory and school canteens, child clinics and youth clubs, hospitals and old people's homes, complement and to some extent replace the labour of the housewife.[17] At times of capitalist boom, such as the quarter-century which followed the Second World War, such an expansion of capitalist enterprise goes hand in hand with a rise in real wages (necessary to buy the new commodities) and with an increasing demand for female labour. In Britain, for example, massive post-war expansion of the processing industry coincided with a leap in the proportion of women over 15 involved in production, from 27 per cent in 1951 to 51 per cent in 1970. Such conditions are favourable to a struggle for "women's rights" which is reflected in limited reforms even at the level of bourgeois legislation; in Britain, for instance, a whole series of legal changes have recently been introduced in favour of the wife in cases of marriage breakdown. Simultaneously, women see the time they spend in production more and more as a permanent part of their lives, and increasingly resist attempts by employers to lay them off or keep down their real wage. The Equal Pay Act, which in Britain will soon make it mandatory for an employer to pay equal wages for equal labour—a real reform, however limited and open to evasion—is at least in part a result of the pressure of women worker militants.

Domestic labour and socialism

What has been said above about the nature and role of domestic labour under capitalism provides a basis for understanding why capitalism cannot carry through the bourgeois revolution in the sphere of reproduction of labour power. The contribution of domestic labour to this process, although indirect, is significant. But why should it be essential? It is true that the existence itself of the bourgeois family, as we have already argued, is by no means brought into question by conjunctural upswings in the cycle of capitalist production. Furthermore, there is an important ideological argument that the family plays an indispensable role through initial socialisation in creating consent to the bourgeois *status quo*. But the real answer lies in the very essence of capitalist production. On the one hand, a free market in labour demands that there be no such control over the labour force as characterised feudalism or slavery. On the other hand, private ownership of the means of production goes hand in hand with inequality (both daily and generational) in the distribution of the social surplus, which in bourgeois society is organised around the family. In advanced capitalism, the education and training of the proletariat can only be institutionalised cheaply and effectively at the level of the nation state. But the intervention of a capitalist state in the reproduction of the labour force, just as in the economy, can only be of a strictly limited nature. In a society dominated by the market, the bourgeois family and domestic labour are spontaneously generated within the working class.

The immediate aim of proletarian revolution is to dispossess the bourgeoisie and socialise ownership of the means of production. But this is only the first step in the creation of a socialist society, which necessarily involves a radical reorganisation of distribution as well: away from its bourgeois form (to each according to his or her work) to a socialist one in terms of needs. That this involves the suppression of the market and of the mystification of the wage-form goes without saying. But that it also involves the suppression of the bourgeois family, into which privatised consumption is inserted, and thus, of course, the revolutionary transformation of all sexual and emotional as well as economic and political relations, still probably needs to be spelled out. The persistence of bourgeois family forms and of domestic labour in the Soviet Union testify to the immense gap which separates simple nationalisation of the means of production from socialism. A planned economy provides a basis for the equality of women in the productive and political spheres only in so far as it provides at the same time a basis for the effective elimination of domestic labour. As the experience of the first workers' state showed in the years after October, the proletarian state, in so far as it destroys the bond of material dependence in sexual and emotional relations, begins the destruction of the bourgeois family as an institution. But it can achieve this only if it creates the material basis necessary to suppress the social division of labour, including that according to sex. Harmonious co-ordination of production and consumption, true equality in distribution, can only be realised once the specific oppression of women, their domestic slavery, has been thrown into the dustbin of history. This is one fundamental reason why the liberation of women is a strategic interest of the working class, and an indispensable pre-requisite for the building of socialism.

Conclusion

What first prompted us to write this critique of Seccombe's analysis was not simply its theoretical inadequacies or mistakes, but rather the spontaneist conception of working-class politics in relation to the struggle for women's liberation which characterises his whole approach. Seccombe puts his faith in "the uneven and combined nature of socialist revolution which affords opportunities for housewives to move onto the historical stage in their own interests and in the general interests of women and of the proletariat. Mobilisations of housewives raising demands for the socialisation of housework, demands against the state, demands for price-watch committees, etc.—such actions can make a tremendous contribution to the advancement of the class struggle particularly if they are combined with simultaneous proletarian initiatives." Moreover, "it is mainly from within this population [of female wage labourers] rather than from the diminishing numbers of women who are still exclusively housewives, that women's leadership will come in the years ahead. Women wage workers and students struggling for full equality with men within unions and in the schools will be in the vanguard of struggles that will diminish sex divisions of the class. Furthermore it will be primarily these women who will inject radical women's consciousness back into the population of women who remain exclusively housewives."[18]

Of course, struggle against inequality within trade unions and schools, struggle against inflation, injection of radical women's consciousness, unity of proletarian initiatives—the cross-fertilisation between these various aspects of the class struggle is undeniable. But there is a great distance between the various instances of women's struggles, actual or possible, and a full revolutionary strategy; between a belief in the necessity of revolution and the working out of its programme in action. Seccombe's initial criticism of the revolutionary left for having "historically developed few strategic perspectives that frontally address the social relations of the bourgeois family"[19] is considerably weakened by his own failure to develop such strategic perspectives.

Such a revolutionary strategy does not flow spontaneously from the immediate economic conditions of working-class existence under capitalism. The fragmented interests of different sections of the working class can only be brought into focus and transcended in the interests of the class as a whole by revolutionary politics, through the intervention of a revolutionary vanguard. For example, when women workers go on strike, there is an immediate clash between the need to maintain the picket line and the need to carry out domestic responsibilities. This clash is made more acute by the absence of public nursery facilities, etc., on the one hand, and in almost all cases, by lack of trade-union support—if not active sabotage[20]—on the other. The employers, given the normal isolation of women workers, are often able to prevent payment of social security benefits to women on strike, through the complicity of the state institutions. Revolutionaries can intervene here by agitating in trade unions and other workers' organisations on behalf of the struggle; by making propaganda in their press and meetings; by helping the strike committee to organise the women's normal domestic responsibilities; by helping to put collective pressure on the local council to provide facilities; by exposing the links between the employers and the state; by raising other demands relevant to, but not directly thrown up by, the struggle in question; above all, by at all times explaining the link between all these aspects of the particular dispute and the overall struggle for socialism. In a modest fashion, the strike for better wages can be transformed into a political action that takes up in practice some of the points outlined above. But, of course, intervention in particular strikes is not in itself sufficient; wider action including on a national level, is indispensable.

But the vanguard of which we are speaking, let it be clear, is not merely the aggregate of the existing revolutionary organisations, or indeed any already constituted social force. Such a vanguard can only emerge fully under conditions in which the working class and specifically oppressed groups within it begin to organise themselves to challenge the structures of their exploitation and oppression. Given what we have shown to be the relative autonomy of women's oppression and the consequent lack of any inevitable short-run unity of interests, this implies that women's self-organisation is a necessary condition for the development of a vanguard that truly expresses the interests of all oppressed groups. The task of this vanguard will be to integrate into its transitional programme measures that will bridge the split in the working class between the home and the factory, that will take up the inequality of women in production, that will fight for women's right to work, that will fight for equality of women within working-class organisations in a society as a whole, that will fight against the sexual division of labour, that will fight for free birth control and free abortion on demand, that will combat sexual repression, and so on (tactical considerations will mean that there are variations from country to country). This is a difficult task, but not an impossible one; for, precisely, it is rooted in the needs of the proletariat, both male and female.

NOTES

1. Wally Seccombe, "The housewife and her labour under capitalism", in *New Left Review* NLR 83.
2. Ibid., note 7, p. 5.
3. Margaret Benston, "The political economy of women's liberation", in *Monthly Review*, September 1969.
4. Mariarosa Dalla Costa, *The Power of Women and the Subversion of the Community*, Falling Wall Press, Bristol, 1972.
5. For Benston, women are "that group of people who are responsible for the production of simple use values in those activities associated with the home and family". Dalla Costa equally focuses on "the housewife as the central figure in the female role. We assume all women are housewives and even those who work outside the home continue to be housewives."
6. Seccombe, op. cit., p. 6.
7. The only gesture at this is found in his concluding paragraphs, where a section of women quite extraneous to his previous discussion, i.e. women workers, after winning their spurs in the struggle for equality within the unions, proceed to "inject radical women's consciousness back into the population of women who remain exclusively housewives". Seccombe, op. cit., p. 24.
8. Ibid., p. 18.
9. Ibid., p. 8.
10. Industrial struggles in which women workers have played a role of special significance have, in Britain alone in the past couple of years, included those at Fakenham, Lucas-Burnley, Branhams, Admiralty House, Salford Electrical Instruments (on two occasions), H. K. Porter, Hawker Siddeley, Maclaren Controls, Armstrong Patents,

BOAC Air Terminal, Typhoo, Imperial Typewriters, Kenilworth Components, Dorothy Gray, Wingrove and Rogers, John Brown, Personna, Vauxhall, Standard Telephone and Cables, Hoover Motors and Associated Automation (see *Red Mole* 45, 49; *Red Weekly* 7, 9, 11, 12, 27, 32, 38, 48, 59, 60, 63, 65, 71–4, 76–9, etc.).

11. Seccombe, op. cit., pp. 9–10.

12. The choice of this example must not give rise to any misunderstanding. On the one hand, the "wives' revolt" at Cowley was a relatively small-scale affair, initiated by conscious strike-breakers, blown up out of all proportion by the press in an attempt to cow the workers. On the other hand, the tendency to unity within the working-class family discussed above soon asserted itself and proved a very much stronger force, provoking the speedy collapse of the "wives' revolt". Nevertheless, with these qualifications, the events in question did reveal a genuine contradiction. For a full account of the 1974 dispute, within the context of the crisis of the British car industry and the specific history of the class struggle in Cowley, see *Leyland in Crisis: Cowley under Fire*, Cowley IMG pamphlet, Oxford, 1974.

13. *The Daily Telegraph*, commenting on the Cowley housewives' revolt, drove this point home: "Trade unionism as it is practised in this country denies to an ever growing extent one of the elementary needs of nearly all wives—regular housekeeping money." Quoted in the Cowley IMG pamphlet, see note 12 above.

14. For an interesting introduction to this question in the history of the German trade-union movement, see Werner Thönnessen, *The Emancipation of Women. The Rise and Decline of the Women's Movement in German Social Democracy* 1863–1933, Pluto Press, London, 1973.

15. But this does not at all mean, as we explain below, that domestic labour can be socialised under capitalism. In this context, Jean Gardiner's analysis of the reasons for the continued existence of housework in terms principally of a balance between its contribution to the cheapness of the reproduction of labour power and capitalism's need for female labour in phases of expansion is quite inadequate. On the one hand, if lowering the cost of reproduction of labour power through domestic labour were indeed central for the accumulation of capital, it would be impossible to explain the process whereby so much of what was previously domestic production was taken out of the family. On the other hand, the continued existence of the sexual division of labour in Sweden, for example, warns against over-optimism as far as the consequences of the full employment of women are concerned.

16. Seccombe, op. cit., p. 17.

17. In this context, the role of the welfare state in relation to the family has been analysed by Elizabeth Wilson, *Women and the Welfare State*, Red Rag pamphlet, London, 1974.

18. Seccombe, op. cit., pp. 23–4.

19. Ibid., p. 5.

20. At a recent strike for equal pay by women workers at the Salford Electrical Instruments factory at Heywood near Manchester, male union members helped to break an occupation of the factory by smashing down the entrance doors. See Ingrid Falconer, "'Divide and Rule' or united in struggle", *Red Weekly*, 12 December 1974.

15

Women's Domestic Labour

JEAN GARDINER, SUSAN HIMMELWEIT, MAUREEN
MACKINTOSH

The kind of theoretical analysis one does is determined by the kind
of questions one asks of it, and one of the hardest problems which
has faced the "Political Economy of Women Group" over the past
year has been to redefine the theoretical questions we were asking
in order that they should address more closely our own political
concerns. We start out with a common political perspective in that
we are all socialists and feminists, but beyond that we are trying to
develop an understanding of our agreements and disagreements in
the process of discussion and research.

This paper presents our views on the problem of domestic labour
(i.e., housework) and its relation to women's total economic role
under capitalism. What we mean by "economic" in this context is
that we are focusing here on production and reproduction as the
material aspects of women's oppression. We examine the in-
terrelations between the different forms of women's work under
capitalism, the material basis of sexism, and the gains to capital
and to various groups of workers from the oppression and exploitation of women. While recognising the ideological importance
of the family, we shall be concentrating on the roles of women in
production; such an analysis is the specific contribution of political
economy to the women's movement. Moreover, in focusing on
domestic labour we are reflecting the view, common to almost all
writing on this subject, that women's role in the home is crucial to
her subordination under capitalism.

The paper is organised as follows. We begin by setting out a
theoretical problem, the relation of domestic labour to the process
by which surplus value is generated within capitalism. We go on to
discuss, in the light of this, the concept of a mode of production,
and its use in analysing the relation of domestic labour to the
capitalist mode of production. We then analyse the nature of the
production relations of domestic labour, and particularly the
relations within the family. Finally we consider the historical
relation of domestic labour to women's wage work and past and

possible future changes in domestic labour in response to the contradictory needs of capitalism.

1. Domestic labour and surplus value

This section identifies the theoretical problem of the relation of domestic labour to the expansion of surplus value. In the process of developing an understanding of this we began with the question of how housework contributes to the production of surplus value, but found that different answers to this question implied answers to certain historically specific questions, such as:

—Why has domestic labour retained a major role in the maintenance and reproduction of labour power in capitalist societies?

—Is domestic labour and the family as we know it likely to be significantly eroded in the current phase of British capitalism?

These are questions which we bear in mind in discussing the relationship of domestic labour to the expansion of surplus value.

(a) Surplus value in Marx

The core of Marx's theory of surplus value is expounded in *Capital*, vol. 1, in the following way. Marx restricts his analysis to the productive relations of a pure capitalist mode of production in which there are two classes: the bourgeoisie who own the means of production and the proletariat who own nothing but their labour power. All labour performed in this economy is engaged in capitalist commodity production. Surplus value is then defined as the abstract labour-time embodied in that part of capitalist commodity production which represents a surplus over and above the commodities purchased with their wage by workers for their own consumption. Since all production is capitalist commodity production, workers' consumption is also exclusively consumption of commodities.

The production relations between capital and labour are inherently antagonistic: capital will strive to shorten the portion of the working day the worker is working for his own subsistence and lengthen correspondingly that portion of the day when the worker is producing surplus value for his employer. The production of surplus value is therefore a process in which class conflict is inherent, around both the wage bargain and the production process.

As far as the wage bargain is concerned, Marx saw the wage for each group of workers as fixed in real terms for a given historical period, identifying this as a historically given level of subsistence. The value of labour power is then the abstract labour-time embodied in commodities making up that level of subsistence at any moment. He could argue that the real wage must be fixed for a given level of subsistence only because he assumed that workers' consumption consisted only of commodities purchased with the wage. In this approach, Marx's analysis abstracts from the determination of the historical level of subsistence, and also from the interaction between this and the wage range. Once one recognises that workers also consume use-values produced by domestic labour (as well as by the state in areas like health, education and social benefits) then the level of wages and the level of subsistence are no longer synonymous.

However, since Marx regarded the level of real wages as historically predetermined, most of his analysis of the production of surplus value is concentrated on the capitalist production process. For once wages are fixed in real terms there are only two ways of raising the rate of surplus value. Either the working day can be lengthened or the pace of work increased, both of which meet with physical limits and organised opposition from the workforce. Or the labour-time required to produce the necessary commodities for wokers' consumption can be reduced.

We feel that in order to develop an analysis of the relation of domestic labour to the expansion of surplus value, the question of wages and the value of labour power has to be explored in much greater depth.

(b) The value of labour power

The dominance of capitalism requires that the mass of producers, men and women alike, be separated from alternative independent means of subsistence, but beyond this, Marx took little further interest in the question of how the subsistence and reproduction of the labour force was transformed by the advent of capitalism. For example, he does not appear to have seen any contradiction between, on the one hand, viewing capitalism as a mode of production in which workers are dependent for their subsistence on wage labour and, on the other, relegating the question of the maintenance and reproduction of labour power to an ahistorical and peripheral terrain:

The maintenance and reproduction of the working class is, and must ever be, a condition of the reproduction of capital. But the capitalists may safely leave its fulfilment to the labourers' instincts of self-preservation and propagation.[1]

However, when the current feminist movement began to focus attention on women's domestic labour and its role in the maintenance and reproduction of labour power, it became clear that the value of labour power—in the sense of the abstract labour-time embodied in the commodities entering into the level of subsistence—was not independent of the other forms of work which went into the total level of subsistence of the working class. Several issues have to be examined as part of a theory of the value of labour power. The first point is that in any period the provision made by capital for the reproduction and maintenance of labour power through the wage paid to workers is premised on the existence of domestic labour and the state historically given in a particular form. The payment of wages to workers does not provide in itself adequate material conditions for their labour power to be maintained and reproduced either on a day-to-day basis or from generation to generation. Secondly there is the question of dependence of the value of labour power on the economic structure of the family. Marx explicitly assumed in his analysis of the value of labour power a family unit in which neither children nor wife worked, although he also pointed to the historical tendency of capital to spread the value of labour power over the whole family through the employment of women and children.

To both of these issues we will return in subsequent sections. There is a third set of questions which need to be examined in developing a theory of the value of labour power. That is how do subsistence needs get determined and change over time; how do needs influence wage levels and wage levels influence how needs are perceived; how do wage differentials get established, maintained or changed over time? We raise these questions but do not explore them further in this paper since they are not directly related to the role of domestic labour.

Before looking in detail at the role of labour in the determination of the value of labour power and hence in the production of surplus value, we first consider the relation of domestic labour to the capitalist mode of production, and the implications of this for our analysis.

2. Domestic labour and the capitalist mode of production

There has been a certain amount of discussion recently of whether domestic labour should be analysed as a form of work within the capitalist mode of production, or as a separate "client" mode articulating with, but outside, the capitalist mode of production.[2] To some extent this has been a question of semantics, but there are some real theoretical issues involved, and we first discuss these in general.

In deciding how the concepts of "mode of production" should be used, we need to distinguish between transitional and non-transitional societies. Transitional societies are those in a process of change from domination by one ruling class, on the basis of one set of relations of exploitation, to domination by another. Non-transitional societies, whatever the fragmentations, fractionating and confusions within them, are not undergoing such a process. So long as this distinction is kept clear one can to some extent choose one's own vocabulary, but we feel that there are good arguments for the concepts we have chosen to use.

Marx does not use the phrase "mode of production" consistently. But he identifies capitalist mode of production and the historical epochs which he contrasts with capitalism: the "Asiatic form", the "feudal dominium" for example, by means of a particular set of social relations defining in each a single contradiction: the relation between the direct producers and the controllers of their labour. The concept of mode of production is thus fundamental to Marx's theory of history; changes in the set of production relations and the development of the productive forces being "in the last instance" the determinant of the historical process. The most explicit passage is the well known one from the discussion of feudal land rent, where Marx contrasts this with the capitalist form of surplus extraction:

> The specific economic form in which unpaid surplus labour is pumped out of the direct producers, determines the relationship of rulers and ruled, as it grows directly out of production itself and in turn reacts upon it as a determining element. . . . It is always the direct relationship of the owners of the conditions of production to the direct producers—a relation always naturally corresponding to a definite stage in the development of the methods of labour and thereby its social productivity—which reveals the innermost secret, the hidden basis of the entire social structure, and with it the political form of the relation of sovereignty and dependence, in short, the corresponding

specific form of the state. This does not prevent the same economic base—the same from the standpoint of its main conditions—due to innumerable different empirical circumstances, natural environment, racial relations, external historical influences etc. from showing infinite gradations and variations in appearance (*Capital*, vol. 3, p. 791).

This it seems to us is the most useful way of using the concept of a mode of production, an inspired abstraction if you like, laying bare the form of the principal contradiction between producers and non-producers.

The dynamic of change in a society can then be explored as the processes of resolution and reinforcement of that contradiction. Thus in any historical epoch, one contradiction is basic to the determination of the laws of development of that society. In capitalism that contradiction is between capital and labour, and therefore our analysis of domestic labour must be situated in relation to the contradictions and dynamic of the capitalist mode of production. It should be noted that we are not collapsing the concept of "mode of production" into that of relations of production. Many different relations of production can exist under one mode, and each of these relations is stamped by the character of that mode of production.[3]

We therefore have rejected the characterisation of domestic labour as a separate mode of production.[4] We include it within the capitalist mode of production, while recognising that the relations of domestic labour under capitalism are fundamentally different from firstly, the relations of capitalist wage labour and secondly, the relations of anything that we might call domestic labour under any other mode.

So we now can make the distinction between transitional and non-transitional societies. While societies in transition are characterised by the contradictory existence of more than one mode of production, this is not so for non-transitional societies which contain only one mode. Modern capitalism is not a society in transition between domestic production and capitalist production (or vice versa). Domestic labour is therefore part of the capitalist mode of production.

One of the implications that has been drawn from the analysis of domestic labour as a separate mode of production is that housewives form a distinct class.[5] This is not an inevitable deduction. Political conclusions do not follow so straightforwardly from theoretical analysis. But there is a tendency to argue by analogy with capital and labour. In all societies, the material situation of women differs from that of men (for example, women's relation to the means of production differs from that of men in even peasant societies) and indeed the categories of material analysis, class or caste for example, are specified in terms of the material situation of men. It is therefore incorrect simply to apply these male-referent categories to the relations between men and women and thus to see housewives (or worse, women) as a class.

This is not to say that women do not have specific class interests, ways in which their material position differs from that of men. There are precedents in Marx for a detailed analysis of the class position of various groups in capitalist society, according to their specific interest, while not losing sight of their position in the division between capital and labour.[6] In carrying out such an analysis, it is essential to recognise that women, like men, of the working class have no control of the means of production. They are potential workers for capital for much of their lives, and most do wage work at some point, including a high proportion of married women. It is only through a recognition of their (actual or potential) double role in production that we can analyse their class position and the tensions within it which lead to change.

3. Production relations and domestic labour

(a) The relations of production within the home

Domestic labour is therefore the production of use-values under non-wage relations of production, within the capitalist mode of production. We now go on to examine the nature of those non-wage relations and their implications for the economic relations between men and women within the home. We shall try to avoid the assumption, so common in the literature, that women are typically full time housewives. Women are most likely to be full time housewives when they have children under five, since pre-school childcare is still almost entirely done by domestic labour. We shall examine this case first, and describe how the relations of production differ for the wage worker and the wife working in the home.

The wage worker sells his labour-power as a commodity for a definite period of time, in exchange for a money wage. The rest of his time is his own and there is a rigid separation of his life into work and leisure. His wages are spent on commodities consumed away from the work place. Thus production and consumption are two separate activities, emotionally and physically. The former is seen as a rigidly timed unpleasant necessity and goes on at the work place; the latter as leisure, supposedly enjoyable, going on in or around the home.

So for the wage earner the home is the place where he consumes but does not work and where his time is his own. For the housewife it is her place of work but she does not go elsewhere for her leisure. So in her life there is no rigid work/leisure distinction either in physical location or in time. She is not paid for her work, and the amount of time she spends is not the direct concern of anyone else, as long as the work is done. This is unlike the situation under capitalist commodity production, where the reduction of time spent on producing any given use-value is the specific concern of the capitalist, since it is he who benefits from increases in productivity, rather than the worker. For the housewife, such pressure as there is to reduce the time spent on particular tasks is of an ideological, non-specific nature rather than direct coercion. This combined with the imprecise definition of her work and the fact that she is not producing for a market means that her work is not under the same kind of pressures for increasing productivity, as is work under capitalist relations. There is not necessarily even a clear separation between production and consumption in her life.

In contrast with her husband, she is a to a large extent in control of her method and pace of working. She organises her own time, given the constraints of fitting in with her surroundings. There is neither division nor practically any socialisation of her labour. All housewives do roughly the same work and they do it in isolation. A few activities, such as shopping, do bring housewives into contact with each other but this socialisation is only that of a group engaging in a given activity together but in parallel. They are not co-operating. The relation between a housewife and her husband is completely different from that between a worker and a capitalist. It is not a relation of commodity exchange. There is mutual responsibility based, at least in theory, on what Engels calls "individual sex-love". Each partner has his or her own realm of responsibility within the relationship usually based on a sex-typing of roles. Thus the relation is not reducible like any monetary exchange to a one-dimensional scale. Also, unlike commodity exchange, the relation is a binding one. The partners are not so free to re-contract exactly as they wish. This means that there is no tendency towards the equalisation of working conditions (compensated by pay differences) that occurs in capitalist commodity production. Since the difficulties of, and prejudices against, dissolving the relationship are so strong, substantial variation in standards of domestic work and time spent on it is possible. Nevertheless, the nature of the relation is such that the adequate performance of the respective sex-roles is seen as signs of love by the rest of the family or indeed society. A good and loving husband is also a good factory worker, one who gets a large wage-packet; a good and loving wife is one who spends much time on domestic work of one sort or another.

Domestic labour is the production of use-values, the physical inputs for this production being commodities bought with part of the husband's wage. The housewife produces directly consumable use-values with them. Some of these use-values are consumed by individual members of the family, some by the family collectively. Most of this work is repeated over a very short period of time since its consumption is practically continuous, e.g., cleaning and the preparation of food. Much of it is of a service nature, rather than the production of physical objects, and so may be unnoticed by other members of the family. She may get some help from other members of the family.

Childcare is the most time-consuming part of the work of full-time housewives. Because childcare is in a sense a twenty-four-hour job, young children requiring constant adult presence, this is part of domestic labour which is the most difficult to combine with wage work. Also because of the almost total absence of socialised substitutes, it is the most essential task performed by the housewife for the continuance of capitalism.

(b) Surplus labour in the home?

There is a knotty theoretical problem which recurs in discussions of domestic labour, and that is the economic characterisation of flows of commodities and use-values between man, woman and children within the home. One approach to this has been that found in Harrison, and in Jean Gardiner's first paper,[7] which used a model of unequal exchange in the sale of labour power, to provide the conclusion that women (often, at least) perform surplus labour which is transferred elsewhere: to the capitalist, or to the husband.

It was assumed that in general the labour embodied in housework would generally exceed the value of the wife's consumption out of her husband's wage packet. She could therefore be seen to be performing surplus labour like any other worker. This surplus labour would then form part of the husband's consumption and if it was seen as part of the value of his labour-power then the capitalist who employed the husband would in fact be paying him less than the value of his labour power. Thus the capitalist would receive surplus value in two ways. First, from his male worker, because the value created by the male worker was less than his subsistence (the value of labour-power, in this way of looking at things) and secondly, from the worker's wife, through her providing part of her husband's subsistence by her surplus labour. This view therefore involves a redefinition of the "value of labour power" to become what we have referred to as the total level of subsistence of the man, measured in labour time. Labour power then appears to be sold at less than its value, and the surplus labour of the housewife is also transferred to capitalist profits.

While this approach represented a real attempt to point out the quantitative economic significance of housework and to connect the benefits derived from it by men to the use made of it by capital, we have rejected it as disguising more than it reveals, and as inadequate on a number of counts.

In particular we do not accept the redefinition of the value of labour power because, to compare domestic labour with wage labour in a quantitative way, is not comparing like with like. However unevenly it operates, the process of value creation within commodity production enables one to talk about quantities of abstract labour in the case of wage labour in a way that is not valid for domestic labour. It is therefore not possible to add together domestic labour-time and wage labour-time in order to calculate the wife's surplus labour because the two are not commensurate.

In addition an approach which equates domestic labour-time with wage labour-time tends to blur the differences from a capitalist viewpoint between the contributions of women's labour in these different forms and therefore fails to expose the forces for change in the relationship between the two. As a result and because, in addition, no account is taken of the wife's potential for wage work, we find this approach static and ahistorical.

The approach we have come to adopt uses a more orthodox interpretation of value theory in that it defines value as socially necessary labour-time embodied in commodities. The value of labour power is therefore defined as the value of commodities necessary for the reproduction and maintenance of the worker and his family. This implies that the value of labour power is not synonymous with the labour-time embodied in the reproduction and maintenance of labour power once one takes account of domestic labour (and the state).

Once we take account of the fact that over half married women are currently in paid work outside the home, we are forced to explore the relation of women's wages to the wages of men and to the value of labour power.[8] We can approach this problem either by an analysis of the value of women's labour power or by examining the role of women's wages within the formation of the value of labour power for the family unit as a whole. Neither approach has been much discussed as yet. We therefore see this as an important area for future work.

The value of labour power is therefore premissed, both on the role of women in the wage economy, and on a particular level and organisation of domestic labour (and state-provided services). The concept of a historical subsistence level of the working class has become somewhat detached from the value of labour power, and has changed somewhat in theoretical status.

What this discussion has rejected is an analysis which calculates a transfer of labour from domestic labour into profits. What it has not rejected is the idea that husbands may benefit from the work of their wives. To illustrate this, let us look at a family where husband and wife are both working, and, for the sake of the argument, are gaining identical wages, but where the wife is still performing all the housework and childcare.

A state of affairs which is by no means uncommon amongst professional married couples and the obvious sense of injustice it generates has pushed a good many women towards feminism. Here the husband clearly benefits from the wife's work, assuming, of course, that they both contribute equally to the family expenses. What this leads us to examine however is also the nature of that benefit. The use-values produced by domestic labour have embodied in them an element of personal service which is dispensed with to a large extent when those use-values are socialised and become commodities. Having your clothes washed for you by someone else is different from washing them yourself, not only in that you do not do the work yourself, but also in that it puts someone into a servant role towards you within the family.

This type of benefit from women's work remains even when the division of labour at home and work is not so obviously in the man's favour. However, where the woman does perform wage-labour, or where the woman is working part time and earning less than the man, the further issue arises of the division of wages between man and woman. There is a lack of empirical evidence on work and consumption within the home, but it appears[9] that in general, women work longer total hours than men, and that in poor families women's subsistence is the first to suffer.

The analytical point here is that there are no forces inherent in family structure working to equalise the division of family resources between men and women. The very fact that much family consumption entails sharing and cooperation means that the real division of resources can be difficult to discern, and also that it is not entirely a ''zero-sum game'' where more for one is less for another. Nevertheless, the housewife role under capitalism can frequently become monetised in a sort of parody of the wage relation: secrecy by the husband about the size of his wage packet and a weekly tussle over the size of the housekeeping money. The expansion of a woman's personal consumption and leisure are often necessarily at the expense of those of men and children, a circumstance which will often prevent her from attending to her own needs.

Some further points can be made about this. Because wages are paid on an individual basis they will tend to be seen initially as the property of whichever member of the family has earned them. Where the housewife is only doing housework she will not be seen to be working because the unpaid nature of housework leads to an undervaluation of its importance even though it is economically essential. In addition because women are responsible for the family budget, even where they are earning wages themselves, they will tend to merge their own individual needs within those of the family rather than seeing the two as separate areas of expenditure in the way that men are more likely to do.

In the families therefore where the wife is either doing no paid work or part-time and low-paid work there are ideological and economic reasons why the division of wages in the family might work against women and in favour of men. Even where in the case of part-time work the women's wages may be contributing an important portion of her own subsistence she will still be economically dependent on some of the man's higher wages in budgeting for the family's needs. From an ideological point of view, as well, the family's wages will not be seen to be equally earned by husband and wife because of the undervaluation of housework. This last factor will not operate in families where equal wages are earned by husband and wife. However, because of the problem of women merging their individual interests with those of the family to a greater extent than men, we might expect women to use or get less for themselves even in this case.

But the division of resources and benefits is not decided merely within the bounds of the family: the undervaluation of women's work and women's needs within the home both influences and is influenced by the undervaluation of women's work in the wage sphere, and by the process by which domestic labour is socialised and women are drawn into the sphere of wage labour. Women, because of the relations of production within the home, find themselves isolated and relatively powerless in the sphere of production. This role and their socialisation into it reinforces their imposed subordination within wage work. The final part of this paper returns to the issue raised in the first section, and examines the benefits to capital of both of these forms of women's oppression in the context of a discussion of the process of socialisation of domestic labour.

4. *The socialisation of domestic labour*

In this section, we examine the process of socialisation of domestic labour, the transference of certain use-values from private production, under domestic relations, to socialised production under capitalist relations. We look at why socialisation of some aspects of domestic labour has occurred but not of all, and consider whether we can expect future socialisation of the remaining aspects.

Domestic labour, largely performed by women, is still essential for the reproduction of the capitalist system. At the present time it provides major services essential for the reproduction of the labour force for which there are no substitutes provided in any quantity by either capital or the state, the most obvious being pre-school child-care. It also provides a large number of other essential goods, such as prepared meals, for which there exist, qualitatively, substitutes such as restaurants on the market, but the price of which has remained sufficiently high relative to the wage to prohibit all but an occasional substitution of the marketed good for the domestically produced one, save for the very rich. So the relation of domestic labour to the production of surplus value is simply that the former makes the latter possible.

Why in that case has domestic labour nevertheless been progressively socialised over the past century and a half? By the socialisation of domestic labour we do not necessarily mean a reduction in the time actually spent on housework by full time housewives: the tendency of housework to expand to fill the day is one of its best documented characteristics. What we mean is the replacement (and at the same time the transformation) of the work done in the home by goods and services produced for the market or provided by the state: laundries and prepared foods, education and health care.

Within the socialisation of domestic labour there are two complementary processes at work. The first is the replacement of some aspects of domestic labour by socialised production (commodities or state services), and the second, the increasing participation of women in wage work.[10] And there are two effects: first an increase in production under capitalist relations of production and hence an extension in the labour force which produces surplus value; second, but a necessary precondition for the first, a reduction in the time which has to be spent in the house for the production of an acceptable standard of living for the family. The concept of socially necessary labour in the home is not analogous precisely to the concept when applied to capitalist commodity production. But in order to grasp the fact that the socialisation of domestic labour is necessary in order to permit women to work in wage labour, we need some concept of the minimum time necessary for tasks in the home, and of the forces permitting its reduction. Thus, though domestic work, as outlined in Section 3, is not subject to the same pressures for speeding up and rationalisation which affect wage labour, the minimum time necessary to achieve a given level of domestic consumption has clearly been reduced by the introduction of certain labour-saving commodities e.g. prepared foods, disposable nappies and washing machines. This process of freeing women for wage labour has gone on to some extent. But it remains true that in a considerable number of working-class families at any one time, the women are full-time housewives. Up to now, capital has been unable to overcome the obstacles to complete socialisation of domestic labour.

A lack of adequate accumulation or of a sufficiently labour-saving technology may be a bar to the further socialisation of domestic labour by capital at any historical moment. The example of this which may be the most relevant at the present time is the socialisation of pre-school childcare, which is extremely costly in labour and initial outlay if socialised provision is to provide an adequate substitute for family care. In state nurseries the required ratio of nursery staff to children is one to five, without taking account of the ancillary and administrative staff required. If one compares this to the average family of one and a half children to one mother with children under five one sees that at least one-third of housewives released from the home would have to be re-employed in nurseries, on the realistic assumption that childcare would remain women's work. Note too that women in families provide a twenty-four-hour childcare service, not just a daytime one. If a complete service were provided the number of wage workers required would be even higher.

It is very unlikely that individual capital would enter into the provision of childcare as a commodity. Its high cost in labour-time would ensure that profit-making nurseries or crèches would have to charge fees which could not be met out of present or likely future female wages. On the other hand, individual industrial capitals might provide nursery facilities, not as a commodity but as a direct use-value, for the children of their female workers. One would expect the capitals that initiated such schemes to be in areas with an existing labour shortage and to be making high profits. In providing childcare directly, no variable capital is "wasted" on women without children, as it would be if female wages as a whole were to rise sufficiently to cover the cost of commodity childcare. For if women with children were paid wages high enough to enable them to purchase childcare services the wages of all other women would tend to rise to the same level.

If one looks at the possible political processes that could bring about the socialisation of childcare, the only large-scale possibility would be for the state to expand its provision. For the same reasons as above, childcare would not be sold by the state as a commodity at its value. State nurseries would be free or, what is probably ideologically more acceptable, heavily subsidised. Since this would add to the costs of reproduction of the labour force borne by capital, this would only be likely to occur in a boom situation, in which there was rapid accumulation of capital and consequent productivity increases. These conditions are not true of the present phase of capitalism in Britian. This is only one example of the way that conditions of crisis are likely to prevent improvements in women's position.

There may also be positive reasons for the maintenance of full-time housework. One example of these is that sections of the working class, both men and women, may benefit from its maintenance. Perhaps, a key component of the conservative ideology of, initially, the male labour aristocracy in the nineteenth century, and subsequently the male working class as a whole was the striving, however partially achieved, for a wage large enough to keep a wife at home to service their needs. Moreover the trade unions' spasmodic and differential success in winning men a family wage was undoubtedly an achievement of organised labour and one that many women as well as men experienced as a benefit, given the arduous nature of domestic labour in this period. Currently however the rising proportion of married women working (now over fifty per cent for those aged 16 to 59) makes the demand for a family wage for men less meaningful, and less likely to be achieved, (especially in a period of crisis), and the ideology of dependent wives whose place is in the home more and more anachronistic. Full-time housework for married women is probably producing increasing strains for families (there is a high incidence of mental illness among full-time housewives) and an increasing burden for husbands in the form of the loss of the wife's earning power. The increasingly common model of the double shift in which women contribute wages to the family and do most of the housework as well is likely to become the most desirable for men in the future, and if it is not to generate resentment among women, and with it strains on the family structure, will require a reorientation of the man's role.

What happens to the value of labour power as the socialisation of domestic labour proceeds is a complex question. On the one hand, the real wage per family is likely to rise, (though not necessarily: in a time of crisis women may go out to work to defend the family standard of living); however, the effect this has on the value of labour power will depend on the growth in productivity in the economy and on the extent to which the value of labour power becomes "spread over" men and women, as discussed above.

We can draw out of this analysis a number of statements with political implications. The first is that the burden of the reproduction of the labour force has shifted proportionally from the family to capital and the state. This is very unlikely to be reversed to any great extent though we are seeing today how, in an economic crisis, an attempt is made to exhort women to work harder, to intensify their domestic labour by, for example, selective shopping or the home preparation of foods for which partly prepared substitutes are available on the market, and hence to try to disguise a fall in the real wage. The last major function of reproduction in the family is pre-school childcare, and if this were to be socialised, the forces keeping the family together would inevitably be weakened.

Secondly, and because of their "primary" role in domestic labour, women have always provided a relatively cheap labour force for capital (often working for low pay, in precisely the areas of domestic production which have been socialised). The value of labour power is spread, not evenly, but unevenly across men and women. But in eroding (not removing) the material basis for the family as an institution and drawing women into wage work, capital has been eroding the material basis for that form of oppression, and it now finds itself faced with demands for setting up the preconditions for equality, such as nurseries, to which it cannot hope to accede, and with demands which, if seriously pursued, could threaten women's role as a cheap labour force. Thus again, the labour process of capital is producing its own opponents.

NOTES

1. Karl Marx, *Capital*, vol. 1, Moscow, 1961, p. 572.
2. John Harrison, "Political Economy of Housework", *Bulletin of the Conference of Socialist Economists,* Spring 1974. Wally Seccombe, "The Housewife and her Labour under Capitalism", *New Left Review*, 83.
3. There are in capitalist society many people whose work is done under production relations other than those of strict capitalist wage labour: for example, artisans, bureaucrats and "professionals".
4. It should be noted that this is not a critique of the use of the concept of the articulation of modes of production in the analysis of capitalist dominance in Africa and Latin America.
5. See, for example, Harrison op. cit.

6. Karl Marx, *The Eighteenth Brumaire of Louis Bonaparte*, Lawrence & Wishart, 1968.

7. Jean Gardiner, "Political Economy of Domestic Labour in Capitalist Society", in *Explorations in Sociology*, vol. VI B, ed. D. Barker and S. Allen.

8. See for example R. and R.N. Rapport, *Dual Career Families*, Penguin, 1971.

9. See for example Audrey Hunt, *Survey of Women's Employment*, HMSO (1968). Lucy Syson and Michael Young in *1974 Poverty Report*, ed. M. Young.

10. Department of Employment, *Women and Work—a Statistical Survey*, Manpower Paper 9.

16

Wages Against Housework

SILVIA FEDERICI

They say it is love. We say it is unwaged work.
They call it frigidity. We call it absenteeism.
Every miscarriage is a work accident.
Homosexuality and heterosexuality are both working conditions . . .
 but homosexuality is workers' control of production, not the end
 of work.
More smiles? More money. Nothing will be so powerful in destroying
 the healing virtues of a smile.
Neuroses, suicides, desexualisation: occupational diseases of the
 housewife.

Many times the difficulties and ambiguities which women express
in discussing wages for housework stem from the reduction of
wages for housework to a thing, a lump of money, instead of
viewing it as a political perspective. The difference between these
two standpoints is enormous. To view wages for housework as a
thing rather than a perspective is to detach the end result of our
struggle from the struggle itself and to miss its significance in
demystifying and subverting the role to which women have been
confined in capitalist society.

When we view wages for housework in this reductive way we
start asking ourselves: what difference could some more money
make to our lives? We might even agree that for a lot of women
who do not have any choice except for housework and marriage, it
would indeed make a lot of difference. But for those of us who
seem to have other choices—professional work, enlightened
husband, communal way of life, gay relations or a combination of
these—it would not make much of a difference at all. For us there
are supposedly other ways of achieving economic independence,
and the last thing we want is to get it by identifying ourselves as
housewives, a fate which we all agree is, so to speak, worse than
death. The problem with this position is that in our imagination we
usually add a bit of money to the shitty lives we have now and then
ask, so what? on the false premise that we could ever get that

money without at the same time revolutionising—in the process of struggling for it—all our family and social relations. But if we take wages for housework as a political perspective, we can see that struggling for it is going to produce a revolution in our lives and in our social power as women. It is also clear that if we think we do not "need" that money, it is because we have accepted the particular forms of prostitution of body and mind by which we get the money to hide that need. As I will try to show, not only is wages for housework a revolutionary perspective, but *it is the only revolutionary perspective from a feminist viewpoint and ultimately for the entire working class*.

"A labour of love"

It is important to recognise that when we speak of housework we are not speaking of a job as other jobs, but we are speaking of the most pervasive manipulation, the most subtle and mystified violence that capitalism has ever perpetrated against any section of the working class. True, under capitalism every worker is manipulated and exploited and his/her relation to capital is totally mystified. The wage gives the impression of a fair deal: you work and you get paid, hence you and your boss are equal; while in reality the wage, rather than paying for the work you do, hides all the unpaid work that goes into profit. But the wage at least recognises that you are a worker, and you can bargain and struggle around and against the terms and the quantity of that wage, the terms and the quantity of that work. To have a wage means to be part of a social contract, and there is no doubt concerning its meaning: you work, not because you like it, or because it comes naturally to you, but because it is the only condition under which you are allowed to live. But exploited as you might be, *you are not that work*. Today you are a postman, tomorrow a cab driver. All that matters is how much of that work you have to do and how much of that money you can get.

But in the case of housework the situation is qualitatively different. The difference lies in the fact that not only has housework been imposed on women, but it has been transformed into a natural attribute of our female physique and personality, an internal need, an aspiration, supposedly coming from the depth of our female character. Housework had to be transformed into a natural attribute rather than be recognised as a social contract because from the beginning of capital's scheme for women this work was destined to be unwaged. Capital had to convince us that it is a natural, unavoidable and even fulfilling activity to make us accept our unwaged work. In its turn, the unwaged condition of housework has been the most powerful weapon in reinforcing the common assumption that *housework is not work*, thus preventing women from struggling against it, except in the privatised kitchen-bedroom quarrel that all society agrees to ridicule, thereby further reducing the protagonist of a struggle. We are seen as nagging bitches, not workers in struggle.

Yet just how natural it is to be a housewife is shown by the fact that it takes at least twenty years of socialisation—day-to-day training, performed by an unwaged mother—to prepare a woman for this role, to convince her that children and husband are the best she can expect from life. Even so, it hardly succeeds. No matter how well trained we are, few are the women who do not feel cheated when the bride's day is over and they find themselves in front of a dirty sink. Many of us still have the illusion that we marry for love. A lot of us recognise that we marry for money and security; but it is time to make it clear that while the love or money involved is very little, the work which awaits us is enormous. This is why older women always tell us, "Enjoy your freedom while you can, buy whatever you want now. . . ." But unfortunately it is almost impossible to enjoy any freedom if from the earliest days of life you are trained to be docile, subservient, dependent and most important to *sacrifice yourself* and even to get pleasure from it. If you don't like it, it is your problem, your failure, your guilt, your abnormality.

We must admit that capital has been very successful in hiding our work. It has created a true masterpiece at the expense of women. By denying housework a wage and transforming it into an act of love, capital has killed many birds with one stone. First of all, it has got a hell of a lot of work almost for free, and it has made sure that women, far from struggling against it, would seek that work as the best thing in life (the magic words: "Yes, darling, you are a real woman"). At the same time, it has disciplined the male worker also, by making *his* woman dependent on *his* work and *his* wage, and trapped him in this discipline by giving him a servant after he himself has done so much serving at the factory or the office. In fact, our role as women is to be the unwaged but happy, and most of all loving, servants of the "working class", i.e. those strata of the proletariat to which capital was forced to grant more social power. In the same way as God created Eve to give pleasure to Adam, so did capital create the housewife to service the male worker physically, emotionally and sexually—to raise *his* children, mend his socks, patch up his ego when it is crushed by the work and the social relations (which are relations of loneliness) that capital has reserved for him. It is precisely this peculiar combination of physical, emotional and sexual services that are involved in the role women must perform for capital that creates the specific character of that servant which is the housewife, that makes her work so burdensome and at the same time invisible. It is not an accident that most men start thinking of getting married as soon as they get their first job. This is not only because now they can afford it, but because having somebody at home who takes care of you is the only condition not to go crazy after a day spent on an assembly-line or at a desk. Every woman knows that this is what she should be doing to be a true woman and have a "successful" marriage. And in this case too, the poorer the family the higher the enslavement of the woman, and not simply because of the monetary situation. In fact capital has a dual policy, one for the middle class and one for the proletarian family. It is no accident that we find the most un-sophisticated machismo in the working-class family: the more blows the man gets at work the more his wife must be trained to absorb them, the more he is allowed to recover his ego at her expense. You beat your wife and vent your rage against her when you are frustrated or overtired by your work or when you are defeated in a struggle (to go into a factory is itself a defeat). The more the man serves and is bossed around, the more he bosses around. A man's home is his castle . . . and his wife has to learn to wait in silence when he is moody, to put him back together when he is broken down and swears at the world, to turn around in bed when he says "I'm too tired tonight," or when he goes so fast at love-making that, as one woman put it, he might as well make it with a mayonnaise jar. (Women have always found ways of fighting back, or getting back at them, but always in an isolated and privatised way. The problem, then, becomes how to bring this struggle out of the kitchen and bedroom and into the streets.)

This fraud that goes under the name of love and marriage affects all of us, even if we are not married, because *once housework was totally naturalised and sexualised*, once it became a feminine attribute, all of us as females are characterised by it. If it is natural to do certain things, then all women are expected to do them and even like doing them—even those women who, due to their social position, could escape some of that work or most of it (their husbands can afford maids and shrinks and other forms of relaxation and amusement). We might not serve one man, but we are all in a servant relation with respect to the whole male world. This is why to be called a female is such a putdown, such a degrading thing. ("Smile, honey, what's the matter with you?" is something every man feels entitled to ask you, whether he is your husband, or the man who takes your ticket, or your boss at work.)

The revolutionary perspective

If we start from this analysis we can see the revolutionary implications of the demand for wages for housework. *It is the demand by which our nature ends and our struggle begins because just to want wages for housework means to refuse that work as the expression of our nature*, and therefore to refuse precisely the female role that capital has invented for us.

To ask for wages for housework will by itself undermine the expectations society has of us, since these expectations—the essence of our socialisation—are all functional to our wageless condition in the home. In this sense, it is absurd to compare the struggle of women for wages to the struggle of male workers in the factory for more wages. The waged worker in struggling for more wages challenges his social role but remains within it. When we struggle for wages *we struggle unambiguously and directly against our social role*. In the same way there is a qualitative difference between the struggles of the waged worker and the struggles of the slave *for a wage against that slavery*. It should be clear, however, that when we struggle for a wage we do not struggle to enter capitalist relations, because we have never been out of them. We struggle to break capital's plan for women, which is an essential moment of that planned division of labour and social power within the working class, through which capital has been able to maintain its power. Wages for housework, then, is a revolutionary demand not because by itself it destroys capital, but because it attacks capital and forces it to restructure social relations in terms more favourable to us and consequently *more favourable to the unity of the class*. In fact, to demand wages for housework does not mean to say that if we are paid we will continue to do it. It means precisely the opposite. To say that we want money for housework is the first step towards refusing to do it, because the demand for a wage makes our work visible, which is the most indispensable condition to begin to struggle against it, both in its immediate aspect as housework and its more insidious character as femininity.

Against any accusation of "economism" we should remember that *money is capital*, i.e. *it is power to command labour*. Therefore to reappropriate that money which is the fruit of our labour—of our mothers' and grandmothers' labour—means at the same time to undermine capital's power to command forced labour from us. And we should not distrust the power of the wage in demystifying our femaleness and making visible our work—our femaleness as work—since the lack of a wage has been so powerful in shaping this role and hiding our work. To demand wages for housework is to make it visible that our minds, bodies and emotions have all been distorted for a specific function, in a specific function, and then have been thrown back at us as a model to which we should all conform if we want to be accepted as women in this society.

To say that we want wages for housework is to expose the fact that housework is already money for capital, that capital has made and makes money out of our cooking, smiling, fucking. At the same time, it shows that we have cooked, smiled, fucked throughout the years not because it was easier for us than for anybody else, but because we did not have any other choice. Our faces have become distorted from so much smiling, our feelings have got lost from so much loving, our oversexualisation has left us completely desexualised.

Wages for housework is only the beginning, but its message is clear: *from now on they have to pay us because as females we do not guarantee anything any longer*. We want to call work what is work so that eventually we might rediscover what is love and create what will be our sexuality which we have never known. And from the viewpoint of work we can ask not one wage but many wages, because we have been forced into many jobs at once. We are housemaids, prostitutes, nurses, shrinks; this is the essence of the "heroic" spouse who is celebrated on "Mothers' Day". We say: stop celebrating our exploitation, our supposed heroism. From now on we want money for each moment of it, so that we can refuse some of it and eventually all of it. In this respect nothing can be more effective than to show that our female virtues have a calculable money value, until today only for capital, increased in the measure that we were defeated; from now on against capital *for us* in the measure we organise our power.

The struggle for social services

This is the most radical perspective we can adopt because although we can ask for everything, day care, equal pay, free laundromats, we will never achieve any real change unless we attack our female role at its roots. Our struggle for social services, i.e. for better working conditions, will always be frustrated if we do not first establish that our work is work. Unless we struggle against the totality of it we will never achieve victories with respect to any of its moments. We will fail in the struggle for the free laundromats unless we first struggle against the fact that we cannot love except at the price of endless work, which day after day cripples our bodies, our sexuality, our social relations, unless we first escape the blackmail whereby our need to give and receive affection is turned against us as a work duty for which we constantly feel resentful against our husbands, children and friends, and guilty for that resentment. Getting a second job does not change that role, as years and years of female work outside the house still witness. The second job not only increases our exploitation, but simply reproduces our role in different forms. Wherever we turn we can see that the jobs women perform are mere extensions of the housewife condition in all its implications. That is, not only do we become nurses, maids, teachers, secretaries—all functions for which we are well trained in the home—but we are in the same bind that hinders our struggles in the home: isolation, the fact that other people's lives depend on us, or the impossibility to see where our work begins and ends, where our work ends and our desires begin. Is bringing coffee to your boss and chatting with him about his marital problems secretarial work or is it a personal favour? Is the fact that we have to worry about our looks on the job a condition of work or is it the result of female vanity? (Until recently airline stewardesses in the United States were periodically weighed and had to be constantly on a diet—a torture that all women know—for fear of being laid off.) As is often said—when the needs of the waged labour market require her presence there—"A woman can do any job without losing her femininity", which simply means that no matter what you do you are still a cunt.

As for the proposal of socialisation and collectivisation of housework, a couple of examples will be sufficient to draw a line between these alternatives and our perspective. It is one thing to set up a day care centre the way we want it, and demand that the state pay for it. It is quite another thing to deliver our children to the state and ask the state to control them, discipline them, teach them to honour the American flag not for five hours, but for fifteen or twenty-four hours. It is one thing to organise communally the way we want to eat (by ourselves, in groups, etc.) and then ask the state to pay for it, and it is the opposite thing to ask the state to organise our meals. In one case we regain some control over our lives, in the other we extend the state's control over us.

The struggle against housework

Some women say: how is wages for housework going to change the attitudes of our husbands towards us? Won't our husbands still expect the same duties as before and even more than before once we are paid for them? But these women do not see that they can expect so much from us precisely because we are not paid for our work, because they assume that it is "a woman's thing" which does not cost us much effort. Men are able to accept our services and take pleasure in them because they presume that housework is easy for us, that we enjoy it because we do it for their love. They actually expect us to be grateful because by marrying us or living with us they have given us the opportunity to express ourselves as women (i.e. to serve them): "You are lucky you have found a man like me." Only when men see our work as work—our love as work— and most important *our determination to refuse both*, will they change their attitude towards us. When hundreds and thousands of women are in the streets saying that endless cleaning, being always emotionally available, fucking at command for fear of losing our jobs is hard, hated work which wastes our lives, then they will be scared and feel undermined as men. But this is the best thing that can happen from their own point of view, because by exposing the way capital has kept us divided (capital has disciplined them through us and us through them—each other, against each other), we—their crutches, their slaves, their chains—open the process of their liberation. In this sense wages for housework will be much more educational than trying to prove that we can work as well as them, that we can do the same jobs. We leave this worthwhile effort to the "career woman", the woman who escapes from her oppression not through the power of unity and struggle, but through the power of the master, the power to oppress—usually other women. And we don't have to prove that we can "break the blue-collar barrier". A lot of us broke that barrier a long time ago and have discovered that the overalls did not give us more power than the apron; if possible even less, because now we had to wear both and had less time and energy to struggle against them. *The things we have to prove are our capacity to expose what we are already doing, what capital is doing to us and our power in the struggle against it.*

Unfortunately, many women—particularly single women—are afraid of the perspective of wages for housework because they are afraid of identifying even for a second with the housewife. They know that this is the most powerless position in society and so they do not want to realise that they are housewives too. This is precisely their weakness, a weakness which is maintained and perpetuated through the lack of self-identification. We want and have to say that we are all housewives, we are all prostitutes and we are all gay, because until we recognise our slavery we cannot recognise our struggle against it, because as long as we think we are something better, something different from a housewife, we accept the logic of the master, which is a logic of division, and for us the logic of slavery. We are all housewives because no matter where we are they can always count on more work from us, more fear on our side to put forward our demands, and less pressure on them for money, since hopefully our minds are directed elsewhere, to that man in our present or our future who will "take care of us".

And we also delude ourselves that we can escape housework. But how many of us, in spite of working outside the house, have escaped it? And can we really so easily disregard the idea of living with a man? What if we lose our jobs? What about ageing and losing even the minimal amount of power that youth (productivity) and attractiveness (female productivity) afford us today? And what about children? Will we ever regret having chosen not to have them, not even having been able to realistically ask that question? And can we afford gay relations? Are we willing to pay the possible price of isolation and exclusion? But can we really afford relations with men?

The question is: why are these our only alternatives and what kind of struggle will move us beyond them?

17

Wages For Housework: Political and Theoretical Considerations

JOAN LANDES

After a lapse of several decades marxists have once again begun to address themselves to the character of women's oppression in capitalist societies. These marxist feminist writers have begun to situate the nature of women's labour within the family. They have approached the various dimensions of women's oppression from the vantage point of often ignored aspects of capitalist relations of production.[1] At the same time, many of these writers have failed to incorporate into their analysis what I take to be the most distinctive methodological and theoretical implications of a fully developed marxist feminist approach.

Marxist feminism, then, begins to express the contours of a dialectical approach to social life. Qualitative changes can be distinguished from quantitative changes; new forms of social life will require new concepts; contradiction not equilibrium will characterise development: historical change will be seen as a constant component of a world already and forever in process.

In my view, marxist feminism proceeds from an approach which Bertell Ollman has termed Marx's philosophy of internal relations.[2] This approach treats the study of social relations as the subject matter of social science. Thus, the study of social reality does not focus on things or essentially isolated individuals but on entire social totalities understood from the vantage point of units abstracted for study, which to a certain extent may be referred to as versions—albeit one-sided or partial—of that totality.

I want therefore to propose that it is possible to view capitalism from the standpoint of the family; that in such a case, the family would constitute a specific mode of production: a definite mode of activity, a definite way of producing and reproducing a way of life. And, this mode of production is an alienating capitalist mode which comes under the law of private property. The family conceptualised as a mode of production is actually a mode of production and reproduction of the working class as a working class. It is a mode of reproduction of the individual worker as a worker; and a mode of reproduction of the housewife as a housewife as well as the reproduction of that same woman as a potential and often employed wage labourer.

Throughout the literature of women's liberation, I have discovered a repeated tendency to attribute conservative qualities to the female houseworker and conservative content to her role within the family. It is now popossible to situate this conservatism in a different way, through applying the method of internal relations.

The family, viewed as a mode of production of capitalism, possesses a class dimension. And this is not merely because it is a reflection of the economic base, but because the reproduction of labour occurs within the working-class family. The family itself is an alienated form of production and reproduction. It teaches workers to sell their labour-power for the sake of consumption which they understand as leisure time; it teaches an instrumental attitude toward work; and it teaches that leisure, and not productive activity, gives meaning to life. As Marx said:

> The worker therefore only feels himself outside his work; and in his work feels outside himself. He is at home when he is not working, and when he is working, he is not at home. [3]

Within the family, patterns of hierarchy (both of men over women, and of parents over children) help to introduce workers to the hierarchical labour patterns to be suffered at the workplace. The ideology of the family helps to teach workers that these patterns are "natural" as well as legitimate. Also, the family absorbs the shock of individuals who fail to achieve the freedom which society promises them through their place in the social division of labour.

Certainly, then, woman's role as a producer of the commodity labour power* possesses a conservative dimension in so far as her labour maintains the worker as worker, and ensures that both

---

*Marx was the first to comprehend that the individual worker—indeed the working class as a whole sells to the capitalist not his or her labour but labour power (or the capacity to labour). In return the worker receives wages. Thus the worker's capacity to labour must be produced and reproduced on a daily basis like any other commodity. Hence, the term commodity labour power. Much of the work of producing the commodity labour power is performed in the family by the woman.

husband and wife will never be anything *but* workers. Hierarchy
and repression are important features of this truly conservative
aspect of the working-class family, and women play an important
role in these oppressive relations. At the same time, the reproduction of the working class is itself founded upon *women*'s oppression within this class.

What, then, are the actual contradictions which are embodied in
the mode of production of the working-class family? The housewife produces use-values within the family, and in this way, her
production possesses a positive dimension:

> . . . within the family women perform useful labour and therefore can,
> under the right conditions, have access to a vision of a life of
> unalienated productive activity. The recent attempts to break down sex
> divisions of labour within the family are providing similar glimpses to
> men. . . . These are only utopian in so far as their partial nature
> remains unrecognised.[4]

Thus, to the extent that the housewife's domestic production is
oriented toward the fulfilment of human needs—and not toward
the production of surplus value—for which she relies upon the
(husband's) wage, she confronts the world of capitalism from a
different perspective from that of the male wage-earner. As Lise
Vogel has argued, for the woman, the world is composed of use-
values waiting to be consumed. Her consciousness—that is, to the
extent that she is a housewife and not also a wage labourer—is
therefore different from the consciousness of her husband, who
sees the world in terms of exchange-values. On this Vogel states:

> Locked in an increasingly brutal division of labour, the two sexes tend
> to experience the relationship between the family and the capitalist
> mode of production from vastly differing points of view. Here is the
> root of the system of contradicitions inherent in the family under
> capitalism.[5]

The production of use-values in the family therefore resembles
the organic, non-rationalised and qualitative dimensions of a
unified work process characteristic of pre-capitalist societies. At
the same time, the family is a solidly capitalist relation. As such, it
embodies dialectic unity between production for use and
production for exchange. Production within the family is oriented
toward exchange-value obtained through the sale of labour power
even though this production is simultaneously the production of
use value for the entire family. Therefore, within the family we are

able to situate one characteristic of capitalist production as a whole: the triumph of exchange-value over use-value production.

The commodity labour power is produced for its exchange-value rather than for the products which it would have to produce under a truly human form of production. The conditions under which labour power's production in the home and the community occurs, are determined from outside the family. Similarly, the sexual potential of both man and woman is subordinated to their capitalist function of producing future labour power. This encourages the objectification of the human sexual potential, so that finally, the development of the labourer as a productive force within capitalism is alienated, one-sided, and brutalised: even the worker's pro-creation exists only for capital.

The way in which workers live, their environment, their life style, are aspects of capitalist alienation. There are no absolute divisions between family and factory in this respect:

> The high-rise apartment building, by virtue of its very structure, forms the residential counterpart of the office skyscraper. Here private life is consciously massified and publicly administered. . . . The standardisation of the dwellings fosters a standardisation of private life that subverts the physical and personal heterogeneity so vital to the give-and-take of meaningful communication. One can only put a limited amount of one's authentic personality into these strictly functional apartment cubicles—and quite often, very little of that personality will be tolerated by the bureaucracies which administer the structures. That the architecture of these developments is featureless, the corridors of the buildings institutional, and apartments themselves nothing more than a suite of offices is not accidental; the developments are bureaucratic institutions for self-reproduction and self-maintenance, just as the office skyscrapers are bureaucratic institutions for commerce and administration.[6]

The preceding considerations begin to sketch the outlines of what might become a full-scale investigation of capitalist society from the standpoint of the working-class family. Such an examination must take account not only of the categories of marxist political economy but also, more significantly, those of Marx's theory of alienation. An examination of capitalist production, as viewed from the vantage point of the family, brings into prominence a series of contradictions.

These contradictions are grouped around, or are aspects of a central contradiction *in* capitalism and *for* it. To say that a contradition exists *in* capitalism is to call attention to a dimension of the system which counterposes its content and its form; to say that a contradiction exists *for* it is to call attention to features that distinguish its mode of being from those within any other social totality and at the same time point beyond it, to its essential transformation. Current marxist feminist literature has focused attention on the role of housework in capitalist production; but at what central and secondary contradictions does the capitalist character of housework point?

(1) The central contradiction *in* capitalism posed by the nature of housework is the fundamental integration of housework into social labour (its *content*) and its privatised, isolated, "non-productive" (for capital, that is) *form*. And just as, in the past, relations of exploitation in the factory have produced demands for unionisation, higher wages, and better working conditions, for example—demands for work reforms within the system—so now the productive character of housework has led to well-intended but mistaken demands for wages for housewives. Those who have raised these demands have failed essentially to grasp the character of the problem. They have not understood that the awarding of a wage, even if it were possible, would neither alter the relations of production nor the fact that the housewife already shares in the wage-packet of the male wage-earner. This is not to say, however, that women should not struggle to force capital to bear an increasing share of the cost of the reproduction of labour power.

(2) Housework's central contradiction for capitalism—which touches upon some broader aspects of alienation—is that between the way it is now performed and a more truly human form of production not measured by labour time. The difficulties posed for post-capitalist societies by this contradiction will be examined below, but a failure to understand it has clouded the vision of the socialist movement and has contributed to the formulation of misconceived strategies which hope to liberate women "for production", ignoring how as housewives, they are already a part of it. As a form of alienated labour, housework cannot be transformed by "freeing" women to enter directly into the labour market. Nor can domestic work provide an alternative to capitalism if it serves to hark back to some earlier mode of production. Housework shows that whereas the subjugation of labour by means of the discipline of labour-time may be the precondition for the emancipation of labour, it is not to be mistaken for emancipation itself. It is only in

this *limited* sense that housework suggests, but cannot in itself offer, the vision of a form of production which is less, not more, alienated than the production of exchange-value under capitalism.

These two central contradictions reveal a number of factors which also deserve serious examination:

(1) In fact, the "socialist" call for "freeing" women for production has been long since heeded by capitalism itself. At the present time, married women are entering the labour-force in record numbers and, in contrast with the early part of this century, they now outnumber single working women. This development has sharpened and extended the antagonism between the property character of sexual relations under capitalism and the capitalist presupposition of a free labourer in a free market for labour. In other words, it has deepened women's consciousness of the contradiction between their status as proprietors of their personal capacities (mainly as sellers of labour power) and as objects of male sexual proprietorship. It is in this sense—and wholly within capitalism—that women's "liberation" from the home has fed potential political opposition to capitalist social arrangements.

(2) Another factor revealed in these contradictions involves the antagonism between the "feminine ideal", which places all women on a pedestal and encourages them to believe they can elevate their social status through marriage, and the *real* exploitation of all working-class women in the labour market. It is at this point that I situate the criticisms of the "feminine mystique" and the emphasis on transforming personal relations within the broader dynamic of social change.

(3) A third major factor in the contradiction between the *form* of woman's work in the home and its productive *content*, is embodied in the housewife's integration into the productive process and her isolation from the point of production of exchange-values. Those who have advocated women's entry into the paid labour market as opposed to their being houseworkers, have often noted the isolated housewife's attachment to conservative neighbourhood institutions like churches, small businesses, schools, bingo clubs, and the like. For them, for the housewife to quit the home and join the union is a first step toward her liberation. Those who have advocated wages for housework, on the other hand, have also noted the potential for the community to become a locus of social struggle. While I have noted the limitations of the wages-for-housework demand, and while I have no objection to women

workers joining unions, my perception that housework is an aspect of the productive process that internally relates factory to community, goes beyond these positions. It challenges movements for social change to examine more seriously the impact of feminist theory upon the formulation of strategies. The nature of productive labour in the family, for me, then, has practical as well as theoretical implications.

As the foregoing remarks suggest, the perspective of the family not only offers a way of situating a range of social contradictions in capitalism—including aspects of those contradictions noted by liberal feminists—but also points to some difficulties faced by marxist feminists in understanding these contradictions *for* captialism. To the extent that the latter have not understood in these antagonisms their implications for examining the entire capitalist social order, they will be forced to fall back on limited, liberal approaches in their effort to effect significant change.

One way of underscoring that point is to project a future in which a purely economic transformation of the mode of production is accompanied by the retention of many liberal *forms* of social relations. Without offering any comment on the postcapitalist societies of the present, I should note that Marx himself, in the *Critique of the Gotha Programme*, made such a projection:

> What we have to deal with here is a communist society, not as it has developed on its own foundations, but, on the contrary, just as it emerges from capitalist society; which is thus in every respect, economically, morally, and intellectually, still stamped with the birthmarks of the old society from whose womb it emerges . . . equal right is still constantly stigmatised by a bourgeois limitation. The right of the producers is proportional to the labour they supply; the equality consists in the fact that measurement is made with an equal standard, labour. . . . It is therefore, a right of inequality, in its content, like every other right. Right by its very nature can consist only in the application of an equal standard; but unequal individuals (and they would not be different individuals if they were not unequal) are measurable only by an equal standard in so far as they are brought under an equal point of view, are taken from one definite side only, for instance, in the present case, are regarded only as workers. . . . Further, one worker is married, another is not; one has more children than another, and so on and so forth. Thus, with an equal performance of labour and hence an equal share in the social consumption fund, one will in fact receive more than another, and so on. To avoid these defects, right instead of being equal would have to be unequal.[7]

Marx, it should be added, felt that in the first phases of communism "these defects are inevitable". He also held that "the narrow horizon of bourgeois right" could only be transcended at the end of the division of labour and "after the productive forces have also increased with the all-round development of the individual".[8]

Now, in the situation which Marx forecasts, there seem to be two alternative ways in which women's needs could be satisfied. The first lies in the institution of something like the radical-feminist "contract" family (or the socialist-feminist "differentiated" family). In either, the woman is "freed" to enter directly into production at the factory and to compete with all other workers for a slice of the existing pie ("from each according to his [her] abilities; to each according to his [her] work"). In reality, of course, given the continuance of competition *within* the labour-force, and the historical legacy of discrimination in the capitalist labour market, women will start out with two distinct strikes against them. Moreover, these might well be taken advantage of by men so that women will continue to be "placed" in lower-paying jobs, with both fewer opportunities for advancement and fewer non-monetary rewards. But even if the obstacles posed by continued sexual discrimination in the labour market are overcome, increased female labour-force participation and contractual family relations might lead to a deepening of social fragmentation, alienation, and competition. For example, in order to prevent being forced back into the defensive housewife position, with no direct, enforceable claim on labour-credits, women will be led to stoutly uphold the principle that all human relations should be viewed as contractual relations. Thus, every detail of the housework contract ("equal duties"—but who will nurse the children?) will have to be upheld to include the smallest of tasks. In this situation—which I have taken to its logical conclusion—socialism becomes universal, competitive egoism, with women forced into the "role" of guardians of the ultimate in social atomisation. In this "role", the woman's social being is forced into contract being, and women are further removed than ever from the chance to develop their fundamental human *capacities*—the promise, after all, of the moral dimension of socialism.

The second alternative wherein women will greet the attainment of socialism as an opportunity to retire from unrewarding labour-force participation is equally unpalatable. Women, for the most part, will return to the home. Once again, they will have no direct, enforceable claim to labour-credits. The struggle between the sexes is now exacerbated and perpetuated within a socialist context. For the man, marriage and the assumption of fatherhood constitutes a definite liability. No matter how much "work" he contributes at the factory, no matter how much he exercises himself, each additional obligation which he assumes toward his family must be paid for out of his earnings. In this situation he can only harbour ill feelings toward his wife and children. And economically, the wife is forced to struggle endlessly against the total deterioration of her position. In such circumstances, bureaucratic functionaries opine that the housewife is nothing but a "parasite", thereby playing upon man's resentment of his wife in order to gain his support for the status quo.

The only escape Marx envisioned from this situation was the increased productivity of labour, so that distribution would no longer have to be tied to quantitative indicators of social worth. With the achievement of social abundance would follow the fact that a woman would no longer depend upon her husband's labour-credit or on his ability to compete, despite unfavourable terms, at the point of production.

At this juncture, marxist feminism must begin to apply Marx's method to problems not considered by Marx. At the same time, it must take issue both with some of the writers in the housework debate who hope to liberate women "into production" and with liberal feminists, as well, who want "equal opportunity" for women at the workplace—that is, with those who believe that equal access to the factory will end the question of who will do the socially necessary labour now performed by women in the family. To admit that such work must be done does not mean that it is necessary to fall back on the unpleasant alternative of the contract family, as envisioned by radical feminists.

This projection of economic socialism, therefore, further clarifies the alienation of the working class, particularly of working-class women, and helps us to understand the alienating alternatives within capitalist society. For, under capitalism, young workers, both male and female, enter the labour-force. Men then necessarily marry and "settle down", and take a woman—but only temporarily—out of production. To grasp this process it is necessary to view the working-class, total reproductive cycle. Under both capitalism and economic socialism, women are already "integrated" into the labour-force, e.g., between school and marriage. Also, after bearing and rearing children, they re-enter the labour-force. Fundamentally, in all their "functions", these women are first, foremost, and always only *workers*, now playing an economically disadvantaged role in the production and reproduction of non-human commodities, now playing a crucial, determinative role in the production and reproduction of labour power. Expressing itself in the battle between the sexes, woman's dual role in the labour market represents a secondary contradiction in the working class under capitalism; and a potentially primary contradiction in the class under economic socialism. Neither radical feminist contractualism nor familial conservatism offers a way out for working-class women and men.

To formulate the dimensions of political change as a restructuring of production within the community *and* the workplace is also to criticise one other version of contemporary socialist theory which advocates "workers' control of production" as a democratic alternative to nationalisation. The proponents of such schemes locate control at the site of the workplace and counterpose it to the "community" where labour power is produced. Therefore even "workers' control of production" falls far short of real control, unless it is broadened to unite control at the plant site with control at the community site, both of which are already internally related as a result of the economic alienation of capitalist society. Such solutions—integrating women into worker-controlled production—will not resolve the economic nature of this alienation. Nor will they overcome the resulting political disadvantages which women will continue to suffer, if only because they will have less *time* to devote to political activity at the plant since they will still also be houseworkers. Like the economic alienation which women suffer, their political alienation cannot be superseded unless there is a strategy which takes into account the dual aspects of production within the factory and community.

The questions which liberal feminists have perceived in terms of "rights" for women and "oppression" of women (in the home) will have to be reformulated by marxist feminists prepared to explore various dimensions of women's oppression within the working class. This will require the application of Marx's method to hitherto unexamined questions. This is only to reiterate that the insights of liberal feminists need to be resituated in an extension of the marxist approach to aspects of women's lives within the family and the workplace: the "woman question" *per se* must be transcended, but its contributions must be preserved.

This analysis demonstrates the inadequacy, even the misdirections, of a political strategy which begins with a demand for "wages for housework" without either analysing the relationship between families and housewives and the requirements of today's capitalist political economy, or exploring the relationship between housework and productive labour performed by working-class women in the commodity producing sphere. Indeed, the housework debate has shown that any implementation of this demand will in fact merely reproduce rather than abolish the sexual divisions between family and economy, between woman's work and man's labour which are exacerbated by capitalist development. Even in the paid labour-force, jobs are segregated on the basis of sex. Wages alone cannot be expected to free women from housework. They may have the very opposite effect, in fact, of freezing women into those jobs. For these reasons, alone, the demand for wages seems to be a shallow one. But there are even deeper difficulties which may arise should this demand be won. For example, the next question, "Who will pay for the housewife's wage?" arises automatically. Certainly not the capitalist! The first remaining choice is, then, the individual wage package, which is already formulated to include a "non-working" or underpaid working wife and will now be formally divided by the boss or by the state. Alternatively, the state will subsidise this additional cost by further taxation of the working class. Either of these possibilities will lead to increased divisions within the working class, divisions which will aggravate already existing tensions between men and women, between husband and wife. Either choice could lead to an additional financial burden for the producing (working) class as a whole. For those who fear that this conclusion merely sacrifices women to the working class we need to ask, "Which women?" We need to propose political strategies which unite rather than divide the various groups (sexual, racial and/or ethnic) within the working class without sacrificing any one group's demands.

Looking beyond this immediate issue, it is possible to identify questions which are not encompassed within the "housework debate", but which are important in any complete investigation of capitalist oppression of women. We need to explore: (1) the purchasing power of the wage, and the role which the housewife performs as a consumer; (2) the important role which sexual objectification plays in family relations and in commodity relations in general, within capitalist society; (3) the situation of women in different sectors of the working class, including the contribution which the employment of male and female migrant labour and Black and Spanish-speaking labour (citizen and non-citizen) may make toward the reinforcement of sexual divisions within the working class. . . . such divisions include reinforcing the housewife status for some women and perpetuating the dual burden of work and home for women who are regular wage earners; (4) the role of the family now and in the future as a locus for community-wide and class-wide organising; (5) the tendency to use working-class women in various ways (i.e., as voluntary layoffs or as means of stretching the budget to meet inflation); and (6) the (related) tendency for housewives to serve as an important flexible component of the labour reserve, providing cheap and easily retractable labour. We can no longer separate women who are housewives from women who are productive labourers, even for the purpose of analysis. We need to understand the inter-relationships between work done in the home and work in production, that is, between production and reproduction. We need to appreciate how both types of labour are aspects of alienated production within capitalist society.

Although these are preliminary suggestions, they point to the directions in which future theoretical work might move. The "housework debate" makes an invaluable contribution for it completes past marxist investigations. That is, in itself the debate is incomplete, but it provides an important complement to earlier investigations. Finally, we need an analysis which can theoretically situate the family as a centre for the reproduction of labour-power as well as personal life, while at the same time clarifying the class relationships which characterise the commodity sphere of capitalist society.

NOTES

1. Margaret Benston, "The Political Economy of Women's Liberation", in Michele Garskof, ed., *Roles Women Play: Readings Toward Women's Liberation*, Belmont, California, 1971, 194–205; Mariarosa Dalla Costa, "Women and the Subversion of the Community", in *The Power of Women and the Subversion of the Community*, Montpelier,

Bristol, 1972; Ira Gerstein, "Domestic Work and Capitalism", *Radical America*, vol. 7, nos. 4 & 5, July–October, 1973, 101–30; Lise Vogel, "The Earthly Family", *Radical America*, vol. 7, nos. 4 & 5, July–October, 1973, 9–50; Wally Seccombe, "The Housewife and Her Labour Under Capitalism", *New Left Review*, no. 83, January–February, 1973, 3–24.

2. Bertell Ollman, *Alienation: Marx's Conception of Man in Capitalist Society*, Cambridge, 1971; and, "Marxism and Political Science: Prolegomenon to a Debate on Marx's Method", *Politics and Society*, 3:4, Summer 1973, 491–510.

3. Karl Marx, *Economic and Philosophical Manuscripts of 1844*, edited with an introduction by Dirk J. Struik. Translated with an introduction by Martin Milligan, New York, 1964, p. 110.

4. Lise Vogel, "The Earthly Family", *Radical America*, vol. 7, nos. 4 & 5, July-October 1973, p. 38.

5. Ibid., p. 33.

6. Murray Bookchin, *The Limits of the City* (New York, 1974), pp. 83–4. Emphasis added.

7. Karl Marx, "Critique of the Gotha Programme", in Karl Marx and Friedrick Engels, *Selected Works* (New York, 1968), pp. 323–4.

8. Ibid., p. 324. Too, as will be immediately noticed, these models have their direct analogues in the literature of liberal and marxist feminism.

Bibliography

HISTORICAL STUDIES

Anderson, Adelaide, *Women in the Factory, 1893–1921*, London, John Murray, 1922. An account of the operation of legislation on women factory workers based on the author's experience as a factory inspector.

Black, Clementina (ed.), *Married Women's Work*, London, G. Bell & Sons, 1915. Recognising the importance of the fact that women's work in the home makes her dependent, this work nevertheless sees the solution in "lifting the domestic burden" rather than the socialisation of household work.

Bondfield, Margaret, "Women as Domestic Workers", in Dr Marian Phillips (ed.), *Women and the Labour Party*, London, Headley Brothers, 1919. A very interesting article demonstrating conflicting attitudes within the labour movement on the significance of domestic labour.

Brittain, Vera, *Women's Work in Modern England*, London, Noel Douglas, 1928. Beginning with an account of the period from the First World War to the beginning of the Depression the book describes the current occupations of women and details attempts to channel them back into domestic service after the war.

Burnet, John (ed.), *Autobiographies of Working People; 1820 to the 1920s*, London, Allen Lane, 1974. Among the autobiographies are those of a number of women from a variety of rural and urban occupations.

Clark, Alice, *The Working Life of Women in the Seventeenth Century*, London, Frank Cass, 1968 (first published 1919). A rich and varied source of information containing an analysis of the shift from "family industry" to capitalised "domestic industry" and the movement of production out of the home.

Davin, Anna, "Imperialism and Motherhood", in *History Workshop Journal*, no. 5, Spring 1978.

Ehrenreich, Barbara, and Deirdre English, "The Manufacture of Housework", in *Socialist Revolution*, San Francisco, no. 26, October-December 1975, reprinted in an expanded version as "Microbes and the Manufacture of Housework" in *For Her Own Good*, London, Pluto Press, 1979; New York, Doubleday, 1978. An account of "150 years of experts' advice to women", primarily in the U.S.A. The first chapter contains clear theoretical account of the character of the change from "patriarchy" to "masculinism" with the development of capitalism.

Engels, Friedrich, *The Condition of the Working Class in England in 1844*, especially the introduction and the chapter on "Factory Hands".

Fussell, G. E. & K. R., *The English Countrywoman: 1500–1900*, London, Melrose, 1953. A detailed study of the domestic routine of country housewives of different classes and of the manufacturing tasks carried on in the home in the pre-industrial period. The cumulative impact of industrial organisation of production on the home is also described.

Gilman, Charlotte Perkins, *The Home: Its Work and Influence*, The University of Illinois Press, 1972 (first published 1903).

— *Women and Economics*, New York, Harper & Row, 1966 (first published 1899).

Hall, Catherine, "A History of the Housewife", previously unpublished paper, 1973 (an extract was printed in *Spare Rib*, no. 26).

Hewitt, Margaret, *Wives and Mothers in Victorian Industry*, Greenwood Press, Westport, Conn., 1975 (first published London, Barrie & Rockliff, 1958). An invaluable study of the problems faced by married women in industry and their children, with an account of the character of public action and legislation.

Hughes, Gwendolyn Salisbury, *Mothers in Industry*, Philadelphia and New York, New Republic Press, 1925.

Jephcott, Pearl, Nancy Seear and John Smith, *Married Women Working*, London, Allen & Unwin, 1962.

Kitteringham, Jennie, "Country Girls in Nineteenth-Century England", Oxford, History Workshop Pamphlet, 1973; also in R. Samuels (ed.), *Village Life and Labour*, London, Routledge and Kegan Paul, 1975. Documents the effects of women's dual work role in the nineteenth-century countryside on the lives and education of their daughters.

Llewellyn Davies, Margaret (ed.), *Life As We Have Known It*, London, Virago, 1977 (first published by Hogarth Press, 1931).

— *Maternity*, London, Virago, 1978 (first published 1915). Letters from women of the Co-operative Women's Guilds in the early twentieth century, describing their experiences in employment, motherhood and household work.

Mitchell, Hannah, *The Hard Way Up*, London, Virago, 1977 (first published London, Faber & Faber, 1968). An autobiography of a working-class suffragette and socialist well aware of the issues raised for women by housework.

Mitchell, Juliet, and Ann Oakley, *The Rights and Wrongs of Women*. Harmondsworth, Penguin, 1976. A collection of essays on aspects of women's lives containing material on health, medicine, work, politics and education in an historical and cross-cultural context.

Neff, Wanda Fraiken, *Victorian Working Women*, London, Frank Cass, 1968 (first published New York; 1929). A classic study drawn from historical and literary sources, of the lives and conditions of Victorian women workers and social attitudes to them.

Oakley, Ann, *Housewife*, Harmondsworth, Penguin, 1977 (first published Allen Lane, 1974). A brief description of the historical changes which led to the present definition of the work and function of housewives with an appraisal of the situation of housewives today. The final pages of the last chapter, "Breaking the Circle", are the least convincing.

Pember Reeves, Maud, *Round About A Pound A Week*, London, Virago, 1979 (first published, 1913, London, G. Bell & Sons). A detailed account based on a survey by the Fabian Women's group of the working lives of housewives in Kennington and Lambeth. An excellent historical introduction by Sally Alexander.

Phillips, Marion (ed.), *Women and the Labour Party*, London, Headley Brothers, 1919. A pamphlet containing several articles about women's role as housewife and domestic worker, indicating the contradictory nature of political attitudes to women at the time.

Pinchbeck, Ivy, *Women Workers and the Industrial Revolution 1780–1850*, London, Frank Cass, 1969 (first published 1930). One of the indispensable pioneering works on the subject of women's work, both inside and outside the home, in manufacturing and agricultural districts in a critical period of change.

Rainwater, Lee, Richard Coleman, Gerald Handel, *Workingman's Wife*, New York, Oceana, 1959. A study conceived mainly as an exercise in determining working-class women's attitudes to consumption, but which, especially in the chapter entitled "Day In, Day Out", describes the situation of white working-class housewives in the USA in the 1950s.

Razzell, P. E., and R. W. Wainwright, (eds.), *The Victorian Working Class*, Selections from Letters to the *Morning Chronicle*, 1849–1851, London, Frank Cass, 1973. Letters from different regions about the lives of different occupational groups showing the variety of home conditions and attitudes to domesticity among them.

Rowbotham, Sheila, *Hidden from History*, London, Pluto Press, 1973.
— *Women, Resistance and Revolution*, Harmondsworth, Penguin, 1972. Two of the first works by the new generation of feminists to attempt to put women's historical role into perspective from a socialist point of view.
Spring Rice, Margery, *Working-Class Wives*, London, Virago, 1981 (first published 1939). A report from The Women's Health Commission of the 1920s on the living and working conditions of working-class housewives based largely on their own words.
Stenton, Doris Mary, *The English Woman in History*, London, Allen & Unwin/Macmillan, 1957. A study of English women from Anglo-Saxon to modern times containing biographies of prominent women and assessments of the social position of women from different classes based on codes of law, patterns of landholding, wills, letters, sermons and other documents.
Thompson, Flora, *From Lark Rise to Candleford*, Harmondsworth, Penguin, 1973. An autobiography of the daughter of a rural artisan from the 1870s, describing the changing attitudes to fieldwork for women, the increasing employment of girls in domestic service and its effect on the attitudes to domesticity and the homes of rural labourers' families.

SOME NINETEENTH-CENTURY LITERARY SOURCES

Eliot, George (Mary Ann Evans), *Adam Bede*.
— *Middlemarch*.
— *The Mill on the Floss*. The daily tasks and attitudes of women from a wide variety of nineteenth-century social groups from artisan to middle class are described with a detailed and critical eye.
Gaskell, Elizabeth, *Mary Barton*.
— *North and South*. Housekeeping among industrial workers and middle-class professionals in mid-nineteenth-century Manchester is described in the context of attitudes to industrialism, class, and different kinds of work for women outside the home.

PERSONAL ACCOUNTS AND POLITICAL ANALYSES

Adamson, Olivia, Carol Brown, Judith Harrison and Judy Price. "Women's Oppression Under Capitalism", in *Revolutionary Communist* no. 5, November 1976.
Barker, Diana Leonard, and Sheila Allen, *Dependence and Exploitation in Work and Marriage*, London, Longman, 1976.
Bebel, August, *Women under Socialism*, New York, Schocken Books, 1971.

Benston, Margaret, "The Political Economy of Women's Liberation", in *Monthly Review*, vol. 21, no. 4, September 1969.

Bristol Women's Liberation Group, "The Oppression of Women in the 1970s", in *International Marxist Review*, no. 2, 1971.

Bristol Women's Study Group, *Half the Sky*, London, Virago, 1979.

Comer, Lee, *Wedlocked Women*, Leeds, Feminist Books, 1974. A descriptive account of the relationship between marriage, women's work, especially housework, and their emotions, often quoting directly from interviews.

Coulson, Margaret, Branka Magaš and Hilary Wainwright, "The Housewife and her Labour Under Capitalism: A Critique", in *New Left Review*, no. 89, January-February, 1975.

Dalla Costa, Mariarosa, and Selma James, *The Power of Women and the Subversion of the Community*, Bristol, Falling Wall Press, 1972, reprinted 1975.

Delmar, Ros, "Oppressed Politics", in *Red Rag*, no. 2, London, 1972.

— "Capitalism, Sexism and the Family", in S. Allen, L. Sanders and J. Wallis (eds.), *Conditions of Illusion*, Leeds, Feminist Books, 1974.

Edmond, Wendy, and Suzie Fleming, *All Work and No Pay*, Bristol, Falling Wall Press, 1975. A selection of accounts by women on their working lives with an emphasis on the demand for wages for housework.

Engels, Friedrich, *The Origin of the Family, Private Property, and the State* (first published 1884).

Fee, Terry, and Rosalinda Gonzalez (eds.), "Women and Class Struggle", in *Latin American Perspectives*, Riverside, California, no. 12/13, 1977.

Federici, Silvia, *Wages Against Housework*, Bristol, Falling Wall Press, 1975.

Firestone, Shulamith, *The Dialectic of Sex*, New York, William Morrow, 1970.

Fonda, Nickie, and Peter Moss (eds.), *Mothers in Employment*, Brunel University Management Programme, Uxbridge, 1976. This selection contains papers on various subjects from analyses of problems created by government policies towards mothers, to attitudes of women and employers towards combining housework with paid work outside the home.

Foreman, Ann, *Femininity as Alienation*, London, Pluto Press, 1977.

Freeman, Caroline, "When is a Wage not a Wage?", *Red Rag*, no. 5, 1973.

Gail, Suzanne, "The Housewife", in R. Frazer (ed.), *Work*,

Harmondsworth, Penguin, 1968 (first published in a *New Left Review* series on Work and Living, 1965–1967).

Gardiner, Jean, Susan Himmelweit and Maureen Mackintosh, "Women's Domestic Labour", in *On the Political Economy of Women*, CSE Pamphlet no. 2, London, Stage 1, 1976.

Gardiner, Jean, "Women's Domestic Labour", in *New Left Review*, no. 89, January-Feburary 1975.

Ginsberg, Susannah, "Women, Work and Conflict", in Nickie Fonda and Peter Moss, (eds.), *Mothers in Employment*, Brunel University Management Programme, Uxbridge, 1976.

Himmelweit, Susan, and Simon Mohun, "Domestic Labour and Capital", in *Cambridge Journal of Economics,* 1977.

Holt, Alix (ed.), *Selected Writings of Alexandra Kollontai*, London, Allison & Busby, 1977.

James, Selma, *Women, the Unions and Work*, Bristol, Falling Wall Press, 1976.

Landes, Joan B., "Wages for Housework: Subsidising Capitalism", in *Quest* (Washington D.C.), vol. II, no. 2, Fall 1975.

— "Women, Labor and Family Life: A Theoretical Perspective", in *Science and Society*, vol. XII, no. 4, Winter 1977–78.

Lenin, V. I., *On the Emancipation of Women*, Moscow, Progress Publishers, 1965.

Mackie, Lindsay, and Polly Patullo, *Women at Work*, London, Tavistock, 1977. A concentrated but lucid study of the relation between women's work at home and in the labour market.

Mainardi, Pat, "The Politics of Housework", Somerville, Mass., New England Free Press, 1968 (reprinted in *Voices from Women's Liberation*, New York, Signet, 1970).

Marx, Karl, *Capital*, Volume I, chapters V, XXIII, XV part 3(a). Especially the discussion of the reproduction of capital.

— *Theories of Surplus Value*, in particular the section on productive and unproductive labour.

Mitchell, Juliet, "Women: The Longest Revolution", in *New Left Review*, no. 40, 1966 (reprinted in E. H. Altbach (ed.), *From Feminism to Liberation*, Cambridge, Mass., Schenkman, 1971). An influential early essay on women's liberation from a marxist feminist viewpoint, examining the interaction between economic, ideological and psychological components of women's situation in the second half of the twentieth century.

— *Women's Estate*, Harmondsworth, Penguin, 1971. A more detailed study containing an account of the development of the women's liberation movement and an expansion of the above.

Moreno, Shirley, "Story", in *Women's Liberation Review*, no. 1, October 1972. A macabre and chilling short story about a loving housewife and mother.

Morton, Peggy, "A Woman's Work is Never Done", *Leviathan,* May 1970 (reprinted in E. H. Altbach, (ed.), *From Feminism to Liberation*, Cambridge, Mass., Schenkman, 1971).

Oakley, Ann, *The Sociology of Housework*, London, Martin Robertson, 1974. An account of women's attitudes to work in the home based on interviews with seventy mothers, with quotations from the interviews and statistical tables based on them.

Rowbotham, Sheila, "The Carrot, the Stick and the Movement", in *Red Rag*, no. 2, 1972.

— *Women's Consciousness, Man's World*, Harmondsworth, Penguin, 1973. This book examines the relationship between the personal dimensions of life and the political, and relates housework to work outside the home.

Seccombe, Wally, "The Housewife and her Labour under Capitalism", in *New Left Review*, no. 83, 1974.

Trotsky, Leon, *Women and the Family*, New York, Pathfinder Press, 1970.

Vogel, Lise, "The Earthly Family", in *Radical America*, July-October 1973.

Warrior, Betsy, and Lisa Leghorn, *Houseworker's Handbook*, Cambridge, Mass., Women's Centre, 1974, 1975. A collection of articles by the authors written at different times which contains a detailed breakdown of the Chase Manhattan Bank estimate of the financial equivalent of a housewife's work.

Williams, Jan, Hazel Twort and Ann Bachelli, "Women and the Family", in M. Wandor (ed.), *The Body Politic,* London, Stage 1, 1972 (first printed in *Shrew*, 1969).

Women's Liberation and Socialism Conference Papers, no. 1, Birmingham, March, 1973; no. 2, London, September 1973; no. 3, Birmingham, September 1974. The immediate reactions and development of the debate about housework in one section of the women's liberation movement are contained in these collections, some of the papers from which were subsequently further developed and published.

Acknowledgements

We wish to express our gratitude for permission to publish the following:

Introduction by Ellen Malos. Copyright © 1977 and 1980. The original version first appeared as an article in *Socialist Review*, no. 37, San Francisco (January-February 1978).

Extracts from "The History of the Housewife" by Catherine Hall published by permission of the author. Copyright © 1973 and 1980.

"The Politics of Housework" by Pat Mainardi is reprinted by permission of the New England Free Press (which publishes "a wide variety of pamphlets on various topics, including a large women's section; for a free catalogue write to them at 60 Union Square, Somerville, Mass. 02143"). Copyright © 1968.

Extracts from "The Housewife" by Suzanne Gail reprinted by permission of *New Left Review*. Copyright © 1965-7.

"Women and the Family" by Jan Williams, Hazel Twort and Ann Bachelli reprinted by permission of Jan Williams. Copyright © 1969.

"The Political Economy of Women's Liberation" by Margaret Benston first appeared in *Monthly Review* in September 1969 and is reprinted here by their permission. Copyright © 1969.

Extracts from *The Dialectic of Sex* by Shulamith Firestone reprinted by permission of William Morrow. Copyright © 1970.

"The Carrot, the Stick and the Movement" by Sheila Rowbotham reprinted by permission of the author and *Red Rag*. Copyright © 1972.

"When is a Wage not a Wage?" by Caroline Freeman reprinted by permission of the author and *Red Rag*. Copyright © 1973.

"Oppressed Politics" by Ros Delmar reprinted by permission of the author and *Red Rag*. Copyright © 1972.

"'The Housewife and her Labour under Capitalism'—a Critique" by Margaret Coulson, Branka Magaš and Hilary Wainwright reprinted by permission of *New Left Review*. Copyright © 1975.

Working-Class Wives by Margery Spring Rice reprinted by permission of Charles Garrett-Jones, Ronald Garret-Jones and Cecil Robertson. Copyright © 1939, 1970. 1970.

"Women's Domestic Labour" by Jean Gardiner, Susan Himmelweit and Maureen Mackintosh reprinted by permission of CSE. Copyright © 1976.

"Wages Against Housework" by Silvia Federici reprinted by permission of the author. Copyright © 1975.

"Wages For Housework: Political and Theoretical Considerations" (originally published in *Quest* under the title "Wages For Housework: Subsidising Capitalism?") by Joan Landes reprinted by permission of the author. Copyright © 1975 and 1980.

Efforts have been made without success to trace copyright holders of the following:

"Women as Domestic Workers" by Margaret Bondfield. Copyright © 1919.

"Women's Work is Never Done" by Peggy Morton. Copyright © 1971.

Index